Tell Me To My Face

Tell Me To My Face

Angelo Mosca

with Steve Milton

ISBN 978-1-105-01836-7

Cover design: Michelle Rechkemmer
Interior design: Hartley Millson
Front cover photo: Brooks Reynolds

Inside photos are courtesy *The Hamilton Spectator* and the Mosca family

Acknowledgements

Throughout my life, I've been fortunate to have been influenced and inspired by a large number of terrific people. It would be impossible to acknowledge them all, but I'd like to thank this core of faithful friends and family who have always supported and encouraged me. This book is dedicated to:

My wife, my best friend, Helen Mosca; my sister Carol Roberg and our other four brothers and sisters; my daughter Jolene Mosca and her husband Bernie Quinn; my son Angelo Junior and Shari; my son Gino and Gill; my great cousin Gary Mosca; my high school friends Ralph Wheeldon and Mike Carme; Steve Milton, whom I really enjoyed working with on this book; my friends from my playing days in Ottawa, Chick and Louise Wolfe; my Toronto friend of 50 years, Mike Palermo; Scott Mitchell, president of the Hamilton Tiger-Cats; Doug Mitchell, former commissioner of the CFL; Lulu.com, and Bob Young, the owner of the Tiger-Cats and the instigator of this book. Thank You!

— Angelo Mosca

As always, I want to thank my "inner circle" of Jess, Toby and Michelle for their support and patience, especially while Angelo and I spent countless hours and days working on this book; my mom, June, who until her very last breath helped me appreciate the beauty of language; Lulu.com for trusting me with Angelo's story; Angelo's family for providing insight into what it's like to live around a legend; and, finally, to Angelo Mosca, for the fun we had while writing this book and for having the faith to reveal to me his most intimate thoughts, memories and emotions. I will never forget that gift.

— Steve Milton

Contents

Foreword   *The Voice*   **9**
Prologue   Passing   **15**

Section One: Growing Up Mosca
CHAPTER **1**   Secret Shame   **21**
          The House on Francis Street   **36**
CHAPTER **2**   Discovering Football   **43**
CHAPTER **3**   Not Your Ordinary Joe College   **57**

Section Two: The CFL
CHAPTER **4**   Welcome to Hamilton   **73**
CHAPTER **5**   Exile   **103**
CHAPTER **6**   Steeltown Forever   **123**
CHAPTER **7**   The Best Team There Ever Was   **143**
CHAPTER **8**   My Last Game and the Year Hamilton
          Will Never Forget   **149**

Section Three: Wrestling and Beyond
CHAPTER **9**   Exhibitions of Strength and Skill   **175**
CHAPTER **10**   King Kong Mosca   **193**
CHAPTER **11**   Life After Pro Sports   **215**

Epilogue   The Last Voice You Hear   **233**
Appendix   CFL Career   **240**
Appendix   Wrestling Career   **241**
Index   **251**

The Voice

By Steve Milton

THE MOST CONSPICUOUS THING ABOUT Angelo Mosca has always been his size. He was a big kid, a big football player, a big wrestler and he is still a big man. Bigger than life sometimes. Angelo doesn't do "small." Not in his body, his face, his voice, his strengths, his weaknesses, his passions, his anecdotes, his history, his secrets.

To those who first meet him and to those who have known him all their lives, the two elements of his size that leave the deepest impression are his face and his voice.

"It's a face that only a mother could love," he says with a huge laugh and, as you'll find out, more than a bit of irony. "I have a unique face. It's a face that's big and that you won't forget. I stand out in a crowd, and I don't mean that as bragging. That's how I still make my money today. From my face."

His face is large and complex, every feature exaggerated. It can light up with mischief and laughter and darken when he's angry or feels he's been wronged. It is a face that can alternately, and quickly, display joy for a good practical joke and disgust for a phony.

It is a face that last graced a football team picture nearly four decades ago, yet it has never left the Canadian public consciousness. "I think he's managed to keep his face out there between commercials and interviews on TV," his wife Helen Mosca says. "And he's always there, people can always approach him. I've never seen him turn away a request for an autograph or a picture. People still remember who he is, whereas with a lot of other football players you wouldn't recognize them if you tripped over them."

Out of that unique face comes a singular voice, and it is that voice which must be heard when reading this book. Angelo is a storyteller, in the most traditional sense of the avocation. He embellishes, but not to the point of distortion. He seamlessly drifts back and forth from the past to the present tense. He swears. He dips and rises as the narrative does. Others could not tell the tales Angelo tells; his story must come from his lips.

In *Tell Me To My Face*, Angelo tells the story of his unusual journey from the hard-scrabble streets of Greater Boston to becoming known internationally for his exploits on the gridiron and in the wrestling ring. His story comes complete with beauty marks and warts, because Angelo Mosca has always done things his own way, for better or worse.

Angelo's voice echoes two childhood accents that will not relinquish their grip: blue collar Boston and second-generation Italian-American. His younger sister Carol, seeking to distance herself from Waltham, Massachusetts, where they grew up, deliberately drove the Boston accent from her speech patterns but says she "can still pahk the cah in the Hahvahd yahd when needed."

But in Angelo the accent lives on, despite a half-century of living in Canada. "I notice it more in certain words than others,"

Helen Mosca says. "Cuba, always sounds as Cube-r. Vanill-er. In car, you can still hear a bit of cah.

"He does have a very distinct voice. He did that commercial for the Ultramatic bed, and my girlfriend said, "I fell asleep on the couch in front of the TV one night and all of a sudden I hear Angie's voice and I thought he was right in the room. That's how distinct his voice is."

A deep and big voice and that can have unintended impact. Angelo Mosca Jr. says his father is funny and loves a practical joke, and you can hear that in his voice: "It's animated but in many ways, it's intimidating too. It's his voice and his demeanor." His sister Jolene calls their father's voice "commanding" but that he can also "be tender with it when he wants to."

In fact Angelo has great control over his voice. He's been a storyteller, a public speaker and an actor — in commercials, TV dramas and on the wild-west stage of pro wrestling — and can change his pitch and tone to suit an occasion.

He also adapts his content to suit his surroundings. In its most natural state — when he's with fellow wrestlers, football teammates or at a card table — his voice is spectacularly robust and heavily laced with jocular profanity. That is understandable for a lifelong athlete and a street kid who was shown the harsher side of adult behaviour early in life. But Angelo is also old-school in many ways and Helen says she never hears him swear around her or other women and that he gets upset when other people do. The voice in this book is partway between those two extremes.

Angelo's coarse language is a product of his upbringing, but also of his playfulness and mischievousness. His son says Angelo employs the practical joke, for which he was notorious in his athletic career, as a vehicle for camaraderie. And camaraderie is very important to him. Those whom he considered elitist or not the right type of teammates — the Ottawa Rough Riders and the legendary Russ Jackson and John Barrow among them — take surprisingly hard knocks in this book.

The jokes also help keep things light. Angelo wants everyone to be happy, partly because he rose out of a youth full of sadness and anger. There is an enormous tender side to Angelo, but he lets few people see it including, sometimes, himself. I've known him professionally for a quarter of a century but it wasn't until we got into the intimate details of this book that I was privileged to see or hear — twice — what very few people ever do: Angelo Mosca crying. Once was in the fall of 2010 in a roadside restaurant when he and his sister started recalling their years in Waltham. The other was in early 2011 when he phoned, sobbingly, to tell me that Bronko Nagurski, a common thread through Angelo's life for 54 years, had died the previous night.

If Angelo Mosca's voice and face are the longest lasting of the many and varied impressions he has left upon people, it's appropriate that, for a septuagenarian, he's so attached to his cell phone. Helen says it was getting so expensive that she had to get him a long distance package. He's regularly calling or being called by old teammates, wrestling foes and business acquaintances. The cell phone replaces the locker room as a forum for camaraderie.

It's fitting that Angelo came of age just as television was moving heavily into his two sports: football and wrestling. During and after his athletic careers TV kept him famous and he, in turn, made good TV. His face filled the screen unforgettably and his it-could-only-be-Mosca voice added to the overall impression.

Angelo Mosca has many faults. He would be the first to tell you that, and he does so in this book. But he is a man with his heart in the right place who is starting to regret some of the pain he caused. He is a guy you want in your corner, and as your friend. And I would tell *him* that. To his face.

Prologue

Passing

EVERY TIME THE WAITER PUT something down on the table in front of me, he paused for a second. And I went on eating, pretending I didn't notice.

I was in Athens, Georgia, dead in the centre of Bulldog country, sitting in the elegant dining room reserved for the alumni and professors at the University of Georgia. It wasn't the kind of place I was used to having lunch in. The silverware was formal and very shiny. There were about six pieces of it at each place and I had to watch how other people were doing it to know when to use each piece of the cutlery. The tablecloth was thick and a very bright white. The napkins were made of cloth and looked like they'd just been ironed. They were as white and thick as the tablecloth.

The day before, I was eating lunch out of a paper bag in the railroad yard in South Bend, Indiana. I was 20 years old and had a job laying down oak railroad ties that weighed close to 300 pounds. I had learned to balance them exactly right so I could carry them myself. It was brutal, hard work and a long way from the wood-paneled dining room at the University of Georgia.

I was sitting with a chaperone who was showing me around campus and introducing me to all the important things the university had to offer, including the other man eating at the table with us. That was Wally Butts, the legendary coach of the Georgia Bulldogs, one of the top college teams in the south. Wally was a little guy, about 5-foot-6, and kind of round-shaped. He had a thick drawl, said "y'all" a lot, and everything about him, everything, was pure south.

It was the winter of 1957, and Wally was trying to get me to come to the University of Georgia to play football. It wasn't the first time he'd tried to recruit me. A little more than two years earlier when I was a high school senior, I did a large tour of colleges, including Georgia, who wanted to sign me. But I chose Notre Dame, because that was *the* place to go. But now I was back on a small recruiting tour because I had just been kicked out of Notre Dame. I was workin' on the railroad all the live-long day, but I didn't want to do it forever.

As I listened to Wally Butts make his pitch, the waiter kept throwing quick glances back over his shoulder at me. He was African-American but since this was 1957 and Georgia, he was called a "negro." To this day I still remember the way he looked at me. He was checking me out with this peculiar, and kind of knowing, look on his face. Like he suspected something. Like he knew I was keeping a secret.

SECTION
ONE

Growing Up
Mosca

ONE

Secret Shame

MY FATHER WAS NOT A good man. In fact, to be honest with you, he was a mean fucking man — a real prick. He was a drunk and a bigot. His name was also Angelo Mosca. He was born in Syracusa, Sicily, and when he arrived in America in 1927 he brought with him his wife and five kids.

At that time, immigrants to America were quarantined at Rikers Island — known mostly for its prison — until their papers were processed and approved. This is where my parents met. My mother, Agnes Wood, worked in the kitchen at Rikers, and after my father's first wife died, he and my mother got together. They were married in 1935 and two years later, when they were living in Waltham, Massachusetts, I was born.

My birthday is February 13, 1937 — my middle name is Valentine because of that — and, of course, I got my first name from my father; just as my son Ang. Jr. got his first name from me, and his son A.J. got his first name from him.

I was the first of six children in my father's second family. My sister Becky was born two years after me, Mike was third, two years younger than Becky. Carol was born fourth, six years after me, June was born a year after Carol, and the youngest, Paul, is 15 years younger than I am.

We never knew my father's other family. After his first wife died the kids were put "on the state," which I now know means that they were sent to orphanages, but at the time I had no idea. My father would almost boast when he spoke of it. He'd threaten us by saying, "I've already put five on the state and I'll put six more." I don't know what became of them all, although I did meet one of his sons much later in life when I was wrestling in Augusta, Georgia. I met one of his daughters, too. Her name was Pauline. Other than those two meetings I more or less stayed to myself when it came to the other family.

My father was an angry man and because I was the oldest, he took his anger out on me. My mother was no help. She was an alcoholic — half meek and half mild. She always made sure I got my ass whipped instead of my dad beating her.

She was a second generation American-Italian. But she was only *half* Italian and that's the story I've held back from telling anyone my entire life.

It's tough, very tough, for me to talk about this, but I might as well start right at the beginning.

My mother was black.

Actually, she was only half-black, what was then commonly called a "mulatto." Her mother was black and her father was Italian, but at that time in the United States, being half-black, or even one-quarter black, was the same as being black. If you had any "negro" blood in you whatsoever, you were black. End of discussion.

Today, being one-quarter black might not seem like something to hide, but at the time, being the offspring of a mixed-race couple could be a curse. And it usually was. My mother had many of the features of a black woman, and if you look at me closely, I have some features people would consider African American, mostly in the nose. It's broader in spots. Other than that I don't really show many black features. My skin is dark and smooth, but that's true of many Italians, too. Still, I knew inside what I had in my background. You can't change your heritage.

America was a very prejudiced country and being black meant, at the very least, that you probably weren't going to get anywhere in life: your chance for success was very slim. Nobody wanted you around. You would be called "nigger," and would automatically be considered a lazy bum. There were "Jim Crow" laws all throughout the southern states that segregated blacks and whites — separate schools, drinking fountains, bathrooms, restaurants, you name it. Even in Boston we would read about the lynching and murders that happened down south.

Waltham is about five miles outside of Boston and Boston has always been well known as one of the most prejudiced American cities outside of the south. The Red Sox were the very last Major League Baseball team to integrate their roster. It was Pumpsie Green who finally became the first black to make the Red Sox, and he did it in the middle of the 1959 season — more than a dozen years after Jackie Robinson made his major league debut for the Brooklyn Dodgers. Even into the late 1990s, black athletes were running into unnecessary hassles with Boston police.

Waltham is a pretty high-tech area now. The city has built a big school on the Charles River and the Boston Celtics have their own training facility there. When I was growing up Waltham was lower working class, and very tough: all Irish and Italian families. I knew we were Italian because we were raised Italian, always ate Italian food. My dad would always be slagging the Irish and the Catholics, and if someone called him a

Wop, he'd fight'em. Me too, right from an early age, if someone called me a Wop then I'd have to fight. That was the racial slur I could defend. The other one I couldn't. It was private, and I wasn't supposed to let anyone know.

I had nothing against blacks, nothing at all. My dad made me feel embarrassed and ashamed about my heritage, so I hid it. He looked at me like I was a little piece of crap. He yelled at me and screamed at me. Right from the earliest times, I can remember him smashing me, cracking me with his belt, kicking me and calling me a "little black son of a bitch." My father made me and my siblings feel like second-class kids. He was the most prejudiced human being I ever met in my life. And to top it all off, his answer to everything was to take a swing at it.

I can remember playing checkers with him when I was about nine years old and I beat him. He reached over and, *wham*! I was knocked clear off my chair. If you were to ask him, he'd say he hit me because a child wasn't supposed to win games when playing against adults. He always gave us this lecture about having respect for older people. I think that's why I never retaliated; I had that respect deep inside of me. He's very lucky that as I got older and bigger I never went back at him; I could have done some real damage. The reason he could get away with all of this was that he brainwashed us kids. It's complicated to understand how to behave when you have your parents telling you not to tell anybody who you are or what you are. And it isn't just the words they would use; it was in all of their actions, too. They browbeat us and belittled us, and the brainwashing I endured as a child kept me thinking there was something wrong with me until maybe 10 years ago.

It wasn't until I was 12 or 13 years old that I found out for sure that I was three-quarters white and one-quarter black.

The realization kind of crept up on me over the years. I didn't understand the situation when I was young. My dad was always screaming at us about our being black. I didn't fully get what was supposed to be wrong with us kids, and I certainly didn't know how the black part fit in. All the kids in the neighbourhood liked us. I even used to organize neighbourhood baseball games where the Italian kids would play the Irish kids, and we never lost a game because a fight would break out and the game would break up. Unfortunately my close friend Harold Kelley — he was half Irish and half Italian — always got caught in between. He played with us Italians, though. And there was Ralphie Wheeldon, one of my best friends right from elementary school. Ralph's parents really liked me. I don't know if they knew what was going on at home — me getting beat up all the time — because I never told anybody about it and I certainly never told anybody about being part black. I'd had that hammered into me, literally. Mikey Carme was my other really good buddy. But he was always hesitant to talk to me later on in life: he thought I was becoming a big shot. These are the two guys who all through high school were my best friends and I still keep in contact with them today. Ralphie had one eye and I called him Cyclops, because I was already developing that street kind of humour. He was a hockey player, a helluva goalie. We made a deal when we got to high school that if he played football, then I would play hockey. He came out and played linebacker — with one eye! — but I lied about me. I never joined the hockey team because I couldn't play. I got away with stuff like that because I didn't mean anything by the things I said and I'm not a mean person. But as a child I ended up confused, and not really believing anything because we were taught to be ashamed of who we were.

To give you an example of how ashamed we were supposed to be, my grandmother lived in Boston and I only saw her once in my life. We used to go into the Faneuil Market in Boston to do the family shopping on the weekends and one time we went to her place which was in Dorchester, the black part of town. My sister and I came inside but we weren't ever actually introduced to our grandmother while we were there. We just sat there. It was an apartment building and it was a real shit hole. A real shit hole. She was a hoarder: everything was stuffed in corners. Clothes piled on top of clothes; shoes, papers, everywhere. The hallways smelled of urine. I think we were in the place for only about 10 minutes before we were told to go back outside and wait in the car

It was in about third grade or so when I first heard someone call me "nigger" but I just ignored it then. When I was a few years older, I started discovering the black-white divide and the hatred that was everywhere in those days. A few classmates even started shouting "Hey Blackie!" at me. Students made accusations of my being black all through my high school years, but I never participated when other kids would show their prejudice against African-Americans. Thankfully teachers and sports writers never made mention of my race.

Two of my cousins on my father's side wouldn't associate with me, because of my mother. The implication was that I had black blood in me so that I was a lesser person. I remember being with another cousin in the early 70s, he and I were driving in a car in Waltham and he stopped outside somebody's house. He said to me, "Just wait here for a minute, I have to go in and get something, I'll be right back." He didn't want me to go in with him. He didn't want to be seen with me. So I said, "Fuck him!" and stopped being seen with him. The funny thing is, I have another cousin who is straight-white on the Mosca side, and all he dates are black girls!

When I look back on it now, I didn't spend too much time thinking about my race or analyzing how I reacted to the negativity projected toward me. It was a way of life. It was the life I knew and I did what I thought I had to.

This is the first time I've ever opened up to the public about my identity. I feel good about it because I know there is nothing wrong with me and that I'm not a bad person. My wife Helen has really encouraged me to tell my story; this book is her idea. Helen is the best thing that ever happened to me. She understands me and gives me the confidence to deal with the past, all these years later. She was the first person I've ever told about the shame that was driven into me, and how I was supposed to hide it. Apparently she already knew about it because my daughter Jolene told her. But it was a big moment for me to share my secret with Helen — from my own mouth. At that point I hadn't even told my kids or their mother; they figured it out on their own.

The reason I'm revealing all of this now is because my family now knows, and I wanted to be the one to tell the outside world. Helen thought it would be therapeutic for me, and it has been.

It's very hard to go your entire life lying. It may not be a lie of commission but it certainly was a lie by omission. I just couldn't tell people about it because I'd been so drilled not to. My mother and father made me feel ashamed of my heritage and myself. I had it worked out in my head that blacks weren't accepted, so I wanted to *only* be an Italian. I had this secret inside of me and couldn't let it out because I was scared of how my reality might change. But, it feels good to get this off my chest, and as Helen keeps telling me, I'm a good person and I have a great legacy to share.

My father was a stonemason by trade and also did menial labour jobs when he could get them. He worked at the New England Mica Company in Waltham, where they lined the insides of toasters with mica. But he had other ways of making money. He used to run a numbers game that was based on the Massachusetts State Treasury Report. My dad would sell tickets, almost like a lottery, and the winning numbers were the last six numbers of the treasury's balance, which ran in the paper every day. My father was working for someone else, who I didn't know, and I'd always see him with big wads of money. Sometimes I'd go out on collections with him and he'd have his gun on his hip. I knew it was there, and I knew what it was for. I never saw him have to use it though. Actually, he was a real chicken-shit, if you want to know the truth. He was only 5-foot-7 or 5-foot-8, which I started to realize as I got bigger and started to get stronger

His biggest racket was organizing local card and craps games. My dad and his cronies had games that they moved from garage to garage every Sunday. I didn't know it then, but they were moving the games to stay ahead of the cops. While my dad ran the games I sold sandwiches to the guys. I'd take the sandwiches (which, if I had to guess, were made by my mother) out to the garage where there would be 10 or 12 guys. The men gambling would give me tips for the sandwiches and sometimes rub my head for luck. I was eight or nine years old when I started helping my dad. It was a pretty good street education, and I learned a lot about how to run a game. Soon, I was running my own card and craps games at school; we'd play for nickels and dimes. I was the "house," putting up the money and I can still remember the odds on each roll: Five and nine were 3-to-2 odds, six and four were 2-to-1, six and eight were 6-to-5. Snake eyes and sevens, you lost your money. Running games is such an easy way to make money that I did it until I was 60 years old. However, today I don't even bother. I live a few miles from a casino now and hardly ever go. I like playing cards and craps, but I'm not a habitual gambler. To make money you can't really be a gambler; and you can't make money if you don't run your games well, either. I used to tell my dad to not serve the players any beer, to just give them food. When you start including drinking, you include problems: guys start yelling, arguing and fighting, and soon there goes the game — and your money. He'd look at me and tell me that I didn't know what I was talking about. But I'd seen enough to know the difference that alcohol makes in a situation.

Both of my parents were alcoholics. When I was nine years old, the family would drive into Boston to do the weekly shopping at the market. We'd get back in the car to head home and they'd pull into a bar. Here we are, me the oldest at nine years of age, sitting in the car and screwing around with my brothers and sisters while we waited for our parents to tie one on! They always drove home drunk, and as soon as they got in the car the arguments would start and they'd continue all the way home and into the house. One drunk goading another. It was terrible. They were terrible.

To help cope with my situation I tried my best to make things humorous. I liked to laugh, and I liked to make people laugh. I'm the same way today. Some people think I'm a prick, but they don't really know me. I say what's on my mind, I tell it like it is and I usually try to say it with some humour. If you don't like it, screw it. That's the way I was, the way I am, and the way I always will be.

Playing practical jokes is a huge part of who I am, even today. It started early, on the street, and continued into the classroom. I used to take a water pistol to public school and while the teacher would be reading to the class, I'd squirt the water pistol at him. And the teacher used to blame the kid that I sat behind. He had to take all the heat, all the time. I was a little devil. I remember this one incident from Grade 5 like it was yesterday. There was an empty room across the hall from our homeroom in elementary school. It was April Fool's Day and this other kid and I — Wallace Wood, I'll never forget his name — took everything from our room and put it in the room across in the hall. We took everything and put it in exactly the right order, we even hung all the pictures in the other room exactly like they were hanging in our homeroom. When the teacher came to homeroom there's nothing in there! He was furious. It was hilarious, and became a famous incident in the school. We eventually had to fess up because they were going to keep the entire class after school and the other kids were going to kick the shit out of us. But I didn't care about coming clean, it was that funny.

I always found myself in funny scenarios. I can remember running errands to Kennedy's, a store near us. They made their own peanut butter and they scooped it into containers right there. I knew I wouldn't get enough peanut butter to eat at home, so I would open the container and eat some. After I was done, I would take the peanut butter and turn it upside down, so it would run to the top and sit against the lid. But when you do that you create an air pocket. At home, my parents would stick the knife in the peanut butter to test it and it would go "thwuuup" with a big suction sound. I'd say, really surprised, "Hey, they cheated us at the store!"

There was another time I was supposed to go to the store and purchase an electric frying pan with the S&H food stamps my parents had saved up. As I was walking through the store I spotted some Oreo cookies, which were in vogue at the time. I'd never had any store-bought cookies in my life, so I thought I'd be pretty clever and I took a package of Oreos and stuck it inside the frying pan, under the lid. When I gave it to the guy at the counter, he flipped it over and all cookies all fell out! Of course the store called home and I got my ass whooped, again.

I wasn't proud of being poor and I was willing to work hard so I wouldn't stay poor. I realize now that as a child I didn't want to be dependent on anyone, how could I? My parents didn't give two shits about me or my brothers and sisters. So, I took care of myself. I began working all the time, and I hustled too, both long before I was a teenager.

By the time I was nine I would raid the lobster traps all the way across town in Gloucester, Massachusetts, and then bring the lobsters back downtown and sell them on the streets at Quincy Market. When I was 11, I had three paper routes, one in the morning, one in the afternoon and another on Sundays, which was the big newspaper day in the United States. I also started working on a farm around then too. Working hard and long at an honest job was much better than coming home and getting beaten, although I didn't think of it that way at the time. So I stayed out and worked. But, you know what? They still beat me — for coming home late, because I was at work!

One Christmas I was collecting the weekly fees for the *Boston Record-American* and this guy gives me a quarter and says, "Merry Christmas, keep the change." The paper cost 21 cents a week. I was a wise-guy kid and said, "Just a minute sir," then gave *him* the four cents back and said, "Merry Christmas to *you*." He called my father and of course my father beat the shit out of me for being a smart ass.

I had the paper routes because I knew that having even a little bit of money was better than having no money. I delivered the *Record-American* in the morning, and the Waltham News Tribune in the afternoon. It was 21 cents a week for the customer and I made two bucks a week for delivering 30 papers. The Sunday route I had was at the Catholic church, selling papers out of a cart. I'd go into the church office and deliver about 20 big, thick Sunday papers at 15 cents per paper. I kept all of the money because I had stolen the bundle of papers. Yeah, it was wrong. I know. I had to make my own decisions and it wasn't easy in my situation. I hate the word "stealing," it sticks to you. I stole for the sake of caring for myself because I wasn't being taken care of. I didn't think there was any right or wrong about it. I just didn't have any money — none at all. I was like Robin Hood: I stole from the rich to give to the poor, and the poor was me.

I've always felt that my theft was for survival. Yes I stole money, but I was also willing to work hard for it too.

Outside of delivering papers, my first real job was picking radishes at Vincent's Farm. The farm was in town about two miles from our place and I'd walk along the railroad tracks to get there. The Vincents had about 200 acres of vegetables, and I worked there all summer long for 25 cents an hour. I remember cutting celery, pulling weeds and working all night long to move the watering hoses to help distribute water to the crops during drought season. My parents kept the money I made, so once in a while I'd erase the numbers on my pay stub and change them to try to score an extra dollar for myself. They'd figure it out right away and they'd kick the shit out of me. The deal was that my money was supposed to be saved away as a college fund. That's what they said, but when I got to college there was nothing. My sister Carol started working when she was 14 and they screwed her out of money, too.

Besides the farm and the games, I tried my hand at a couple of other jobs. For a couple of years, I'd hitchhike into Boston and sell hot dogs at Fenway Park. Hot dog boys made about a nickel for every hot dog sold. But I wasn't very good at the job because I loved watching baseball so much. Ted Williams was a huge hero of mine, and I'd watch him through the screen during batting practice along with two other of my favourites on the Sox, Bobby Doerr and Dom DiMaggio. One day a supervisor pulled me aside and asked me if I planned on selling any hot dogs that day. I asked him why, and he said, "I gave you a full tray an hour ago and you still have the originals." It was totally unlike me to not maximize the profit on those hot dogs. That's how much Ted Williams mattered to me.

I heard from some of the guys that you could make good money being a caddy at the golf course, so naturally pretty soon I was out at the golf course. The very first time I'm caddying the guy asks me for some advice on club selection: "What club do I use here?" he said. "I don't know," I answered. Then he asks, "How long is this hole?" and I answered, "I don't know." Then he said, "You don't know much do you?" and I said, "Neither do you. What the hell are you doing out here playing golf?" I didn't caddy for long.

My type of humour also fit really well into my story telling. It started out on the street, where a bunch of us would always be hanging around making cracks and it continued right through my adult life in football and, especially, wrestling. For instance, at Christmas time we'd have the food in our house — everything was centred around food — but there were no toys. One thing I never got, and still don't, is how after the holidays teachers would make you write a composition, or stand up and tell the class what you got for Christmas. I call that downright cruel. I wasn't really proud of being poor, so I'd make stuff up about what I got. And I made up some doozies because my parents never gave us anything. I'd tell completely fabricated stories about the way my dad was, to play him up and make him look good. Like, I'd say, "My dad gave me a shotgun for Christmas. And I was on the street and traded it for a watch and when I went home my dad said, 'Hey where's a-you shotgun?' And I said, 'Hey, papa I traded that beautiful gun for a beautiful watch.' He said, 'Whatsa gonna happen one-a day you get-a married and come-a home and you-a find your wife with another man? You gonna say, 'Scusa…time is up?' Yeah, I made it up completely out of the blue. I'm probably 13 or 14 at time. I told a pretty good story and I liked the audience too, even back then. I'd tell lies, make up stories about my life. I've always said that a story not worth colouring is not worth telling and I've taken that to the *n*th degree. On the block, there'd be a bunch of kids, eight or ten of us, always on the street making a move, whistling at the girls. I can remember telling crazy stories when we were young about broads — sorry, that's what we called girls and women in those days and in that crowd — and about how ugly they were and the way we treated them. There was a lot of chatter around the card games when I was a kid too and some real characters at the table, so I absorbed a lot of that kind of talk at a very young age.

My life at home was the shits and I think, now, that I developed story telling as a way of covering it up.

By the time I was a teenager I was beginning to realize that I couldn't live at home any more. Not if I wanted to survive. My father was still beating me, but he was becoming leery of me. I had starting playing football at high school, and I was working out in the Waltham Boys Club like a maniac. No one else worked out back then, but I had an idea in my mind of being totally independent, and becoming stronger and tougher was part of it. Being good at sports became my rebellion. Sports were becoming my guiding light, without them I'd have probably ended up in jail.

When I was 16 I finally got tired of getting beat up and made the decision to leave the house for good. I got a room upstairs in my aunt's house. Her name was Fiona Dinapoli, and she was my father's sister. She said I could come and live with her family; they were the cousins who ignored me, but she liked me. My aunt knew her brother and knew what the problem was. I thought my father was going to kill me for leaving, but it turned out he didn't give a damn where I was. My mother? She never said a word.

I didn't see my parents much after that. I later heard my dad would be in the bar when I was at Notre Dame and our games were on TV, bragging about my football playing. I'm sure it was only so the other guys would buy him beer. He never once came to see me play: not in high school, college or pro.

My dad died 25 years ago. I didn't go to the funeral. And when my mom died a few years ago, I didn't go to her funeral either. I had no reason to go, I raised myself. They treated me like I was a "nigger," in the most ugly and hateful sense of the word. Once I left home I had no respect for my parents. They didn't want me, so I didn't want them.

The House on Francis Street

Angelo's sister doesn't remember the exact day her big brother left the house. "I've probably wiped that out," says Carol Roberg. "There's big blocks of my childhood I don't remember. I like to characterize my whole childhood as a toxic shame. I was ashamed that I had a big nose, I was ashamed that I had big feet, and I was very ashamed of the black part of me, the way my mother looked, the way she talked, the way she acted. She was not educated at all. She should have never had children because she taught us things that were opposite of what was real.

"What our parents said about Angelo after he left, was 'Oh, he's a big shot. He doesn't care about anybody.' That was hard for the rest of us kids because he was our hero. I remember when he was living there, ironing his pants and he'd give us a dime or a quarter.

"If I could get a dime," Angelo chimes in.

Carol, the fourth of the half-dozen children, is six years younger than Angelo and is by far his closest sibling. In fact, they both say they're the only members of the family who have a real relationship. "I think it was the football," Carol says. "Ang would have me up to Hamilton — I'd drive all the way in my new '63 Chevy — and I remember what a star he was there. He also took me to the Schenley Awards one year. When we were kids, none of us got really close because every one of us was just trying to survive."

Like her older brother, Carol describes a Mosca household simmering in alcohol, anger, fear and shame. Unlike Angelo, over time she recognized the relationship between her upbringing and her actions later in life, and has spent a great deal of time analyzing it. Angelo, on the other hand, preferred to bury his pain and drive right through it. "The past is the past," has been one of his lifelong mantras. According to him, it was only in his early 70s that he began to draw the connection between his upbringing and the adult Angelo Mosca. Even then, if he mentions his childhood too often he feels like he's making excuses for his behaviour. Angelo wants to take responsibility for his life, not blame it on someone else. But there is no doubt that the conditions on Francis Street were not emotionally healthy.

"It was absolutely chaotic," Carol says. "The alcoholism. We'd be driving home from the market after doing grocery shopping on a Saturday and they'd take us all into a bar, and all six of us kids would have to sit at a booth with our hands folded. It happened so many times.

"Our house on Francis Street was a Cape Cod style and divided into four units, left and right, up and down. We had one of the upstairs apartments and our bathroom adjoined our neighbours' bathroom. We could hear everything that was going on in there. There were three bedrooms: our mother and father had a bedroom, the boys had a bedroom and the girls had a bedroom. There was an eat-in kitchen but no living room. And that was it — for eight of us.

"After getting groceries, our parents would be fighting all the way home, yelling and screaming and the kids would all start crying. We'd traipse upstairs with the groceries, but not before our father would threaten to drive us all into the ocean. We kids would all be hungry, so we'd start lining up as my father sliced the bread and sliced the provolone. We were like a bunch of animals, lining up to be fed, and all of a sudden he would go off and throw all the groceries on the floor and stomp on them and start beating us. This is a man that didn't just have anger, he had rage. You've heard of blind rage? I can remember one time when he was beating one of the kids — it might have been Angelo — he slipped between my father's legs and my father was still beating the floor.

"My mother was as bad as he was. We had a field not far from us and she would make us cut down the switches from the field and then she would beat us with them. I think my mother was mentally ill, looking back on it. She must have had agoraphobia because she hardly ever left the house. She sat in the window and made the children do all the chores. And she was a provoker: she'd hit my father, and also tell him stories about how bad we were so he'd hit us. The cops were down to our place a lot. My mother would provoke my father and many times he'd be on top of her with a knife at her throat.

"They had the weirdest ideas. They could yell and scream at the table but the kids had to be silent. The expression they used, and I don't know where they got it, was 'You're competing with God when you eat.' What in the world does that mean? Angelo sat to the right of my father. Ang would say something when we weren't supposed to talk at the table and he'd backhand him, and there'd be blood coming out of his mouth and all of us kids would be whimpering, crying in our spaghetti. My father would say 'Shut up or you'll get it too.' He'd flinch and raise his arm just for fun, to get a reaction out of all of us. There were times when he'd throw the meal out of the window if the spaghetti was cooked too much. It had to be al dente. Chaos, just chaos. And we were always told that nobody wanted us in their house. We weren't allowed to go into friend's houses or anything like that because they didn't want anyone coming into our house because it was such chaos."

Being taught to hide and be ashamed of their African-American heritage had varied effects on the Mosca children. Angelo crammed it into the recesses of his memory and never told anyone about it, not even his wives. Carol essentially told them, on his behalf. Angelo practiced what was then called "passing." That is, passing himself off as purely white when he actually had significant African-American bloodlines. Carol began working in a soda fountain at age 14 and like Angelo, gave all her wages to her parents. She later was in the military, sold real estate, studied at college and had a responsible job for a major corporation that eventually sent her to California. "I had a lot of things going on," she recalls. "Racing, racing, running away from everything." She eventually found a higher calling, went to Bible college and started her own urban rescue mission and is starting another one in Los Angeles with her husband Jerry. "I was very ashamed, and I'm ashamed of some of the things I've done regarding the family," she says. "And I'm sure Angelo was too, but big bro has always kept it locked up inside. Our sister Becky is the shortest one in the family, only about 5-foot-2, and a terrific woman. She got married very young and she had six children. But she chose to tell people she was black from when she was very young. She thought it was very cool. She could be taken either way, by the way she looked. She came out to

California to visit me one time, and introducing her to people I never said, 'This is my sister,' I'd just say, 'This is Becky.' And of course she knew what was going on. I apologized to her, but her kids never forgave me. And we were all ashamed of my little brother, Mike, because he looked African-American. Nobody wanted anything to do with him. And then my sister June, a year younger than me, was probably ashamed of me because she was really fair skinned. She changed her name and cut ties with the family altogether. She and I had an apartment together before I moved away. She came to see us before I got married (29 years ago) and I didn't hear from her again until she surprised me by phoning me in August of 2011."

The Mosca children toed the line as much as they could because their father was continually threatening to abandon them as he did his first family. "He kept saying 'I already put five on the state and I'll put six more on the state,'" Carol recalls. "We didn't know what the state was but as bad as it was at home we didn't want to be put on the state."

Carol recalls Angelo as a good student who didn't really have to study because he had a photographic memory. She was impressed by the way he was always working and like her siblings, wept when he was locked out of the house, then beaten, after coming home from working two or three jobs.

"I think he was pretty angry as a young man," she says. "And so he got into some fights and stuff like that. He also got married at a pretty young age and I think he was looking for a mother figure. I'm pretty sure that was it. She was a wonderful, wonderful, woman and she was a mother to him.

"I'm very proud of his accomplishments, but I'm most proud of the way he's created family, the blended family and the grandkids. And how he's recently become more open about his past. He was never like that."

Carol also thinks the abuse at home actually may have made Angelo a better football player, because he could aggressively channel his anger in an acceptable pursuit. His first line coach, Tony Zullo, feels the same way. "He's one of the best football players I ever coached," says Zullo, now retired on Long Island. "He was half-white and half-black, but the kids on the team never picked on him for that, I wouldn't permit that as a coach. I think it was actually good for our team. At that time there weren't many mixed kids like that. He was very tough and always did more than we expected. He was a hard-working kid. It was his ability which made him such a great player, I don't think he used being a mulatto as a way to increase his ability, but I think he maybe felt more at home on the field than at home and it also helped make him tougher. And he was a very tough kid."

Angelo's parents never saw him play football, in fact they never came to any of the kids' schools, not even for parent-teacher interviews. And that was fine with their children. They had been taught to be ashamed, and they were ashamed of their parents.

"It was bizarre," Carol says. "We were known either for the drunkenness, the alcoholism, or for Angelo's fame. We were really proud of Angelo because he was a big star. I never thought consciously of it, but it made you a bit of a somebody to be Angelo's younger sister. He was the legend around town."

CHAPTER TWO

Discovering Football

THE LEGEND AROUND TOWN WAS not living at home and, believe it or not, I was working at the police station. I don't know if the people at school or that I knew in town were even aware of where I was living.

I didn't tell the teachers or the principals that I wasn't living with my family and they couldn't figure out anything wasn't right from looking at my academic performance. I was a good student, and my marks were unbelievable — 90 or 95 per cent — and I don't know why. I didn't study much. None of us ever had any help with learning from our parents. We never got help with homework and we were never read to. In fact, my parents couldn't really read or write themselves. One thing I do find unbelievable is that my parents did eventually teach themselves to read, on their own. And then my dad read every detective novel he could get his hands on.

I used to fill in all the permission forms from school myself, and then sign my parents' names. I couldn't care less if they could read or not, I just knew that they wouldn't fill in the forms. They just wouldn't. So, for instance, when I wanted to play football I brought the papers home from school, because

I was still living at home in grade nine, and I filled them in myself.

There was no such thing as Pop Warner football, or minor football, when I was growing up. It was all street stuff in the neighbourhood; the Italians against the Irish. Organized football started in high school, and that is when I started playing, in Grade 9 at Waltham High School. By then I was a 6-foot-3, 215-pound kid. The coaches saw me and asked me to come out and play. From the very first hit in practice, I was sold. I loved every minute of the physical contact. When I look back on it, the physicality was probably a way for me to retaliate and get even with my father. The thought would never have occurred to me at the time: I just loved the hitting. But it makes perfect sense when I think about it now.

I didn't think about football as a way to keep me straight or keep me disciplined, but now I'm sure it was football that kept me out of deep trouble. Some very tough guys from my neighbourhood ended up taking the wrong turn. When we were 17, two of my pretty good friends, Hal Kelley and Tom Giralumo, robbed a house and ended up murdering a guy. They were lucky they didn't get hanged, but they did get life in jail. That was more than 50 years ago and both of them are still in prison. Football kept me on the straight and narrow — although I still hustled, so it wasn't that narrow. I loved the game and I liked the idea of having responsibility on the field and to the team.

And I liked the whole conditioning aspect of football. I was before my time when it came to working out. What gave me the idea to work out was seeing the "Strong Man" lifting weights at the circus. I was never sure if the guy was lifting real weights, but some of them had to be real, and I was impressed. So I began lifting weights when it wasn't even fashionable; even when I went to Notre Dame I would go into the weight room and find dust on the barbells.

I remembered seeing the Charles Atlas ads that would run on the back of comic books. The ads were in a comic book style and featured some version of the story where a 98-pound weakling would get sand kicked on him by a big tough bully at the beach — right in front his girlfriend. The 98-pounder would then send away for the Charles Atlas kit, and soon enough he would beat up the guy who originally kicked sand on him — right in front of his girlfriend! So, I wrote away to Charles Atlas for the information. What I got back was written instructions on how to work out, like: how to bench-press, how to squat and how to make weights out of cement. We didn't have weights at Waltham High, so some of my buddies and I made them ourselves with the Atlas guide. I first saw real weights at the Boys Club in Waltham. The boxer Jack Dempsey had given the club money for the weights, but there weren't too many of them.

But weightlifting was never enough. I met a guy named Martin Cavanaugh at the Boys Club who convinced me I needed to run in addition to lifting weights. He was a marathon runner, but I was way too big for that. By the time I went to Notre Dame I was doing 11 miles in my runs. I was in great shape. I used to run the stadium steps at the high school, and later they made us do that at Notre Dame. In fact, when I first got to Hamilton I used to run those long steps up the mountain at Wentworth Street.

I further supplemented my workouts with a job I got at a cement block factory. Mortar weighs 70 pounds a bag, and ordinary cement weighs 90 pounds, a difference I learned from my dad. I'd unload the cement cart and I'd carry two bags of cement at a time — that's 180 pounds, multiple times a day! I knew that if you were strong, it helped you be independent so I did a lot of things when I was young to make that happen. I'd do the physical labour at the Vincent Farm, which was owned by my friend's family, and right after I moved into my aunt's place I got a job at the Waltham Police Station as a janitor. It wasn't as much physical labour as some of the other jobs but it was 35 hours a week and I had to go to school and then sometimes have football practice after school, sometimes basketball practice. I suggested to the police that I have my own hours. I really wanted that job. I got up at 4 a.m. to work at the police station and sometimes I would have to go back after practice, as long as I put in the 35 hours. I had a helluva motor and I've never really slept in my life. I was making 40 bucks a week and that's big money in those days. My father was probably making only two dollars an hour, maybe $2.20. Plus I was doing some work on the farm too. From the time I'm 16, I'm carrying school, football, and basically a full-time job, plus whatever other work I can scrape up. But I liked my fun too, which did lead to the occasional jam. One summer I was driving from the farm implement company back to the Vincent Farm with a tractor on the back of the truck. It's summer and I see an air force guy from the local base hitchhiking so I pick him up. I don't realize it but when the guy climbs into the cab of the truck, he hits the lever for the back of the truck and it starts dumping the tractor. They just spent about a thousand bucks on the tractor and I was dumping it on the highway! I got my ass in some hot freakin' water on that one. You weren't supposed to have anyone in the truck with you at all, so I made up some real crazy story and got away with it.

I was a big kid in high school, and it was difficult to find equipment for a player my size, especially shoes. In Grade 9 I was already a size 15, but the largest football cleats they had were 13. So, I squeezed into them for nearly three years. My feet were sore all the time in practice and in games, which you didn't think about as long you could kick the shit out of somebody on the field. But during my senior year, Waltham High purchased a brand new pair of shoes from the Wilson sporting goods company. They were custom made and cost $27, which was a lot when shoes normally cost about $7. The funny thing is that I never really got to wear them because they were my backup pair and weren't broken in yet. After the season the Waltham Citizen's Bank put them on display in their front window where they would usually display art. The Waltham paper wrote a story after I had graduated about the Waltham trainer, Ken Harding, keeping my shoes and using them as an example whenever a new player came in and wanted special equipment. Ken would show the shoes to the player and say, "When you can fill these shoes, then you'll have a talking point." And I was a talking point in high school. Even 15 years after I left, my shoes made the paper again. Somebody called from Vermont in the fall of 1970 needing shoes for one of their players. The Wilson company got my shoes from Waltham High School for them and the school got three brand new pairs back in exchange.

The team I played for at Waltham was named the Red Crimson, and football was pretty big in the area. The booster club for the Waltham team, which was made up of town citizens, had more than 500 members; we had 10,000 or more fans show up to our big games. High school football is a different, bigger animal in the States than it is in Canada, and that was especially true when I played.

Waltham's head football coach was Joe Zeno, who played at Holy Cross and also played some pro. One time near the end of my high-school career he was quoted in the paper saying, "Angelo Mosca was the greatest schoolboy lineman I ever coached."

Our line coach was a very rugged guy named Tony Zullo. Tony was 29 years old, 5-foot-6 and about 285 pounds. He'd do the drills with us. I remember in line drills that he would get down underneath you and then he'd fire up and pop you in the nose with his knuckles. In the '50s we didn't have face-masks; our faces were wide open. Tony would get right in your face with his hands, and it would hurt — he made you want to get even with him. And that's the way he projected football to be; that's the way he wanted it: physical. We were taught to spear and to hit with our head. The message was to hit into an opponent's chin with your helmet. No one worried about head injuries.

Tony always said that his style of coaching embodied that old Marine adage, "to kill or be killed." It was Tony who taught me how to play like that. A lot of my success in the CFL I owe to Tony Zullo.

Many players didn't like my style because I played very phys-ical and very, very aggressive. But Tony taught me sound fun-damental techniques as well. When I arrived at Notre Dame they wondered where I had learned all of my techniques and fundamentals because what Tony had taught me was beyond what the Fighting Irish were doing. Tony taught me things like how to pull and use my leverage to my advantage, as well as how to use my hands effectively without holding. I had developed really quick hands that I used for the head slaps that became a huge part of my style in the CFL.

At Waltham I wore No. 31 and played tackle on both offence and defence. We had some really good teams. Most of them had a really big line and I was the biggest and toughest. I was named an All-Scholastic tackle three consecutive years from 1952–54, and in 1954 I was named co-captain of the All-Scholastic Team. Waltham never really had a city championship because we didn't have playoffs, but we played 11 or 12 games every year and never lost more than three. Our big game was on Thanksgiving, and we always played Somerville, our big rival. During the season we also played against Malden, Weston and Arlington. The main guy from Arlington was Tom McNeeley who ended up playing football at Michigan State and then boxing Floyd Patterson for the world heavyweight championship. I was All-Scholastic tackle in our league for three years running and when I made it for the second time in my junior year, the All-Scholastic quarterback was Don Allard of Somerville, and I played against him in the CFL about a decade later.

I was getting a lot of ink for playing football and basketball. My father, though, wasn't proud of me for it. He never liked when any of the kids received attention because he was worried that someone might find out that we were black — he wasn't worried for us, he was worried for himself. He was ashamed of himself for having a mixed-race family and he made all of us kids ashamed of our black heritage. Excelling in football created a lot of attention, and he didn't like that.

By the time it came to decide where I'd go to college, I had 60 scholarship offers. I had no help from any family members in choosing where I went to school. When the colleges would send a recruiter to town, I had them visit me at my aunt's place, or I'd meet them down the street from my parents' house. I lied all the time to recruiters about why my parents couldn't attend the meetings. I made all the decisions myself, and one of the decisions I made was that I'd take the colleges up on their offers and visit as many of them as I could. They were paying for it and it was a good chance to travel and see a bit of the world outside of Waltham. That's how I ended up going all the way out to California to visit USC. I was really nervous because it was my first time in an airplane, but when I got there, they set me up with girls because they really wanted me to come to USC.

The two big Boston Catholic schools, Boston College and Holy Cross, were after me too. When I was visiting these colleges as a high school senior I didn't have any money for new clothes and I was still growing like a weed. Holy Cross had me up to a banquet and the only clothes I had to wear were too small and worn out: I wore a size 48 jacket with the sleeves coming only about halfway down my forearm; I had a 19-inch neck but I was stuck wearing a 17-inch shirt, my pants had a hole in the crotch and my socks had holes in the heels, even the shoes I had were busted; they were what we used to call "dunlaf" shoes: done at the top and laughing at the bottom.

I wasn't used to eating in restaurants or at fancy affairs like banquets and when they brought the food I wasn't sure whether you held your fork in the left hand or the right; no one ever taught me these things. But I was smart enough to watch the people around me. I always had to figure out what other people already knew by looking around and not making a mistake. One thing I didn't quite figure out was that you don't order seconds at a banquet. When the food came at Holy Cross I just put my head down and went right at the steak. I finished it in a hurry, and then asked for a second one. The coach looked at me for a second and then yelled, "Bring this kid another steak!"

But getting a second steak wasn't enough to get me to Holy Cross. Notre Dame sent their scout, Joe Restic (who later became head coach of the Hamilton Tiger-Cats for a year) to come and see me. There was a guy I knew of from Natick, in the Boston area, named Frank Verachioni, who had played offensive tackle at Notre Dame and went on to play for the Pittsburgh Steelers for about 12 years. Since I was also a tackle, that was another selling point, and Joe made sure Frank spoke to me about accepting their offer. Notre Dame also had an Italian quarterback that I really liked. His name was Ralph Guglielmi, and he took a liking to me. When I was in South Bend touring the campus, he took me into his room and showed me the life of a Notre Dame footballer. Another major draw that Notre Dame had was that they were the only college in America to have all of their games on national TV. So, with all of that, in February of 1955, I accepted Notre Dame; after all those years of playing in the playgrounds against the Irish, I was now joining them.

A month before I decided Notre Dame was where I'd play my college football, a newspaper reporter interviewed me and told me that I'd been chosen as a high school All-American by The Sporting News. The magazine published a list of the 60 best high school football players from the entire country. Not only was I on the list, but they sent me a plane ticket to come later in the year to Memphis, Tennessee, where there was a banquet honouring the All-Americans and a showcase game to play at Crump Stadium: the 30 Eastern all-Americans against the 30 Western All-Americans.

That game was going to be played in August, after I graduated and just before I was supposed to start at Notre Dame. In May, I had a horrible accident at school. It was pretty close to graduation and I was running down the corridor to go get my tuxedo for the high school prom. I was excited, I guess, and I missed the doorframe when I went to open it. My hand went right through the glass on the door and sheared my forearm like a peeled banana. It took 88 stitches to close the cut, and I was lucky I was ready to play in the All-American Game. My parents didn't have the money to pay the doctor, Dr. Cohen, but he was such a good guy that he took care of me for free. He was wonderful to me. I'd never had my own suit jacket in my life — one that fit — and he bought me one. He did it so that I could take a prep course in derivatives and calculus in Washington, D.C. It was a six-week cram course, and it was an entry requirement for the Naval Academy, who were trying to recruit me. You needed a personal note from the State Senate to take that exam, and I got it and passed the exam. I had already accepted at Notre Dame, but decided to take the course because the Academy was paying for it and I thought it would be good experience. I liked learning things.

After we took the exam they brought us across the Chesapeake Bay into Annapolis, Maryland and as we're walking I heard this drum roll. *Budda bum, brrrdudda bum. Budda bum, brrrdudda bum.* "What's that?" I asked the coach. And he said, "They're marching to dinner." When I left the coach I said, "Nobody's going to tell me to march to dinner. I'm marching my ass right out of here." And I did.

A couple of weeks later I took a plane to Memphis for the All-American game. We made a stop in Chicago and while I was walking through the airport I saw another guy about my age. He just looked like a football player. Our eyes met and I said, "Hey, you goin' to Memphis?" And he was. He was wondering the same thing about me, too. I had all black clothes on and I guess I looked the part to him. He was a lineman from International Falls, Minnesota, and his name was Bronko Nagurski, Jr. It was a very famous name in the 1950s because his father Bronko Sr., had been a legend at Minnesota, where he made All-American at fullback and defensive tackle, and he was a huge star for the Chicago Bears. Bronko Sr. became a charter member of the Pro Football Hall of Fame, and he wrestled pro, too. Not only was Bronko Jr. going to be in the same high school All-American Game that I was in, we ended up playing together at Notre Dame and for the Hamilton Tiger-Cats, too. In fact, he married a Hamilton girl, Beverly Cudmore. All of our lives he used to laugh about meeting me for the first time in the airport and me grunting, "Hey, you goin' to Memphis?"

Bronko and I flew to Memphis and took a taxi downtown to one of the world's great hotels: The Hotel Gayoso. I remember it like it was yesterday. It reminded me of the hotel in Richmond, Virginia, with the big, sweeping stairway where scenes for *Gone With the Wind* were shot. I thought this was really cool. It was the first time I ever got to stay in a hotel. There was a bunch of old-time southern people sitting around the lobby in white suits, dressed to the nines. It was a classic scene and one that was very different than what I was used to. And that's when I first noticed the signs on the drinking fountains. Coming down to Memphis I knew that the south was really prejudiced against blacks, and I knew about the Jim Crow laws, so I wasn't surprised that there were signs enforcing the laws, but I was surprised by the way the signs looked. They weren't big like I had imagined them; instead they were just big enough to get your attention. The wording got your attention, too. The signs said, "Colored" instead of "Black." Needless to say I followed the instructions of the "White" signs.

Bronko and I checked in, and it turned out that we were roommates — like it was fate that we'd already met and hit it off. Bronko was supposed to play on the Western side, but he wasn't able to play because he injured his arm playing baseball. He was a farm boy and I was a city slicker. After we got comfortable I decide to pull a rib on him. I used to be really good at ripping phone books in half. You have to have strength but there's also a trick to it, and I used to show off once in a while. I'd make a big production out of the whole thing, making it look like it was really difficult. So, I took our phone book off the desk and tore it right in half and threw it out the window. Bronko gets this look on his face like he can't believe what I just did and he yells, "Noooooooooo!" as he scrambles to save the book from falling out the window. Turns out his plane ticket home was in the book! All I can remember is the look on his face, I can't even remember if he ever got the ticket back. He did get home, I know that much.

Bronko and I had a wild time in Memphis. I got the bright idea to set off a smoke bomb in the hotel lobby to piss off all the southern suits. I put it behind a statue and suddenly the whole lobby was loaded with orange smoke. Everyone started coughing and the firemen had to come in. It was one hell of a commotion.

One day in downtown Memphis two girls picked Bronko and I up in their car. The car wasn't working properly and I suggested that they needed to take it to a garage. "What do I tell them?" the girl who was driving asked. "Just tell them there's something wrong with your foo-foo valve," I said. I thought

Bronko would fall out of the car laughing. "What's the foo-foo valve?" she asked. And I said, "It's right next to the Finnegan pin." I made her repeat it to me several times so she got it right. She drove into the garage and said "foo-foo valve" and "Finnegan pin" and I thought I would freakin' die.

The entire time I was in Memphis I practiced "passing," which means passing as if I were white. I drank out of the white fountains, ate at white restaurants, sat at the front of the bus, rode the white trains. The experience gave me a really strong idea of what it was like to sit on that side of the fence, and believe me, it was a fence — a real barrier. I wasn't nervous about it, in fact I was very confident, and I attribute that to my athleticism and my size, as well as the fact that I acted a gentleman in those situations. I found it hilarious because I'm having the greatest laugh in the world fooling every fucking hypocrite in Memphis. My sister and I joked about how we could make a movie out of it. But I knew it was serious.

I played tackle on both sides of the ball in the All-American game, and they chose me as captain of the East team. Crump Stadium was sold out at 25,000 people for the game. We won, and I made the first tackle of the game. I was listed at 234 pounds and I was playing over a defensive tackle who was 6-foot-3 and 230. They ran behind me for the first touchdown, and in the third quarter I tackled a guy downfield on a punt, he fumbled and I recovered. I thought I was away but they got me from behind.

Notre Dame coach Terry Brennan was the principal speaker at the All-American luncheon afterward, and he said that I played really well. There were seven players in that game who had been accepted at Notre Dame: Gene Saxon who was from Memphis, Frank Geremia from Sacramento, Jim Just of

Milwaukee, Bob Wituska of Minnesota, Jim Schaaf of Erie, Pennsylvania — a longtime friend of mine who later worked for the Kansas City Chiefs for 22 years, including 12 as general manager — and then there was Bronko and me.

That game in Memphis was the last time I played football before college. And it was at college that I started to get into trouble.

THREE

Not Your Ordinary Joe College

I WAS 18 YEARS OLD WHEN I left Waltham, Massachusetts, for South Bend, Indiana, and the most famous football campus in North America: Notre Dame. It was *the* school at the time for recruiting, and you felt important just because you were at Notre Dame on a football scholarship. Every Catholic boy wanted to play there. And it wasn't like just anyone could get selected: for sure you had to be a good football player, but you also had to have decent marks. Notre Dame was the only college that had all of their games televised, and there was even a movie about Notre Dame's legendary coach Knute Rockne — everyone wanted to "win one for the Gipper." The Fighting Irish had a rabid fan base, from coast to coast and around the world. Today, kids say Notre Dame isn't such a big deal. All the other big schools are on TV, but back then, Notre Dame was *it*.

Frank Leahy wasn't head coach when I started at Notre Dame, he had passed the job to Terry Brennan, but he still had an enormous amount of power at the school. Leahy played for Knute Rockne in the late 1920s and coached some great Irish teams in the late '40s and early '50s. He was incredibly influential on Irish football. In fact Rockne and Leahy still stand one-two in winning percentage for Division I football coaches. We also had an assistant coach named Jack Zili, who oddly enough was a coach with the Tiger-Cats in 1972, my last year. The football world can be a small place.

When I arrived at Notre Dame I was boarding with a teammate, but I eventually had my own room in a dorm. All of our meals and our courses were paid for and we ate together as a team at the training table. No one was paid any money, which made me feel a little uncomfortable; from the past few years in Waltham I knew that to have any kind of independence you needed a little cash. I wrote home and asked my parents for the money that they were supposed to have put aside for me for college. My dad wrote back and told me not to ask for money. In the envelope they stuffed twenty bucks. After all those years of hard work, the only thing I had to show for it financially was $20. I should have known better than to think my parents were actually going to save my money for me.

I was a pretty good student and was passing everything. I was taking regular classes in a general arts course. Math was going to be my major. I had never gone to Catholic school growing up, so Notre Dame was really different for me and I was already losing interest in the classroom. I was bored. I used to tell the priests, "I gotta go to Heaven, because this is like going through Hell."

Football and religion were everything on campus. The football team had to go to mass twice a week. I was familiar with church because my parents sent me when I was young. They didn't go, however, and then I started skipping it myself. I learned Catholicism on my own because I knew that blacks weren't Catholics. But I never really enjoyed church. Mass at Notre Dame was compulsory, but I suspect the coaches knew that I probably wasn't going to go, so they made me an altar boy. I hated it at the time, but I see the humour in it now: me, an altar boy! I brought some humour to the job to help pass the time — at least I thought I was funny — I used to drive the Notre Dame priests nuts. Notre Dame was pretty traditional; during communion when the priest put the host on the tongue of a parishioner, the altar boy had to hold a tray underneath the parishioner's chin. When it came time for me to hold the tray and the football players were taking communion, I would drive the tray up and hit the guys in the throat. They would always start gagging and one guy almost choked. The priests wanted to kill me. But somehow they always liked me. I guess it was my sense of humour that got me by. Six or seven years after I left Notre Dame I went back and was walking across the campus when I ran into one of the priests. "Remember me Father?" I asked, and he said, "How the Hell could I ever forget?"

As a freshman, I couldn't play on the varsity team because of NCAA rules. You only had three years of eligibility and it wasn't until a long time after that that you could play all four years at college. So, we practiced against the varsity every day, and that was tough. Practices started at 4 p.m. (so you could go to school) and lasted for a couple of hours, and the varsity squad used to really beat the crap out of us. One of the halfbacks on the varsity was Paul Hornung, and the next year, when I did get to play, he won the Heisman Trophy.

One day, we were in a scrimmage and I was playing offensive tackle. We were working on pass blocking and I missed my block. The defence bounced right through and sacked the guy we had at quarterback. Leahy came steaming out. When I crouched into my stance for the next play he gave me a hard kick in the ass. Then he moved me back seven yards to where the quarterback would normally be. He called off the other offensive linemen and he had the front four converge on me while I was standing there all on my own. The guys all crushed me and I was black and blue all over. Leahy said, "Now you know what it's like back there when you miss your block."

It was really tough not playing all year. All my years at Waltham I never missed a game and now as a freshmen I just had to watch. It was brutal. During the home games, the team gave the freshmen the job of selling programs at the stadium. Everyone was supposed to take a package of 40 programs, but I'd pick the one with 50, sell them all and only give back enough money for 40. Good Catholic boy, eh? But, do you think I was the only one?

It sucked having to be on the sidelines, but at least the games we were watching were good: the 1955 varsity team didn't allow a point in their first three games. And, until they got clobbered in their last game of the season, 42–20 by USC in California, they were, 7–1.

The next year, as a sophomore, I got to play. Prior to the season Coach Brennan had come to Boston for a coaching conference and told the Waltham newspaper that our freshman squad was one of the best ever at Notre Dame. He also said that I had done a good job on the practice squad: "We expect big things of Angelo. I don't know what he can do and for that matter, I don't think he knows what he can do yet himself. I know Mosca has got a little more serious and he seems to be maturing."

Unfortunately, we lost our first game in my sophomore year, 19–13 at SMU, and we didn't do too well after that, going 2–8 on the year. We won our next game after losing to SMU, which gave us confidence, but we lost five in a row, including two drub-bings: 40–0 by Oklahoma and 48–8 by Iowa. Given our record, I was very surprised that our halfback Paul Hornung won the Heisman. Jim Brown finished fifth in the voting and he did everything at Syrcause but peel the ball and eat it. Syracuse was the best team in the East, and despite the fact that they lost the Cotton Bowl, Brown was still named MVP of the game. But, there had never been a black player win the Heisman. The next season, Ernie Davis — who was also at Syracuse — became the first black player to win the Heisman, but Brown should have won the year before. Hornung is still the only Heisman winner to have played for a team that lost more than seven games.

While I was playing football at Notre Dame I met a woman named Darlene Goodrich. She was from South Bend and had come home from Indiana University. One thing led to another and before you know it, we were married; I can't even remem-ber whose idea it was. I didn't have to get married. I think I was just a lonely young guy and I thought I was in love. I needed somebody who loved me and I had never got any love at home, that's for damned sure. We got married at the end of the 1957 school year in the church at Notre Dame. What a dumb thing to do. Nobody came from my family because I didn't invite them. I made an excuse to Darlene and her family about why they couldn't come. I was living a dual life: in one half I'm get-ting married, in the other, I'm dealing with being mixed-race, and feeling ashamed of myself and upset with my parents. I couldn't even bring myself to tell my wife about my family.

What a great lady Darlene was, and she became the mother of my three children. She was sharper than I was, and I sure didn't appreciate her enough. She died of cancer in 1989, but we'd been divorced for a long time by then.

My marriage to Darlene was one of the things that ended my scholarship. Notre Dame didn't want its scholarship athletes to be married. They weren't a coed university, and it was a stipulation of my scholarship that I couldn't be married. I can't remember if I knew that at the time. Lots of schools allowed you to be married and have a football scholarship, but not Notre Dame.

Notre Dame was against something else I was doing with my life, too.

I was running card games on campus and making book on pro football games for the other students, which I also learned how to do from my father. I did the bookmaking with a partner and we had about three or four hundred customers, so the odds were pretty good in our favour that we'd win. I was making more money than I knew what to do with, and I was pretty open about it because I was so young. Cards and bookmaking had always been a presence my life and I never really thought of it as illegal or wrong. It was the world I knew and it was just natural for me to do it. What I didn't figure on was someone squealing. When the school found out, I got in trouble, big trouble. Father McGregor, the chief disciplinarian, called me to his office and revoked my scholarship. So, I only played one year with the Irish.

It was before the start of what should have been my third year, before football practice had begun, and I found myself with nowhere to go. I was married and I had got kicked out of school. I had a summer job on the railroad in South Bend, just labour work, putting logs on a tram and pushing them into the spot where they made railway ties. The logs were made of oak, and let me tell you, they were fucking heavy! Then I got a job working for a guy named Julius Tucker who was a big backer of Notre Dame football players and was very supportive of all the players, including a guy like me who got kicked off the team. The players used to go to his house to eat and play cards. Julius owned a stationery store in South Bend and I worked there from four in the afternoon until nine at night. But I was also working for the city clocking traffic, getting an average count of cars per hour in certain spots. I'd go in at 7 a.m., do my shift, then go over to Julius' store, so I was getting double ended pay. I was a sharp kid learning how to make money. Besides his connection to Notre Dame Julius Tucker also had a lot of contacts with the National Football League and the Canadian Football League and was kind of an agent for Notre Dame players. But, at the time I don't know a thing about Canada, and wasn't even thinking about the CFL.

But I knew I had two years of college eligibility remaining, and I figured out pretty soon that I was a hot commodity. I was basically a free agent, and people knew I could play: I was a 295-pounder that could run. I had interest from seven or eight schools, but only visited about four of them on my second "recruiting tour" in three years. One of them was Georgia, where I ran into that suspicious waiter while I was eating dinner with head coach Wally Butts. I didn't want to play in the south, though. I couldn't stand the bigotry, so I ended up choosing the Wyoming Cowboys in Laramie, coached by the now-legendary Bob Devaney. Things were about to take a very interesting turn.

The NCAA rule then, just like now, was that you couldn't pay athletes any money. But Wyoming was giving me all kinds of money on top of my scholarship. The school provided housing for Darlene and myself, and the school was paying me close to $1,200 a month, which is more than many people were making at their jobs. They even got Darlene a job working in a bank. The money was welcome and also quite needed as Darlene was pregnant with our first child, Jolene. (Wyoming eventually got caught by the NCAA for paying players, including me, and weren't allowed to play bowl games for a couple of years.)

I never played a formal game for the Wyoming Cowboys. Because I transferred from Notre Dame, I wasn't eligible to play in my first year, so I red-shirted on the practice squad. But that wasn't what kept me out of the lineup.

In Wyoming I started doing all kinds of illegal stuff. I was making money and didn't give a shit about school. Almost as soon as I got to Wyoming I met Bob Marshall, who was also on the team. He was a Portuguese kid from Rhode Island who had played defensive end for Tennessee with Doug Atkins, who went on to the NFL. Bob had been kicked out of Tennessee, and together, we were kind of on the run. Bob and I ran card games, and we stole. My poor wife was from a wonderful family and this stuff was all very foreign to her.

When I came to town Bob already had some things going in Laramie with some people out of Chicago, and we became partners. To be honest, the people out of Chicago were gangsters, and Bob and I represented them. We ran card games and operated illegal slot machines for them. The money was good, and I needed it with a baby on the way.

I also had a partnership going with a guy named Martin Strube. Actually, I couldn't remember his name, or I'd blocked it out, until recently when someone researched it and found it for me. Strube was from Lance Creek, Wyoming, and he was wealthy. He had more money than he did brains, and together we stole typewriters and sold them on campus. I used to walk right into business machine stores and walk right out with a typewriter. I had got to know the girls in the store, so they didn't suspect anything. We also stole typewriters from cars, trucks, anywhere really. One night in December of 1957 we stole a typewriter from a pickup truck, and also took some clothes and an electric razor. I didn't think anything of it — it was just another small job. But in January the cops nabbed Martin for the truck robbery and he turned state's evidence on me. In those days, anything over $50 was grand larceny, which is a serious charge, and now I've got a warrant for my arrest hanging over me.

Bob Marshall knew a guy named Porky Padillo in Casper, Wyoming, who had a lot of connections. I met with Porky and he set up a meeting for me with a district attorney. The attorney should have had me arrested on the spot, but I told him about my nine-month-pregnant wife and he simply advised me to go back to Laramie and give myself up. I guess he figured they'd go light on me.

I drove back to Laramie at night, and just before town, four cops stopped me on the highway. Right around that time a guy named Charles Starkweather and his girlfriend went on a killing spree in Nebraska. He killed 11 people including his girlfriend's parents and the movie *Natural Born Killers* was based on the two of them. They were on the run and had crossed over into Wyoming. I was a fugitive and the cops were very nervous because of what was going on with Starkweather, so they all had their guns drawn and it was quite a scene. I was laughing because I thought it was a joke and I asked them, "What is this all about?" They weren't laughing, though. They arrested me and immediately threw me in jail on the typewriter charge. A police sergeant was quoted in the paper the next day saying, "Apparently he is coming back to give himself up."

Devaney obviously caught wind of it all and cancelled my football scholarship immediately. He told the papers it was for "scholastic deficiency and disciplinary reasons."

My "partner" posted the bail of a $1,000 for himself but I couldn't post my ass. That was a lot of money. I ended up staying in the slammer for five days — my first, and only, real time in the joint. It was awful. Darlene gave birth to our daughter , Jolene, while I was in jail. I'll never forget the other guys inside the jailhouse. I was half-assed crying and they're saying, "Yeah, yeah, we know, another innocent guy in jail." You know how these hard line guys can be. I told them to fuck off, and I eventually smashed one of them who wouldn't let up. That seemed to prove a point.

If anybody asks me about that time of my life, I say I'm not proud of it. I also say stealing was salvation, a way of getting me and my family, with a baby coming, some money. I don't regret much in my life, but the stealing bothers me a little. I didn't steal for the sake of stealing, I did it to transfer into dollars and cents, which eventually became food.

When it came my time to go to court, I decided to plead not guilty to the grand larceny charge. The reason I did was because of something my friend Julius Tucker told me. While I was in the joint I reached out to Julius. As I mentioned, he had a lot of contacts with the National Football League and the Canadian Football League and he wrote back and asked me if I had any interest in playing pro in Canada. The NFL wasn't going to be able to draft me until my college class graduated, which, for me, was the following year. The Philadelphia Eagles had already expressed interest in me, but I would have to wait to play there.

In fact, they did take me in the 30th round of the 1958 NFL draft, but by then I'd already played a year in Canada. So, based on Julius' advice, I decided that Canada was the place to go. The only problem was that if I had a criminal record, I wouldn't be able to get into the country, meaning I couldn't play. Pleading guilty might have made more sense, but I pled not guilty because, up until this point, my record was clean.

Martin painted a horrible portrait of me in court — he made me sound like the worst human being, the worst criminal in the world. When it was my turn to speak I told the judge about my wife and Jolene. The judge then deliberated for two hours in his chambers. When he reached his decision, he looked at me and said, "Mr. Mosca, we are finding you guilty and I'm going to give you one year…" My heart dropped right to my feet. He held that pause and then continued, "…suspended sentence." That prick *had* to pause. He loved it. He wanted to give me the willies, and boy did he ever! I wanted to fucking kill him for playing with me like that, but I also wanted to kiss him.

The suspended sentence meant that I could travel to Canada and play professional football there. So Darlene and I quickly packed up, left Laramie with Jolene and started to drive back to South Bend. I'll never forget the night we left. It was snowing really hard and as I'm driving I peer through the wall of snow and I can make out a yellow 'W' at the side of the road. I know it's got to be a Wyoming student hitch-hiking and we pull over to pick him up. It was Bob Marshall! He had gotten himself in big trouble, worse shit than I ever did, and was on the run. We picked Bob up and we drove him all the way to Chicago. We would stop at a bar to warm up the baby's milk bottle, sit there and have a couple of beers, then jump back in the car and keep driving. My poor wife never saw anything like the two of us guys. She came from a very good family, and just had a sister, no brothers. Unfortunately, Bob is in jail today in New Jersey. I don't know what he's done to get there, but he's become institutionalized: he's been in jail probably 35 of the last 40 years. I still talk to him and in May of 2011, I got a letter from him.

When Darlene, Jolene and I got to South Bend, I went to see Julius Tucker and he told me that he had negotiated a contract with something called the Hamilton Tiger-Cats for me. The contract was for $10,000, with a $2500 signing bonus! That was very serious money and the Canadian dollar was worth 10 cents more than the greenback at the time, so I was very happy. I'd never even heard of Hamilton or the Tiger-Cats and wondered how they had heard of me. In the end it turned out that Jim Trimble, who was then head coach of the Tiger-Cats had come to the team from the Philadelphia Eagles, and so did his assistant coach Ralph Sazio. I figure that must have been how the Ti-Cats knew about me; the Eagles had been scouting me. Signing with Hamilton was really a lucky break, and I was incredibly fortunate to have Julius in my life; he was such a good man. I came completely clean with him on the whole typewriter story and just laughed about it. I don't think I was the first college guy that Julius knew who got in trouble.

In South Bend we were staying with Darlene's parents, and they knew what had happened. My mother-in-law certainly wasn't in love with me, but she and my father-in-law loved their grandchild.

The Korean War hadn't been over for long, and with the soldiers coming back work was hard to come by. I decided if I was going to play ball in Canada then I should go up to Canada to work before the season started. The plan was for Darlene and Jolene to come up to join me once I got settled. The only thing I knew about Canada was that the Toronto Maple Leafs and Montreal Canadiens came to the Boston Garden to play hockey. I was about to learn a whole lot more, and little did I know that coming to Canada would turn out to be the biggest break of my life.

SECTION TWO

The CFL

Welcome to Hamilton

I DROVE TO CANADA IN MY 1949 Oldsmobile that cost me $125. I bought bulk oil for the trip from the A& P store and when the heaters didn't work right, I'd put a piece of cardboard on the grille to force the engine heat back into the car. I had $300 stuffed into my pocket, which was all the money I had left to my name. It was only a six or seven hour drive from South Bend, Indiana, to Hamilton, Ontario, maybe 400 miles in total. But, when I was driving up, I thought I was going to the end of the world. I drove all the way to Buffalo before I took a room for the night. I was thinking Canada was going to feel really foreign to me. I didn't know a thing about the country. I thought everyone spoke French because there were a lot of French-Canadians around Boston when I was young. "Le Blanks" we called them, after the Leblanc surname.

I drove into Canada at Fort Erie, about an hour from Hamilton. It wasn't hard to cross the border in those days, I just had to show them my birth certificate. As I started driving toward Hamilton I'm thinking, "Shit, this ain't any different than the United States." This, of course, is before Canada went metric so the speed limit signs were still in miles per hour. The further I got into the country the stronger my curiosity grew about Canada. That's what always drove me to find out things: curiosity. And I got my ass in trouble a lot of times because of it.

The Queen Elizabeth Way (QEW), running from Fort Erie to Toronto, was not really a highway in 1958, and every one of the bridges you see today on the QEW had traffic lights then, so it was a much slower drive than it is now. I stopped in what I know now was Burlington, near the bridge, and got a motel for the night. The next day, I went straight to the Tiger-Cat offices.

The first person I met was Len Back, who I later learned, had been managing Hamilton football teams for decades. The Ticats treated the new guys pretty good and Len was the guy who showed everyone around the city. Len helped me get a job and an apartment. He was real good to me. I've been lucky that way. I didn't realize it while I was a kid in Waltham, but for my whole childhood I just wanted to leave, and I was very fortunate to get out, and have people who helped me get out. I've met some very wonderful people along the way who believed in me.

And Jim Trimble was one of them

The very first time I met Jim Trimble was at the Ticat offices shortly after I arrived in Hamilton. He was in a very small office with a wood floor, sitting behind a table. The whole set-up accentuated his size. I didn't know anything about Big Jim: I never had heard of his playing days or his coaching background, I learned about all that later. I didn't look at *him* so much as I looked at the size of the man. He used to rub his hand across his chest all the time and because of that, and his size, we called him "Bwana." He was a great character. He spoke with me almost like a father would, although my own father never talked to me the way Jim did. He gave me confidence right from the first time we met. He said, "I've heard all about you, we've been tracking you." He knew about all my Notre Dame and Wyoming problems, too. Julius Tucker had explained everything to him.

I didn't know whether to sit down or stand up, and he said, "Sit down, son." And I'll always remember that: he said, "Son."

Jim wasn't overly tall, maybe 6 feet, but he was a very wide guy. He really presented himself as what a professional football head coach should be. Jake Gaudaur was the general manager, Ralph Sazio was the line coach and "Indian" Jack Jacobs, the guy who really made the forward pass popular in pro football, was the other coach. He could still throw the ball as well as anyone who was playing. Just three coaches, that's all they had in Hamilton.

It was mid-April, and in those days CFL training camps didn't start until July, so I needed to work. The Cats had contacts with Hamilton businesses, and after a week they got me a job at Stelco, the steel company. Jobs in 1958 were really hard to come by and I was very fortunate to get this one. I went to work every day, working a regular day job. I referred to it as slave labour. My job was to clean up the spilled, molten steel with a shovel. It was very hot and incredibly dirty. But I learned the process at the mill really quickly: sit down and go to sleep. Dofasco and Stelco, the steel companies, had maybe 20,000 people working for them. The steel mill was *the* place to work in Hamilton.

I figured that I would be playing for the Tiger-Cats in a couple of months, so I started to promote myself around the city. I walked into *The Hamilton Spectator* newspaper and did an interview with Bob Hanley, the sports columnist. Then I went to the radio station and did an interview with Norm Marshall. They were the two big guys in sports in Hamilton at that time, and I thought it important to meet them. *The Spectator* even ran a picture of me: the new guy in town sort of thing.

My apartment was in the east end, and I'll always remember that I was told not to touch anything in the city's north end, which is the harbour side of the city. The north side was supposed to be nothing but old houses and bad neighbourhoods, but right away I liked it.

One of the first Sundays I was in town, I went to St. Patrick's Church off Main Street, a beautiful church in the east end, and I meet the singer Fern Viola (he still occasionally sings the national anthem at the Ticat games). He recognized me from the article in the paper. Fern took me in and introduced me to the priest and a whole bunch of other people. That same week I started working out at Mahoney Park and I met Marty Martinello who played with the B.C. Lions. He was seven years older than me, but we became workout pals. (Later in our careers, I convinced management to trade for him and we ended up winning a Grey Cup together.) Right from the beginning, I really liked Hamilton.

I got to know the north end really well. It's basically Little Italy, so I was well accepted there. It was a rugged end of town, but it was full of a good bunch of people. I don't think anyone will now be upset, or even shocked, to learn that I am one-quarter black.

I was getting to know the guys that had card games, so I'd sit in with them. I played poker as many times a week as I wanted: there were all kinds of games going on around town. Bootleggers too. Hamilton was a very vibrant city in those days. Downtown was un-be-lieve-able. On a Friday and Saturday night, it was bumper to bumper: people…and lots of them were women. The season hadn't even started and I was already moseying around town with different girls. When you're 20 years old, 6-foot-4 and have a 34-inch waist, you think you're the cock of the walk. I was always 300 pounds once I came to Canada and 300-pounders in those days were not looked upon as being in good shape, but I was in really good shape and I thought I was the king.

In 1950s' Hamilton, you wanted a card game, you could get a card game. You wanted booze after hours, no problem with that. On Saturday night, the bars were closed at 11:30 because of the Sunday Blue Laws. But I got to know every bootlegger in the city pretty quickly. I'd ask the guys in the north end, and they'd show me different bootleggers. I still drive by their houses and have a memory flashback to over 50 years ago. I think the booze cans declined once the liquor laws relaxed in the early 1970s. There was a booze can on Cannon Street and they closed that. The other big one was down on Sherman Avenue. I can tell this name because he's dead now: Mike Baker. The telephone system had operators in those days and if you couldn't remember Mike's number, they would know exactly what you were after and the operator would give you the number to dial. That's how well-known Mike Baker was. He had a place right beside the police station. He would sell you a case of beer for five bucks that cost three bucks at the beer store. And a taxi would deliver it to wherever you were. I loved the city right away, and I loved the people, the real people.

I fit right in with the lifestyle of downtown Hamilton and I was obviously not ready for the responsibility of family life. Just before training camp started I picked up Darlene and Jolene and brought them back to our apartment in Stinson Court.

When training camp started, I took a leave from Stelco and reported to the field. Training camp was held at the H-Triple-A grounds, which stood for the Hamilton Amateur Athletic Association. It was an old field where they had had a Grey Cup game in the 1920s. The junior teams played there in the '60s and now it's a city park. It was a nice little area. There was a writer from *The Spec* that lived in that area and he and his wife rented rooms to a lot of the football players, which I don't think you'd see in this day and age.

When camp started, I was cocky. And even though I was new to the team, the city and, for that matter, the country, I wasn't scared or nervous. I always had confidence in myself. It's a confidence I cannot describe. Jim Trimble knocked me down a small peg though when he told me that the team could only keep 11 Americans — there must have been 30 of us in camp. Until then I thought I was one of the chosen few. Nobody had explained to me that there was an American limit, what they now call the import ratio, and that in professional football you actually have to *make* the team. I also didn't know anything about Canadian football — not even the fact that there were only three downs. The size of the field caught me by surprise, and so did the 20-second huddle. That was half what we had in college. And the end zones were huge, although that didn't affect linemen much. In the States, the end zones were 10 yards deep. In Canada they were 25 yards deep (they were shortened by five yards in the '70s). I've been in Canada long enough now that I think the Canadian game is the way football should be played — it's logical to have deep end zones.

I really only knew one thing about playing ball in Canada: the money was good, better than what the NFL was paying, and I knew I had no choice but to make the team. I felt sorry for the guys in training camp with me, because I hit everything that moved.

I did a few sneaky things, figuring that not making the team simply wasn't an option. In drills and in scrimmage I would purposely blow offside and completely bury my opponent. One time in practice, the count was on three and I blew off as soon as the quarterback said, "one." I completely clobbered the other lineman. The guy complained that I was offside. I shot back, "Tell that to my daughter."

Another way to cheat that I think most players used was that in the CFL you had to play a yard off the ball but, if you were good, you could line up three-quarters of a yard off the ball instead of the full yard. This allowed you to get up under the guy's face. That helped a guy like me on both offence and defence.

I'll always remember Vince Scott, who became a good friend. He was short as he was wide and he'd always say challenging stuff like, "Nobody here can knock my ass down!" In one practice, Vince held up a blocking dummy and I charged him, but instead of hitting the dummy I came right across his head. Knocked him right on his fucking ass.

I was aggressive, but I had to make the team to make some money, and physicality was my best attribute. Showing that off was important.

Just 27 players were allowed on the final roster. Hamilton had just won the Grey Cup in 1957 over Winnipeg and it was going to be tough for a new player, especially an American, to make a championship team. As it turned out, I was the only American rookie who made the team right out of training camp. I found out the week before the season started that I made the Tiger-Cats. Jimmy Golla of *The Globe and Mail* wrote, "the guy who virtually has cracked the lineup of the defending Grey Cup champions is Angelo Mosca. Silently but surely he has found himself a spot on the vaunted Tabbie line." Actually, I didn't think I was that silent, and my teammates sure didn't.

The team gave me a $500 advance on my contract in training camp and Trimble had said to me earlier, "You're a wild guy, I'm putting you under Eddie Bevan's wing." And within two weeks any bootlegger in town I didn't already know, I met through Eddie. Trimble didn't realize that he was a wild guy too.

We had a pretty good football team. Dave Suminski, Eddie Bevan and Geno DeNobile were guards; Chet Miksza was the centre. I played right tackle and John Barrow played left tackle. I met John in training camp and I had no idea what "Barrow and Mosca" was going to come to mean in this league, on both sides of the ball — we were a force to be reckoned with. We ended up playing together for most of the next 11 years. I found John to be a very arrogant guy. I noticed that right away. He was one of those "All-American" kind of guys from Florida. But that was John. And he was a real good football player.

Barrow was one of the appointed captains, but the real leader on that team was the other captain, quarterback Bernie Faloney. Bernie was one of the most unorthodox guys I've ever seen play QB, especially the way he ran: slew-foot. He didn't run foot over foot like most people, both his feet would kind of stick out to the side. And when he threw the ball it often went end over end, but it got there — it was definitely not a perfect spiral. Bernie had just come off a great Maryland team a few years earlier that had won a national championship and produced a lot of great players who starred in the NFL. He was a first round draft choice of San Francisco in 1954, but he never played for the 49ers. When Pop Ivy came up from Oklahoma to coach in Edmonton, he called Bernie, who had beaten his team in the Orange Bowl. Edmonton offered Bernie a lot more

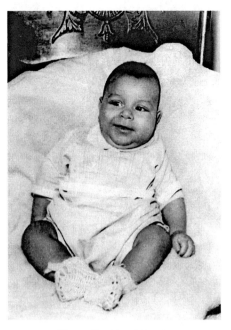

Six months old and already
looking like a defensive end.

Seven years old: from the smile, you
can see I always got the joke.

Grade 3 at Plympton Public School. I'm the big guy at the far right of the third
row. My half-Italian, half-Irish friend Harold Kelley is on the third row far left.

My sophomore year at Notre Dame, while I'm still in the school's good books.

My rookie picture with the Ticats. I'm 6-foot-4, 295 pounds. I became associated with No. 68, but my first two years I wore No. 62.

Just before flying to Vancouver in 1958 for my first of nine Grey Cups. I'm almost hidden in the back right of the middle row. Somebody told me I looked like Hoss Cartwright from Bonanza.

Wearing 60 in 1960 for the Ottawa Rough Riders. I hated playing for that team. I didn't belong in Ottawa.

The moment that made my reputation: I go flying over Willie Fleming and Joe Zuger and became the "Football's Dirtiest Player."

My first Hamilton Grey Cup championship team. The 1963 Tiger-Cats broke the hearts of all of British Columbia by beating the Lions in their first Grey Cup appearance.

Wrestling with anger as my career starts to build in 1965. I'm a heel, through-and-through. I never liked working as a "baby face" later in my career.

The 1965 Hamilton Tiger-Cats, the winners of the Wind Bowl. That Grey Cup game resulted in a rule change about safety touches.

CANADIAN WEEKLY

PUBLISHED BY TORONTO STAR LIMITED FOR
TORONTO DAILY STAR FOR AUGUST 8, 1964

ULCERVILLE
The town where most
of us live

A dog that gets a
kick out of soccer

THE VEGETABLE
DAWN PATROL

When Jules Verne
came to Canada

GARDENING
The Madonna lily

Sports editor Jim Hunt interviews

CANADA'S MEANEST FOOTBALL PLAYER

Angelo Mosca, 272-pound tackle
of the Hamilton Tiger-Cats

Canada's Meanest Football Player. This magazine cover ran in
newspapers across the country in 1964. In the late 1960s the two
most recognizable names in Canada were Pierre Elliott Trudeau
and Angelo Mosca.

The muscle of the Greatest Team of All Time, the 1967 Hamilton
Tiger-Cats. From the left: John Barrow, Gene Ceppetelli, Bob Steiner,
Jim Reynolds, me, Ellison Kelly, Ralph Sazio, Bronko Nagurski, Billy
Ray Locklin, Chuck Walton, Richard Gibbs, Dave Viti, Bill Danychuk.

The Greatest Team in CFL history: the 1967 Tiger-Cats won the Grey
Cup in Canada's Centennial Year.

I never was much
on winning a
championship belt.
I'd rather lose the belt
and win the crowd.

Mazda 1800 Pickup.

**We built it for
Angelo Mosca.**

A player's toughness is sometimes compared to the toughness of a truck. Here the truck's
toughness is compared to me! This ad was shot in the end zone at Civic Stadium.

money than San Francisco did, so he came north for a year, then got drafted into the U.S. Army. (I had a deferment because I had a kid, which is why I never served). When Bernie got out of the service, Trimble jumped on a technicality (what we'd call free agency today), and signed him in 1957. He took the Ticats to the Grey Cup championship in his first year.

When you got into the huddle with Bernie, he somehow made you believe that you were going to score a touchdown, or win the game, and he just made you believe that everything was going to go just right. After he called a play in the huddle he'd look you right in the eye and say, "It better fucking work!" If he was calling the play over you, he made it your responsibility that it was going to succeed. He wasn't the greatest quarterback that I've ever played with, skill-wise, but he could score touchdowns and make teams believe in themselves. When you were at the 10-yard line, Bernie somehow made it feel like the one-yard line. We believed in Bernie, and as a result, we believed in ourselves. He was a terrific guy to be around, on and off the field.

Bernie and I became good friends and we were both named to the top 50 players in CFL history. He died of cancer in 1999 and I'm still good friends with his wife Jan. She's a lovely lady, still going strong.

When I came to Canada, Americans would play both offence and defence. On defence, I played left tackle and Barrow played right tackle — flipped from offence. There was always a man over centre, the nose guard, and that's what Vince Scott played. He was not the prettiest human being I've ever seen in my life and I always joked with him about that. I called him "Neanderthal Man." I'll never forget him. He was about 5-foot-6, and 250 pounds.

That year Gerry McDougall was a pretty good halfback for us, playing at 6-foot-3, 230. He was in the spot vacated by the great Cookie Gilchrist. Cookie was a great halfback who had played in '57 and eventually became the star of the first Buffalo Bills teams. He was probably one of the greatest athletes that ever played in this country but also had a very interesting life off the field. I guess the city of Hamilton wasn't big enough for the two of us, so they traded him to Saskatchewan before I joined the club.

Jim Trimble ran everything. He would yell at the assistant coaches and it would even make me feel a little bad for them. Trimble came from the Philadelphia Eagles and he was one of the youngest coaches to coach in the NFL at that time. He and I eventually became really good friends and he left me with a lot of good memories but I really tested him in my first couple of years with the Ticats. Jim had a Doctor Jekyl and Mr. Hyde personality. When he got on the gridiron it turned him into a vulture: yelling and screaming at the players. He had great expressions: "You're like a dog shittin' razor blades," was one of his favourites. "You're no bigger than kicking two ducks in the ass," was another. Some of the Canadian kids weren't used to this kind of individual. I wasn't scared of him because Tony Zullo from my time at Waltham High was the same way.

The Globe and Mail called Jim Trimble the most controversial person in Canadian football. He always made headlines trying to drum up interest for the team and the league and had a lot of innovative ways to use the different rules of the Canadian game.

Jim was big. He was a Stelco-type guy, so he was well-liked around the city. Jim came from the Pittsburgh area, another steel district, so the city of Hamilton just embraced him. They really did. Off the field he was really a nice man. He was a real gentleman and he became kind of a father to me.

No one ever talked to the head coach on the field. Jim remained aloof from his assistants, he remained aloof from his players. It was not an easy position to be in. As a head coach you can be a nice guy if your assistants are tough, but most of the time the head coach is the bad cop. Jim had Ralph Sazio as his line coach and the only other coach was "Indian" Jack Jacobs. He was one of the greatest at throwing a football that I ever saw, even when he had finished playing. Jack was a great quarterback for the Green Bay Packers before he came to Winnipeg and starred there. What a great guy, a real good person. I always thought he got the raw end of the deal because he was Native-American, and I would tease him about it. He could take it.

Ralph Sazio was pretty tough too. He was the line coach so he was the guy I worked most with. I had him on both sides of the ball. Everybody was a yeller and a screamer in those days. I can remember telling Ralph, "Don't yell at me" even though I was used to it and could take it. I just knew it bothered me, but I wasn't thinking about why. Now I know that it reminded me of home.

What is now the CFL Eastern Conference was then officially called the IRFU (Interprovincial Rugby Football Union) and nicknamed the Big Four. The west was called the WIFU (Western Interprovincial Football Union), this was all before both leagues officially merged to become the CFL in 1958. To play in '58 we had to sign a Canadian Rugby Union contract. We played the other three eastern teams four times each, twice at home, twice on the road and we had one extra road game against one team, and one extra home game against another team, which made up the 14-game schedule. When we went to Ottawa or Montreal, we got dressed in the hotel in their big conference rooms and then we'd get on the bus and go to the stadium. When we played in Toronto, we got dressed in Hamilton at the HAAA grounds and took the bus, just like in high school.

We only played 14 regular season games in those years, plus four or five exhibition games and I always remember the first one. We played the games at Civic Stadium, which was Ivor Wynne Stadium's former name, and we'd get dressed at the HAAA and take a bus across town to the stadium. We even did that during the regular season. To kick the point-after in the exhibition game, we'd turn around the other way and kick it from the end zone toward the field of play so we didn't lose the football. It wasn't until two or three years later that they built the south stands and a couple of years after that they rebuilt the north stands. I'm coming from a stadium that holds 60,000, where they don't kick converts from the end zone, and I'm wondering what the hell I've gotten into here.

My first official CFL game was August 19, 1958 in Montreal, at Molson Stadium on the McGill campus. The Alouettes had really good players and always sold out — 29,000 people crammed in the stadium, everyone spoke French, and the sidelines came right up against the crowd. Some fans were practically sitting on the field. Bernie Faloney was described in the papers the year before as dull and methodical at quarterback, but our first game he threw four touchdown passes and we won 27–14. The most memorable part, though, was that partway through the game the referee blew his whistle and yelled for everyone to get off the field. I looked up, and there was a helicopter hovering overhead. After the players walked to the sideline, the helicopter landed at midfield and paramedics rushed a patient on a stretcher over to the neurological hospital right next door to the stadium. I said to myself, "What kind of fucking league is this?"

Four days later — four bloody days: I was figuring out this wasn't U.S. football — we played Ottawa at home and beat them. Then eight days later on September 1, I had my first experience with Labour Day.

We beat the Toronto Argos by a touchdown and the fans at Civic Stadium (now called Ivor Wynne) went crazy. You'd think we just won the championship. Labour Day really meant something in those days in Toronto and Hamilton — it still does in Hamilton — because it was kind of a symbol of the two cities. Toronto was fancy and rich, and Hamilton was blue collar and gritty, just like where I grew up. Our team played gritty, too. That was our trademark, and that's why the city loved us.

We were a very good team, which you'd expect for a club that won the Grey Cup the previous year and didn't make too many changes. In fact, Trimble said later that the 1958 team was 25% better than the 1957 team.

We won our first five games, and the fifth, in mid-September, was the most unique CFL regular season game played up to that point. It was our home game, against Ottawa, but we played it in Philadelphia. It was the first Canadian football game to be played in the U.S. and the last one until the league got into that stupid, and I mean stupid, American expansion in the 1990s.

The game was in Municipal Stadium, which could hold 102,000 people, but even though the organizers were hoping to sell 40,000 tickets and said they had 20,000 advance sales, less than 15,000 people showed up (about 3,000 of those were people who drove down from Ottawa or Hamilton). It was supposed to let Americans see our game and also raise money for the Children's Hospital in Philly, but the organizers needed to sell 17,000 tickets to break even, so I guess they didn't raise anything for the kids. The organizers were trying to promote the big American star quarterbacks, Bernie and Ottawa's Hal Ledyard, who played at Chattanooga and was well known. Trimble, and Ottawa coach Frank Clair, whom a lot of Americans knew from Ohio State and the Washington Redskins, were also supposed to be fan draws. But not many people came.

The field looked weird, because it was only 100 yards long, like in American football, but it had been widened and the end zones were made deeper. The problem was that the track around the field cut the end zones near the sides to only eight yards deep. We won 24–18 but the American media never took to the game. They counted the 31 punts and said three downs was a real problem in developing offence. You couldn't blame them, they didn't give a damn about our game; they were close minded. But I found out when I got to Canada that the CFL is almost always more exciting than the NFL.

After the fiasco in Philly we went back into Montreal, tied the Alouettes and then won three more. So it was our 10th game before we lost, and did we ever lose.

We had beaten the Argos at Civic Stadium 28–15 and then got hammered 39–0 at Varsity Stadium in Toronto two days later. Dave Mann was a big factor for the Argos. It was his first year in the CFL and I remember him from when I was at Notre Dame. Dave played up the highway in Chicago for the Cardinals and was a real star. They never won much but the Cardinals had a great backfield with Mann and Ollie Matson (who got traded to L.A. for *nine* players in the late '50s).

We finished first in the Big Four by six points that year at 10–3–1 and got a bye into the conference final which was a two-game, total-point series. Ottawa, which was only 6–8, upset Montreal in the semifinal for the right to play us.

I was making a real name for myself in the papers and with other players. I think that meant that I pushed the envelope right to the edge, and a lot of people didn't like it — mostly football players. On the field, you'd push it to where you almost got a penalty. I never trash-talked; although we didn't describe it that way back then. But opponents trash-talked me. They'd practically call me "asshole." My game was about striking fear into the opponent, and I think it really worked. I used the fear factor for 12 or 13 years, and it got me a long way.

The referees didn't really pay enough attention to the lines, and despite the rule that you had to give a one-yard restraining zone on defence, I learned how to gain an advantage: I guess you could call it cheating to win. I'd move up a little closer and on converts I used to blow offside on purpose, to hit the center. In today's game they penalize you on the kickoff for going off-side on a convert attempt, but when I played they just let it go if the convert was good. I learned how to utilize the rules to my advantage. Now you can't even hit the centre. I couldn't play today. I'd get penalized on every play. You can't slap, you can't collar a guy — I used to clothesline guys. As I rushed the quarterback, the back would be standing trying to sneak out of the backfield behind the QB and the tackle, but when I saw him running by I'd stick my arm out and snag him with a clothesline. If you studied the film long enough, you knew where the backs were going to go and on what plays you could hit them.

Everyone used to talk about the way I would head slap, which I learned in high school. I would come off the line of scrimmage on defence and slap the offensive lineman on the side of his helmet with my open hand — my hands are always sore today from the head slaps. Then, I'd do the swim move: I'd take my hand up and over the lineman's elbow, stopping him from raising his arm, and giving me free rein to push him away and open the lane up for myself. Another move I used a lot was to drive the heel of my hand right up under the chin of the opposing lineman. Then I'd use the swim move again.

The things that I saw back then: even from some of the doctors. The way they'd test you for concussions was to ask you, "How many fingers am I holding up?" If you got that right, you played. I can only recollect one concussion I ever had. And let me tell you, what a horrible feeling. I still don't really know to this day what happened. I remember trying to figure it out at the time, but I couldn't. I gave out a few concussions myself though. That was the pride you had in the game, when you hit so hard you hurt people. Can you believe that? When I look back on it, it's absolutely ridiculous, but that's the way we were taught: hurt people, be physical. It fit me to a "T."

I played my entire career at 300 pounds. People made a big deal when "The Fridge" played for the Chicago Bears at 300 pounds in the early 1980s, but I was the original big guy. I never told anybody I weighed that much because people thought 300-pounders were fat and slow. Jim Trimble always said I had great speed, but he never knew that I would get on that scale and cheat: I'd drop one of my feet off so I wouldn't hit 300. Or I'd tell Sandy Sanderson, the trainer, I only want to weigh 290, and that's what he'd tell Trimble. I bought the trainer, really. And those trainers weren't really training us. Jimmy Simpson was a great football player for the old Tigers, but I would never let him tape my ankles. I was scared to death that this guy might choke off my ankles and I'd never get them right again. So I'd tape myself, or three or four of us would tape each other. It wasn't compulsory that you had to tape but if you had a little problem you'd tape it to stabilize it.

In those days, we'd start practice at five in the afternoon so the guys could work during the day and then we'd practice for maybe an hour and a half. But it would become a two-hour practice if guys were making mistakes. After practice we were fed in one of the rooms under the stadium stands. I call that the original *Animal House*. It was crazy with pranks. I think that really kept the team together. Offensive guys are usually very passive and it's the defensive guys who are the fucking characters. We'd glue guys' shoes to the ceiling, that kind of thing. We'd have ice cream fights all the time and you'd always be looking for the things that bothered other guys when they were eating. Garney Henley was a queasy eater; his stomach would turn at anything. So Gene Ceppetelli and I would stick raisins up our noses and then say "Hey, Gar, look at this!" and we'd blow the raisins out of our noses like snot. Garney would just turn white. The coaches were right in the next room, but never bothered us because they knew it was building team spirit. It was a tough room. We always said that if you could make it in our dressing room you could make it on the field.

Playoffs brought an edge to our team. During practice the week before the first game of the conference final I got into a fight with one of our backfielders, Milt Campbell. Milt wasn't a great football player, but he was one of the greatest all-round athletes ever. He finished second to Bob Mathias in the 1952 Olympic decathlon and in 1956 at the Melbourne Olympics he became the first African-American ever to win the decathlon. But because he came between Bob Mathias and Rafer Johnson, people kind of forgot about him. I had played college ball against him when he was going to Indiana. Then he played with the Cleveland Browns before joining the Tiger-Cats. I heard that he left the Browns because the owner, Paul Brown, didn't like Milt's mixed marriage. Naturally, I found that interesting.

Milt was unbelievable. He weighed 230 pounds and he could run: world-class speed. When the fight happened we were working out hard and physical, and with tension things happen. Ralph jumped in the middle and broke it up and we all forgot about it.

We clobbered the Rough Riders in Ottawa 35–7 in the first leg of the conference final, and then hammered them back at Civic Stadium 19–7 to secure our spot in the Grey Cup. Including the pre-season, we played Ottawa seven times that year and only lost once.

The Grey Cup was played in Vancouver, and it was only their second time hosting the game because the BC Lions only joined the league in 1954. I remember that the flight out there took us nine-and-a-half hours: non-stop. It was before jet engines were common.

The Vancouver papers were writing about how I was the fastest lineman and heaviest player on the team, and how the Bombers were supposedly motivated because Trimble had run up the score in the 1957 Grey Cup by going for a meaningless touchdown late in the game. Trimble then really gave Winnipeg something to talk about. When a reporter asked how we'd do, he said, "We'll waffle 'em. We'll leave 'em with lumps on the front and the back." One of Trimble's nicknames was "Jungle Jim," partly because he said all kinds of controversial stuff. The "waffle" comment became part of Trimble's image the rest of his time in Canada.

The 1958 Grey Cup has been voted one of the top-10 of all time. At the time, they called it the greatest ever, and I'd have to agree.

We went up 14–0 after only seven minutes and had the game well in hand, but then, Jim Van Pelt went to work. He had one of the finest games I've ever seen a quarterback play. Van Pelt came from the University of Michigan and was another one of those guys, like Bernie, who got drafted into the NFL but came up here instead. He replaced Ken Ploen at quarterback when Kenny got hurt earlier in the season, and he played so well Winnipeg left him in there. One game against Calgary, he hit Ernie Pitts with a 107-yard touchdown pass, which was a league record. Van Pelt could do everything: play quarterback, defensive back and place kick. And he did it all against us.

Van Pelt and Leo Lewis combined on a trick play where Van Pelt pitched the ball to Lewis, then Lewis threw it back to Van Pelt who ran 29 yards for a touchdown. We were still up 14–13 late in the first half when Trimble decided to punt from deep in our own end instead of hanging onto the ball, or conceding a safety. Norm Rauhaus blocked the punt and fell on it for a touchdown and we were down 20–14 at the half. I told the papers later that it was a coaching mistake, and it was.

Ralph Goldston, who had scored one of our touchdowns, was ejected from the game late in the first half. One of the officials said that Ralph punched Leo Lewis and tried to grab his facemask. It wasn't necessary to throw Ralph out of the game, and it probably had an impact on the final result. He was one of our best players.

The game went back and forth in the second half, and we traded touchdowns until Ploen scored on a one-run dive to make it 35–28 for Winnipeg. They were driving again with two minutes left when Vince Scott recovered a fumble at our own 25 and we got a life. Bernie hit Harry Lampman around mid-field with a minute and a half left, and we had a chance to score the touchdown that would send it into overtime. But a couple of plays later, with about 30 seconds left on the clock, Bernie was picked off at the Winnipeg five-yard line by Kenny Ploen. Van Pelt ended up with two touchdowns, four converts and two field goals. Twenty-two points by himself. The next year, Ploen would be the quarterback against us in the Grey Cup, because Van Pelt was hurt. And after that, Van Pelt was gone from football. He was drafted into the U.S. Air Force, had to serve three years, then decided to retire when he got out of the service.

The Grey Cup was played on Saturdays in those years and we were supposed to leave on the Sunday, but had to stay over because the weather was so bad we couldn't get out. They were being extra cautious because two years earlier a plane crashed coming out of Vancouver after the All-Star Game, and all 62 people on board were killed. At the time it was the worst air disaster in Canadian history and five of the victims were players. The trophy for the western Canadian lineman of the year is named after two of them, Mel Beckett and Mario DeMarco. I played against one of the others, Cal Jones, when he was at Iowa. So, we stayed over an extra day in Vancouver, which we didn't mind. Naturally, we partied most of the night and had a great time.

When we got back to Hamilton they took us directly to the HAAA Grounds. It was a really cold night, but there were still a couple of thousand people there waiting for us. And we had *lost* that game. The fans were great, and, knowing exactly what happened in the Grey Cup game, they hoisted Ralph Goldston up and carried him around on their shoulders. It was a pretty moving scene.

That's the kind of love Hamilton had for the players on that team. And most of the players loved the city right back — some of us, a bit too much.

CHAPTER
FIVE

Exile

MY CLASS FROM NOTRE DAME graduated between the 1958 and 1959 seasons. Naturally I didn't graduate, although I told a lot of sportswriters over the next few years that I paid my own way to go back to South Bend in the off-seasons and graduated in math. You can even find some newspaper stories where I talk about teaching math in high school for four years. None of it ever happened of course, but I was trying to make my past look good because I embarrassed about it. I also told reporters that I was drafted by the Red Sox. I don't even know if there was a baseball draft in those days. I played around with writers, pulling their legs, and I fantasized. Part of it was that I was creating a legend for myself. If you didn't know anything about the background of the stories I told, you would have believed me too. I sugar coated a lot of things. I was always telling writers about advice my dad gave me as a child, and the sayings he had. What was I supposed to do? Come out and say, "My dad was a fucking jerk?" I wanted to make everybody believe that I had a good childhood. It seemed everyone I met in training camp had some great childhoods. The reporters could have found out that I was lying, if they just checked, even a little.

When my class graduated I was eligible for the 1959 NFL draft, and Philadelphia took me, although pretty low: 30th round, 350th overall. That was long before they let underclassmen leave and play in the NFL and by the time the NFL could take me I was already playing, and starting, in Canada and making more money than they would have paid me. But it was another example of the connection between the Eagles and the Ticats in those days. Trimble and Sazio were both from the Eagles, we had a handful of American players who had played for Philadelphia or at least been to camp with them and we played that game in Philadelphia during my rookie year with the Ticats. That's probably where the Eagles decided to take a chance on drafting me.

My old friend Bronko Nagurski, whom I met at the high school All-American Game in Memphis was part of that graduating class at Notre Dame, and the New York Giants took him 114th overall in the NFL draft. His dad had been retired from his glory days with the Chicago Bears for 15 years, but Nagurski was still a big name at the time. I was never impressed that his dad was famous. In fact I was never impressed with anything like that. I don't care who your parents are; it makes no difference to me.

The Tiger-Cats wanted Bronko, especially after they found out that he could play as a Canadian because his dad was born in Fort Frances, Ontario, right across the border from International Falls. So, because I knew him the Ticats gave me $300 to go down to South Bend, take him to dinner, entertain him and convince him to come up to the CFL. I bought him a milkshake and kept the rest of the money. But he still decided to come to Hamilton! I showed him around the city and showed him all the ropes. He was a really terrific guy and he and I became really close friends and stayed friends the rest of his life. Bronko had a pretty good career in Hamilton, he played eight years with the Ticats and went to six Grey Cups. He also met his wife Bev in Hamilton, and when he was finished with the CFL they went back to International Falls and he got into the paper industry, mostly in what they now call human resources.

Our 1959 lineup featured Bronko at offensive tackle — because he was Canadian — and I moved out to defensive end. I played offensive tackle too, switching off with John Barrow. We had a pretty damn good group at tackle.

John Barrow was always getting press, and he believed in his press clippings. Don't get me wrong, John was a great football player, but he was not a teammate, he was strictly an individual. And he couldn't physically handle my ass. I used to love to play against him the two years I wasn't with the Tiger-Cats. I'm a prick when it comes to that kind of thing. I am going to show you what the fuck I could do. I think he used to shudder when he had to play against me. That's the way to keep people if you're an opponent...on edge.

John and I never socialized. People talk about us in the same sentence because we played together for so long and had such success. We were a great team together but we were different guys. Our coaches made John out to be a god. Trimble had him calling signals and even Sazio had him calling signals. I found that unbelievable. John didn't know anything about coaching defences. I never heard of a defensive tackle who called the defensive signals — anywhere on any team. Defensive linemen don't know what's going on behind them. Normally a middle linebacker would call your defensive signals, or a secondary guy. I used to tell John to go fuck himself. I said to him one

time, "John, you and I have learned this game altogether differently. You're one of those pretty boys from Florida. I'm a street
kid from fuckin' Boston. And we'll kick your ass all over town."

I felt that John Barrow was for John Barrow, and I told him
that. John wasn't a real good teammate, to be very fucking
honest. But I really appreciated that he could play the game.
He was an Eastern All-Star on both offence and defence
four straight years, he was All-CFL six times and he won the
Schenley Award as Most Outstanding Lineman in 1962.

John and I keep in contact, and when he comes to Hamilton
we have lunch. Recently I blew-up at him. I told him, "John I'm
tired of hearing all about you, it's 40 years later, so fuck off with
this stuff." That's the way I am. I tolerate him and I think he
probably feels the same way about me.

John and I both had pretty good years in 1959 and we finished first again at 10–4. John was one of the captains and
Bernie was the other. Bernie was a good guy, and a really good
teammate. I haven't found a quarterback who could win like
him. That's what he did best.

In 1959 we were the best team in the Big Four at the end
of the regular season with a 10–4 record. We lost twice to
Montreal, and twice to Ottawa, but we never lost two games in
a row during the regular season.

We had lost the last game of the regular season, and we lost
our first game in the playoffs, giving us our first two back-to-
back losses. The Eastern Conference final was a two-game,
total-points series, and Ottawa beat us at Lansdowne Stadium,
17–5. We weren't worried heading into the second game of the
series. We were playing at Civic Stadium, and Ottawa always
had trouble against us at home. Maybe it was too rowdy for them
but whatever reason was, we usually seemed to beat them there.

We won the second leg of the East final 21–7 to win the two-game, total-points series by two points to advance to the Grey Cup. It was Hamilton's third consecutive trip, and my second, to the Grey Cup, and each time we played against Winnipeg; Bombers vs. Tiger-Cats was quickly becoming *the* matchup in the CFL. Only once in the six years, between 1957 and 1962, was the Grey Cup not Winnipeg vs. Hamilton — in 1960 the Ottawa Rough Riders and Edmonton Eskimos made the final, and I was in that game too.

The 1959 Grey Cup was the first of 12 Cup games that would be played at The Canadian National Exhibition Stadium, otherwise known as Exhibition Stadium, or its more deserving moniker, "The Mistake by the Lake." The Stadium was right beside Lake Ontario, and the lake made the weather unpredictable, and often miserable.

Jim Van Pelt was having another good year for Winnipeg and set a Western Conference record by throwing seven touchdowns in one game. Unfortunately for him, he separated his shoulder late in the season. Ken Ploen took over at QB — when a team can replace a guy like Van Pelt with a future hall of famer, you know that team has depth!

I always worked hard in practice, and while getting ready for the Grey Cup I got into a hard collision with Dave Suminski. I came off the ball on offence and pulled the wrong way, Dave pulled the right way and we clocked each other. The collision opened a gash over my eye — I still have a scar from it. The eye swelled completely shut but it went down a bit by game time, so I could play. Even so, I essentially played the Grey Cup game with just one eye. During the game one of the Blue Bombers' defensive linemen, I can't remember who, hit me so hard with a head slap when I was trying to block him, that my head was on a swivel. I just kept swinging. To this day, I don't remember where I was.

There were over 33,000 people at the game, which was a Grey Cup record, and the play-by-play guy on CBC was Norm Marshall of CHCH-TV, the guy who did one of my first interviews when I came to Canada. On the very first drive Winnipeg went down field and Gerry James kicked a 21-yard field goal. A few days later, he'd return to Toronto, because he played hockey for the Maple Leafs after the football season.

We couldn't capitalize on any breaks. Vince Scott blocked a punt in the second quarter and the ball went into the end zone, but Vince couldn't recover it and they brought the ball out. It was only 3–1 at halftime, and we could have taken control in the third quarter but we were marooned at their four-yard line and had to settle for a field goal. We led 7–4 into the fourth quarter but then we had to go into the wind, which was really picking up. Gerry McDougall fumbled just inside our half of the field, then Kenny Ploen hit Farrell Funston with a pass all the way to our two, and Charlie Shepard ran it in on the next series. Shepard kicked three singles with the wind and Ploen made a long pass to Alan Pitts late in the game to put it away for them. We lost 20–7. So, two years in the league and I'm 0–2 in the Grey Cup.

I was developing a reputation with the Tiger-Cats, and downtown Hamilton was my Mecca. People who only know downtown Hamilton today probably would not believe what it was like in the 1950s and '60s.

It was just like old-time Chicago of the 1930's, and I thought it was the greatest town I'd ever seen. There were card games, lots of bootleggers, and some really good bars downtown.

People were shoulder-to-shoulder on a Saturday night. I knew all the action in town, and there was a *lot* of action. When you play in a smaller city where the team matters, you get treated like a god, and we Tiger-Cats could do anything, the people loved us! We were tough and gritty, just like Hamilton itself.

I was tailor-made for the Hamilton. There were about five really good bars downtown and if you couldn't end up with a chick to take to the bootlegger's once the bars closed, there had to be something wrong with you. And I always made sure there was nothing wrong with me. We were kind of the Tiger Woods of our day but there were no computers, no cell phones; I knew I wasn't going to get caught. I'm laughing about it now, but those things happened. I was young and full of myself. It was really hard on my wife, Darlene, and that's the part I really regret. She was taking care of our first child, Jolene, and we had another one coming, Angelo Junior. Even with all of this, I'm chasing everything in town that moves. The last thing I wanted to do was push a carriage around when I was 22 years old. I made things very hard on Darlene. I was disrespectful to her. How many times can you come home with lipstick on your collar? We separated four or five years into my CFL career, and she was sharp enough to nail me to the cross. What's that old saying? Alimony is the screwing you get for the screwing you got? I tried to make sure I took care of my obligations. I wanted to take care of my children the way my father didn't, and I felt like I never left them high and dry. I've talked to my wife Helen about this, and she understands what I did and what I went through. I wasn't mature enough to be a husband and a father at the time.

My lifestyle was hard on the Tiger-Cat organization, too. When I look back on it now I feel bad for Jim Trimble. About once a month he would get a call from the cops about some kind of trouble I was in: fighting, being caught in booze cans. I wasn't a heavy drinker but I was a barroom-brawler type. I'd punch guys out who would bother me. Guys at the bar would all want to take me on to see if I was as tough as was reported in the papers. I'm not very proud of my brawling, but that was 50 years ago. I don't think you could get away with what I did, today. But the cops liked us and only took me in when I went way over the line.

There was a great bar named the Grange Tavern and the owner's son, Harold Lee, liked me a lot. Ronnie Hawkins used to play there pretty regularly and I got to know him well. He always had great bands backing him, and one of them eventually became The Band. They started as Bob Dylan's touring band and went on to have some big hits of their own. Ronnie was from Arkansas and came to Canada in the '50s about the same time as Elvis Presley was making it big. He came up here with Conway Twitty and they toured together. I was sitting with Conway Twitty one night in another Hamilton tavern, The Flamingo Bar, when he wrote, "It's Only Make Believe." I had no idea what he was writing down that night, but it became huge hit — and he wrote it on a fucking napkin! We stayed in touch and when I wrestled down south later in my career I told some of the guys I was going over to Conway Twitty's house. No one believed me, but it was true.

It is a good thing Harold at the Grange liked me. The most outrageous thing I did there was when I was with my teammate Don Paquette. We were driving past the Grange and I told Don to get out and hold the doors of the tavern wide open. I drove up over the curb and right through the doors into the lobby of the tavern. Harold immediately rushed over and yelled, "What the heck are you doing?" And I said, "Harold, I need a drink to go." The cops showed up, but like I said, they liked me and they didn't take any action.

But there were times they did bring me in and Trimble was getting tired of it. One night there was a brawl in a bar downtown and I knocked a guy down a flight of stairs. He weighed about 260 pounds and I'll never forget the big fat fingers on him. They were huge, and somehow I've never forgotten the sight of those big fingers rolled into a fist. I was charged that night, and when the cops phoned Trimble at his home I could hear him scream over the receiver, "Lock him up!" I yelled back, "Fuck you!" I was able to post my own bail, and eventually the charges were dropped.

A week and a half before the first game of the 1960 season, Jim called me into his office for a meeting. "We're trading you to Ottawa," he said. I had no idea it was coming. I was traded for Hardiman Cureton, a guard from UCLA who had played in two Rose Bowls. Trimble told me, "I didn't trade you because of your playing ability. I don't want to trade you, but we've gotta straighten you out. I have to get you off these streets."

His exact words at the end of our meeting were, "One day, we might bring you back." I thought he was an S.O.B. for trading me, but I respected Jim. He was kind of a street guy himself, so he understood where I was coming from, but he had a team to coach and I understood that, eventually.

While I was playing for the Tiger-Cats, I got a phone call from a wrestling promoter in Montreal named Eddie Quinn. Eddie owned the rights for wrestling in the old Montreal Forum and for all of Quebec. When I first got the call, I didn't have a clue as to who Eddie Quinn was, but he knew me quite well. It turned out that Eddie was from Waltham. He was a big Irishman who owned a bunch of cabs in Boston. He sold them all and moved to Montreal to get into wrestling promotion. He followed my football career and knew my entire background. He saw something in me that he thought would make a natural transition to wrestling. I guess he had looked at my character, and what I was doing on the football field. I played angry and I was pretty demonstrative: I was also pretty dramatic.

I wrestled at high school, but that was completely different than professional wrestling, which I didn't know a thing about. This all came out of the blue to me and my immediate reaction was to look at him like he had six heads and say, "Are you kidding me? I don't want any part of that fake, phony shit!" Eddie didn't really acknowledge what I said, but instead answered "Well, you can call it what you want, but it's made me a helluva living." He told me that I was a character guy, and that the business needed people like me. By character, he meant the way I played on the football field. I was a hidden 300-pounder. During the 1960s, wrestling really started to go to guys who looked more like athletes, so they went after football players. I came along right at the start of that, so I was a very fortunate guy. Right place, right time. There was myself, Ernie Ladd out of Grambling who became a big name with the Kansas City Chiefs, Bobby Duncum, Black Jack Mulligan, and Ed "Wahoo" McDaniel, who was a full-blooded Indian who went to Oklahoma and wound up playing for the New York Jets. And here's how small a world it is: I played with Wahoo McDaniel in that high school All-American Game in Memphis in 1955.

We didn't talk actual dollars and cents, but I told Eddie I'd go home and think about it. Darlene didn't particularly like it, but I knew deep down that it was tailor-made for me. So, in January of 1960 I went to Montreal and started training.

I did most of my training in the Montreal Forum where they had a ring set up for us. All of Eddie Quinn's guys would workout there. The trainer, Eddy Auger, helped me quickly learn some things.

I had only been training for a week-and-a-half before I had my first bout. I learned everything from working on the road and watching how it was done. The veterans that I worked with in the ring helped push me up toward the top. These were guys that had never been Main Event wrestlers, but they realized that I had some talent and could become a really good heel — bad guy — if I kept at it. Before I got into the game, I didn't realize that wrestlers talk to each other in the ring, but all the veterans told me, "Just listen to me. I'll tell you what to do." Timing is everything in that business and I was a natural, but they taught me what to do and I'm grateful for it.

Monday was wrestling night in Montreal and there were about 10,000 fans in the Forum for my first bout. It wasn't a Main Event, of course, but I was still fighting a well-known wrestler, a guy from New York named Angelo Savoldi. Angelo was pushing 40 and I thought he was near the end of his career, but he's still alive, maybe 96 years old today, and they call him the world's oldest wrestler. Before I wrestled him, he held the National Wrestling Alliance (NWA) World Junior Heavyweight Championship three times, working as a heel named "The Vampire." Everybody seemed to have more than one nickname, depending upon the area you were wrestling in, and Savoldi also went by Little Jumping Joe, a play off of the fame of Little Jumping Joe Savoldi, another wrestler who had played fullback at Notre Dame in the 1920's. That Savoldi was expelled from Notre Dame for being secretly married, so I kind of felt a connection there.

Strangely, I wasn't scared or nervous before our match. I was the "good guy" that night, but it was the second match of the card, and it didn't matter as much who was good or bad because it wasn't the main match. I wore was a pair of trunks, nothing fancy. A guy from Hamilton made my boots and he made them for 99% of the guys in the business. He's still up on King Street in Hamilton.

When it came time to fight, they announced me as "Angelo Mosca." I didn't have a nickname yet, and the fans half cheered and half booed — I'm pretty sure it had to do with my football reputation. The boos were from those who knew football and the way I played. The cheers were from those who wanted to cheer on a "Canadian" (I was American, but known well in Canada) instead of Savoldi, who was an American.

When the match began, Savoldi whispered in my ear, "listen to me kid." I'll always remember him saying that. He took care of me just like I was a baby. He'd say, "throw an elbow at me," and I'd throw an elbow at him. At this point I'd practiced a bit and knew how I was supposed to make contact, but when I got in the ring I was pumped — it was like a street fight for me. I almost knocked Savoldi out with that elbow. I'm pretty sure he was just trying to survive *me* that night. Savoldi more or less built up the match and carried me. He was a good heel and would do some dirty things to me, like the old eyeball trick: he looks like he's ripping my eyeball right out, but his fingers aren't really in the socket. He would get me in a headlock and then punch me in the neck. He'd parade me around in the headlock and show all the fans what he's going to do. It was up to me to sell it. On the offensive, I was going too far, too hard. Angelo whispered to me, "You'll never last in the match." I learned quickly that it wears you out if you do everything as if it's real. I could never have lasted 25 or 30 minutes in that match because I was working way too hard. Down the road, though, 30 minutes was nothing. It kept me in shape for football, and football kept me in shape for wrestling. It worked out really well that way.

The big finish, because Savoldi suggested it to me just before the match, was going to be my bear hug, which I had developed to play on my size and brute strength. The match was supposed to last 30 minutes, but when you're new to the ring you have no concept of time. Savoldi told me that he'd let me know when it was time for the finish, and wrestlers do that by saying, "it's time to go home."

Toward the end, Savoldi was controlling the match, he was doing all this stuff to me and I was reacting dramatically, and finally we got into what they call, "coming back," which means I start to rally just when the crowd is getting antsy about the heel pounding me. Savoldi was telling me, "throw a punch to my stomach," so I would, and he'd sell it and the crowd would go nuts. Then Savoldi said it: "Let's go home." I threw him into the ropes, and when he bounced back to me I hoisted him up. He has momentum off the ropes and he's also jumping up at the same time that I hoist, but it appears like I'm this big, powerful guy because I have him high in the air. The ref counts us out, "1–2–3," and that was it. I won my first bout and the crowd was cheering like crazy.

Eddie and I never talked money at the start, there was no such thing as getting paid by contract then. You just shook hands and that was the way it was. My first paycheck for that night in the Forum against Savoldi was $250. I don't remember my second or third bouts, just the first, but I ended up working five nights a week all over Quebec that winter. By the end of my first month in Quebec, I made over $3,800. It was great money. My contract for the whole season with the Tiger-Cats was

$11,000 and that was good money too, the NFL wasn't even paying that. But this was *incredible* money. You'd drive your car everywhere you wrestled and they'd even pay you two cents a mile, and gas didn't cost you that much.

I wrestled part-time for 13 years while I was still playing in the CFL but I wouldn't start until December, after the season was over. The Tiger-Cats would never have gone for me wrestling during the season, even though I probably could have. Ralph Sazio didn't like me wrestling. One time after he became head coach he said to me, "Why are you in that phony business?" And I said to him, "If you give me a contract that equals what I make in wrestling, then I will quit on the spot." And that was the end of that conversation.

Once I got really going on my football career, I'd wrestle right up until it was time to go to training camp. One year in the mid-60's I wrestled at the Cow Palace in San Francisco and good loyal old me drove back to Hamilton 48-hours straight in order to make training camp. When I got there I found out five of our guys hadn't even reported to camp. Here I am with two jobs and I'm being more diligent about football than some of the guys who don't have anything else going on but football.

It was during the training camp after I got back from my first winter of wrestling, that Trimble traded me. So in my third year in the CFL, I became an Ottawa Rough Rider. I no more belonged on that Ottawa team than the man in the moon did, and I don't consider that time a very big part of my life.

All I can say is that Ottawa had a weird fucking football team. Frank Clair was the head coach and they called him "The Professor." He was really wary of me, and I don't know why.

Someone must have told him some stories about me. He never, ever talked to me. Frank was scared to death of his own shadow and he hated thunder. When thunder came up, he'd yell at us to get off the field. Eventually we started hearing thunder all the time, "Hey, I think I hear thunder. We better get off the field!" Bill Smythe was the guy who really controlled that whole football team, and he was a heckuva coach.

I wasn't cut out for that team or that town. Ottawa is a very different city than Hamilton. I found the city to be too clean, too boring.

Russ Jackson was the starting quarterback, and I was never a big fan of his. I found him egotistical and I didn't like the way he treated certain players. In 1974 Bill Hodgson bought the Argos, and the next year it was like he had an orgasm when he got Russ Jackson to come in as his head coach. I had retired a couple of years earlier, and I thought with Russ there that I might have an opportunity to get back into the league in some kind of front office capacity. Russ says to me, "Send me a resume." I was shocked. I sent him a resume all right, I wrote, "Dear Russ, I played in the CFL for 15 years, and I'm the guy who knocked you on your fucking ass over 200 times in your career." I signed my name and everything, but I never heard from him, of course.

I'm not saying Russ couldn't play football. He was a great quarterback, and a lot of people from that era think he's one of the two or three best quarterbacks to ever play in the league, but I think he always had a better supporting cast than a guy like Bernie Faloney had in Hamilton.

When I got into the Ottawa locker room, Russ had his little clique with Ronnie Stewart and Kaye Vaughan and those guys.

I used to dress right beside Russ and I'd mimic him all the time. I liked it when the whole team was one big group, like it was in Hamilton. But that wasn't the case in Ottawa. We had another really good quarterback named Ron Lancaster. He was a rookie who had beat out Babe Parilli for the backup quarter-backing job. But, right from the first game the coaching staff began alternating the two of them. It became a big controversy in town, splitting the football fans into the ones who supported Lancaster and the ones who supported Jackson. And it split the team in some ways too.

There was a lot of talent in Ottawa, with Stewart, Vaughan, Joe Poirier. Dave Thelen was the fullback and he was terrific and Bobby Simpson was the tight end. As a matter of fact, Bobby was kind of a clubhouse lawyer and he's the guy who hustled the league to give the players more money for the Grey Cup. We were taking a pay cut for the biggest game of the year: getting only $500 dollars for the Cup Game. Bobby got us an extra $250 in 1960. He was a tremendous athlete and not many people know that he played basketball for Canada at the 1952 Olympics as a member of the famous Tillsonburg Livingstons. He bought a bar in Ottawa from Paul Anka, and we used to hang out there. I lived with a defensive back named Doug Daigneault in Wakefield, which is across the Quebec border, about 30 miles from the city. My wife and family were still back in Hamilton so it was a crazy place, naturally.

We finished second that year at 9–5, two points back of the Argos who were loaded with Tobin Rote from the Green Bay Packers and Detroit Lions at quarterback. We beat Montreal in the semifinals and beat the Argos 33–21 in the first game of the two-game Eastern final. But we had to go back and play in Toronto, where the Argos were really tough.

The entire game was back and forth, and with seven minutes remaining, we were down six points in the game, but still ahead in the series. Our offense was stuck inside the 10-yard line of our end, and as I recall, after a dive play, Bobby Simpson got up slowly and started walking toward the sidelines and got in behind the official. Ron was at quarterback and told the guys to hurry back up to the line of scrimmage. Bobby had got up so slowly that nobody saw him over near the sidelines. Ron hit him with a pass and Bobby took it all the way to Toronto's 18-yard line. Bobby's sleeper play not only got us out of trouble that could have cost us the series, we scored a touchdown and won that game too, by one point. The league changed the rules right after the season to prevent sleeper plays.

We won the Grey Cup in Vancouver 9–6 over the Edmonton Eskimos. The field was really sloppy because of rain, and that really helped the defence. Kaye Vaughan recovered a fumble for the only touchdown of his entire career, and I was now 1–3 in Grey Cup appearances. And by the way, Hamilton, which traded me in the summer, finished last that season and missed the playoffs.

In the off-season I was continuing my new wrestling career, and my family moved to Ottawa that year. But I wanted to be playing somewhere else. Mike Holleback, who tried to recruit me at Boston College, was going to be coaching the Boston Patriots of the American Football League which was just getting started that year. I went to see him and offered my services for a no-cut, no-trade, three-year contract. He wouldn't give it to me, so I had to stay in Ottawa.

The 1961 season wasn't too memorable. We finished 8–6, and got mangled by Tobin Rote and the Argos in the Eastern semifinal. The Ticats got back into the Grey Cup, but lost yet again to Winnipeg, this time in overtime. It was the fourth time that Hamilton had been in the Grey Cup since the Hamilton Wildcats and Hamilton Tigers merged in 1950, and all four times they played the Blue Bombers.

The biggest thing that happened that year was that some of the players got together to try and start a union. A few players from each team meet in Hamilton with Johnny Agro, a lawyer who was also kind of like an agent, even though agents didn't exist then. The union was Ralph Goldston's idea, and he was really vocal about it. There were 26 guys in the room and we put in $100 apiece to start the players' association. Don Shull, a quarterback from Toronto hated management so much that he put in $200. The drive for a union lasted a little over a year before management around the league squashed it. I think that some of the guys were threatened with losing their jobs. As union backers, we couldn't get anything done. It was very hard to get other players to join. That's a big reason why I had an axe to grind with John Barrow, he didn't back our union. Football has never had the strongest unions. And they have a weak one now. And the NFL isn't much better. I get a pension through the union, $250 dollars a month. My pension will be running out soon. I think someone is making some dough on that.

When I think about that '61 Grey Cup, the first one I didn't play in since I came to Canada, I think about Paul Dekker, a tight end I played with in Hamilton before and after I was in Ottawa. He scored a 90-yard touchdown in that '61 game on a pass from Bernie, which tied the Grey Cup record, and ended up playing one more year for us before retiring. Paul unfortunately passed away with Lou Gehrig's disease about 10 years ago. It's just like Tony Proudfoot, who died from ALS just after Christmas in 2010. Now they're finding out through a lot of the research that Tony worked so hard to bring out into the public that football players get Lou Gehrig's far more often than the regular population. We had the running back Ed Buchanan in Hamilton in 1969 and '70, after he'd been a big star in Calgary and Saskatchewan, and he also died of Lou Gehrig's in 1991. He was only 51 years old.

In 1962 I went to training camp with the Rough Riders, but Frank Clair soon traded me to Montreal. He never even called me into his office to talk to me when he made the trade. I was glad to get out of Ottawa, I never felt at home there in the first place. They had the 50th reunion of the 1960 Cup team in the fall of 2010 and I didn't even bother going. I just never felt like I belonged with that team.

I get to Montreal and I meet Perry Moss, who was the head coach. He wanted to make me a linebacker and that was not my position, even if I was pretty fast. I wanted out of Montreal so bad I could taste it. Moss was an egotistical guy who I didn't want to play for, and it showed.

I created a stir one day in practice. In line drills, the defence would hold the blocking dummies for the offence to block against during practice. I didn't have one in my hand and Moss yells out, "Hey Mosca, get a dummy." So I said, "Come here!" and I grabbed him and put him right in front of me — I had my dummy. Moss yelled at me to get off the field and to see me in his office the next morning. The next day he informs me that the team is fining me a game's salary. So, I told him I had a better idea, and that was to release me. It was a ballsy move.

The next thing I did was call Jake Gaudaur, collect. I joke that that was the only time the Ticats had ever accepted a collect call. I told Jake to watch the wires because I might be available.

So, after two years in the wilderness I came back where I belonged. To Hamilton. I proudly wore that black and gold No. 68 for 11 more seasons.

Steeltown Forever

JIM TRIMBLE CALLED ME INTO his office when I returned to Hamilton in 1962. It was a speech similar to the one I received before I was traded. He reminded me that I was talented, but that the team needed stability, and that things were no different this time around. I told him that I understood. I was sure glad to be back in Hamilton, but in hidsight, I'm not sure his speech made any difference to how I acted. When we hit the field I learned of Jim's plan for me. I'm not sure if it was his way of trying to keep me on the straight and narrow, but he put me on every conceivable team there was: kickoffs, punting, defence, offence. I thought, "Holy fuck, this guy is going to kill me."

Once again, we had a pretty good team. There were a few new pieces to the puzzle since I last suited up as a Tiger-Cat. Joe Zuger had just arrived from Arizona. He was another player who turned down the NFL to play in Canada. The Detroit Lions drafted him but he came to Hamilton instead and played defensive back, punter and was the backup quarterback to Bernie Faloney.

Joe was a guy who could do anything on the field and so was Hal Patterson. Hal had come to the Tiger-Cats while I was in

Ottawa. For seven years before that he and Sam Etcheverry were the best passing combination in the league with the Montreal Alouettes. Sam would always get the ball out there, and Hal would climb the ladder and get it. In fact, that's how his career ended. Playing for us in 1967, he went up for a ball, got hit and ruptured his spleen. Hal was such a good guy that everyone called him Prince Hal, but Etcheverry usually referred to him just as Harold. He's one of the greatest athletes who ever played in Canada. He not only was a star in football at Kansas, he was a big rebounder on their basketball team, which lost the 1953 NCAA championship by only one point. I remember playing against Montreal in my rookie season and Hal ran back a kickoff for a 110-yard touchdown. The referee called the play offside, so we kicked it off again and Hal ran it all the way back a second time! I'd never seen anything like it in my life. Hal was not only a tremendous player, he was a tremendous guy, and I've never met a better teammate in my life. Hal was the kind of guy who would go in for a contract and say, "Don't give me all that money. Give some of it to the young Canadian kids who don't make much." In 1960, while I was in Ottawa, the Alouettes traded Etcheverry and Patterson to Hamilton for Bernie Faloney and Don Paquette. Hamilton finished last in 1960, the only time since the old Tigers and Wildcats joined together in 1950 that they didn't make the playoffs, and I guess they were looking to shake things up. But Etcheverry had a no-trade clause that he stuck to, and he ended up leaving the CFL to play with the St. Louis Cardinals, killing the main part of the deal. Bernie wouldn't report to Montreal, either. So the trade became Paquette for Patterson — pretty uneven. They hated the trade in Montreal, and some of the fans burned cars in protest. The Tiger-Cats ended up keeping Faloney and now he had Prince Hal to throw to.

We started the season off 5–1–1 before we hit a real bump. It was just the second year of inter-conference play and we lost at home to Calgary, then lost on the road to Ottawa and Toronto. Bernie was hurt and Joe Zuger, the rookie, was replacing him at quarterback.

While we typically relied on the running game, which was led by Bobby Kuntz (he could really hit a hole hard), we began throwing the ball for as many or more yards as we were running it. We played Saskatchewan at home after we'd lost three-in-a-row, and Zuger really took to the air. He threw eight touchdown passes that day, a CFL record that still stands. And remember, Trimble has me playing on just about every unit we have, including the kickoff team. I was bagged, so I said to Joe, "You throw one more touchdown pass and I'll fuckin' kill you!" He looked at me and wondered who this animal was.

When I look back, we didn't play with the greatest quarterbacks in the world in Hamilton, but they were mentally tough guys who knew how to win. Joe Zuger was a tough, tough player. He was a linebacker too, so that tells you something. I'd say that for seven or eight games, in my last year, Chuck Ealey was probably the most talented quarterback we had with the Tiger-Cats and Frank Cosentino, a Canadian, was probably the closest thing we had to a real quarterback. He had great form, but I don't know that he could win: he didn't get a lot of chances to, with Faloney and Zuger around.

After we killed Saskatchewan we won our last three games of the season and finished first in the East with a 9–4–1 record. We were the only team in the East that didn't have a losing record that year. We took out the Alouettes with no trouble in the two-game, total-point, Eastern final to make it five straight wins as we made our way to the 1962 Grey Cup in Toronto.

For the fifth time in six years, and the third time in my three years in Hamilton, it was going to be the Tiger-Cats and Blue Bombers in the championship game.

Anything could happen when you played at Exhibition Stadium in Toronto. CNE Stadium was always having trouble with weather ruining games which is why Toronto people always called it The Mistake By the Lake. The Grey Cup was still being played on Saturdays and that morning it started out cool, but really humid, which was pretty rare. As game time approached it was getting pretty warm — maybe 50 degrees Fahrenheit (it was before Canada starting using Celsius) for December 1, and a lot of the fans were wearing sunglasses. Late in the first quarter it began: small wisps of fog started drifting in, and by halftime you couldn't see the field from the stands. The game has lived on in infamy as "The Fog Bowl." I read somewhere that Jackie Parker drove up from Tennessee for the game and called it, "The greatest game I never saw." I love that line.

The media in the press box, which was way up near the roof of the stadium, had no idea what was going on the field — and what was going on was a phenomenal display by our flanker Garney Henley and Winnipeg's running back Leo Lewis. Garney took a pass from Joe Zuger 74 yards for a touchdown. He also ran for another touchdown, and by the end of the game he had 100 yards in pass receptions, 119 yards rushing, 47 yards on kick returns and two touchdowns. He could have, and probably should have been MVP, but that went to Leo Lewis, who scored two touchdowns, one of them on a 64-yard kick return, and also threw a touchdown pass to Charlie Shepard. They used to call Lewis the "Lincoln Locomotive" and Shepard's nickname was "Choo-Choo." You just don't get those great nicknames in football anymore.

We led 21–19 when we broke for halftime and Sydney Halter, the league commissioner was so worried about the fog and the TV reception, that he ordered the referee to shorten the intermission by five minutes. It was getting to be that you couldn't see and the punt returners were telling us that you had to listen for the ball to land and then go try to pick it up.

We were trailing early in the fourth quarter, 28–27, partly because Don "Sudsie" Sutherin had missed two converts. Sudsie was one of the best ever at kicking the extra point and he accepted the blame for those misses, which he said cost us the game. He was, and still is, a real stand-up guy. He became a helluva defensive coach in this league. It was his defence that was the core of Hamilton's last really good teams in the late 1990s, and I truly believe that he could still be a defensive coordinator in this league today.

With 5:31 gone in the fourth quarter the commissioner and the two general managers decided to postpone the game until the next day. I still think that was a mistake, and the game should have been finished. We'd already played that long, what was another nine minutes? But they decided to call it.

Despite all my partying, I was never one to cheat the team by going out and breaking curfew before a game, but in my mind that game should have already been over. (And we should have won). That night we were staying out in some dump on the Lakeshore not far from the CNE because somehow they couldn't get us rooms downtown. I said to Bob Minihane, my teammate, "Hey we can do nine minutes standing on our head," and we decided to go downtown. We go outside the motel, and flagged down a cab but when we opened the door, there's Trimble, Sazio and Joe Restic sitting in the back seat! There must be 10,000 taxis in Toronto and all three of them are in that one! Trimble asked us where we thought we were going and we said "Out for a soda", and Trimble barked at us, "Soda my ass! Get back to your room!" So we went back to the room, waited a while, and went right back out and joined the party downtown. That should have been the party night; that game should have been over.

The next day, there were only about 15,000 fans in the stands, instead of the 32,000 who were there the afternoon before. When we got to the stadium the players found out Joe hurt his ankle the day before and couldn't play quarterback, he could only punt and even that was going to be hard. We had nine minutes and 29 seconds left, and Frank Cosentino, who was actually our third stringer behind Bernie and Joe, came in to play quarterback for us. He had a good game and, as I recall he rushed for 128 yards. We completely dominated the Sunday part of the game but we kept making mistakes at the wrong time, and nobody scored. Joe tried to kick a single, which would have put the game into overtime, but he couldn't get anything on it because of his ankle and it hardly reached the goal line. We lost by that single point, which was my third Grey Cup loss to the Bombers in three trips. It was getting a little old, if you want to know the truth.

After the 1962 season Jim Trimble, the guy who brought me to Canada, moved to Montreal to take over the Alouettes. The Ticats promoted Ralph Sazio to head coach, and he was murder as a bench boss. He was very tough, but he knew defence like nobody else. He could still coach in today's game. Sazio was always in complete command, because he kept it simple to understand. I've seen Sazio move a player just a little bit on the field and that would make the difference in making a play. Once I saw him tell Bobby Krouse to shift six inches over, *six inches,* and then he told Bobby, "Now that's how you cover the guy."

With Sazio at the helm in 1963 we finished the year 10–4, two points up on the Rough Riders, who had a pretty good team. The standings don't really paint a true picture of that season, because it wasn't as close as it looked on paper. Our four losses were all on the road — we were undefeated at home until the last game of the Eastern final, when it didn't really matter. And like always, we finished strong, winning the last six games of the schedule to head into the playoffs on a roll.

In the Conference final we absolutely murdered the Rough Riders in Game 1 at Ottawa, 45–0. They won the second game at Civic Stadium in Hamilton, 35–18, but it didn't mean anything at all. By then we were hardly even thinking about them, we were already looking forward to going to Empire Stadium in Vancouver for the Grey Cup.

The B.C. Lions were representing the West, so it was the first time the Tiger-Cats would play somebody other than the Blue Bombers in the Grey Cup. It was only B.C.'s 10th season in the league, and second time in the playoffs, and here they were in the Grey Cup in their hometown. Vancouver was going nuts. The 2010 Olympics in Vancouver reminded me of how the city was going crazy for the Lions in 1963. Sure it was a smaller scale, but the Lions were Vancouver's only real pro team in any sport at the time, so the whole city was pretty well crazy for the team. The Lions had a good team, including Joe Kapp, who went on to play for the Minnesota Vikings three years later and is the only person ever to play quarterback in the Rose Bowl, Grey

Cup and Super Bowl. Tom Brown was B.C.'s defensive star, and the heart of their offence was running back Willie Fleming.

Sazio had said during the week leading up to the Grey Cup that the key to the game for us was stopping Willie Fleming. He rushed for over 1,200 yards that year and he averaged 9.7 yards per carry, which was unbelievable in the days of two-back sets. He was really hard to stop, and sometimes impossible to bring down, so Sazio was right to be worried about him.

Bobby Kuntz blocked a punt and Gene Ceppetelli recovered the ball in the first quarter, giving us a great chance to score, but the Lions stopped us on their three-yard line. Willie Bethea later scored after a long drive to give us the lead, and Art Baker got another touchdown and we led 14–3 at the half. But nobody remembers any of that, because late in the second quarter Fleming took off on a sweep to my right, and headed down the left sideline. Ceppetelli and Zuger played on that side and they kept fencing Fleming in. I continued running after Fleming as fast as I could from behind. It ended up being one of those bang-bang plays. Fleming ducks and goes down right when I come over the top of him. My knee caught the back of his head and Fleming stayed down. I think, after all that running, Fleming gained exactly one yard on the play. It was not an illegal hit, and there wasn't a penalty on the play. Fleming was in bounds, and it was just one of those plays. Even if I didn't hit Fleming, he still would have been hit by Ceppetelli or Zuger who had him boxed in. As a matter of fact, I think I hit Zuger on that play too.

Nobody tried to get even with me, nobody retaliated: because that's the way the game was played. I didn't help Fleming up, either. I never helped anybody up — in fact, I told the Ticats' Otis Floyd in 2010 that he shouldn't help players up off the field — I just walked away.

But the crowd wanted my head. It happened so fast that it probably looked like he was out of bounds and that it was a late hit. Plus, Sazio had been talking all week about how important Fleming was to their offence, so maybe that's why people thought I did it on purpose. But I wasn't trying to hurt him, that's just the way I played, full speed. Fleming had to leave the game with a concussion, but he didn't actually go to the hospital as the papers reported. The crowd booed me every time I made a tackle for the rest of the game.

Hal Patterson scored another touchdown for us in the second half, and B.C. didn't score until the dying moments of the game. We won 21–10. But, the only score people remembered was Mosca 1, Fleming 0.

After the game Jake Gaudaur grabbed my arm and held it up like I just won the world heavyweight boxing title or something. I laughed about it and said, "That's show biz!" Long after that, I told the writer Earl McRae that "I didn't mean to hit him, but I did hit him and that's football. I always pushed things right to the legal limit. If I saw a guy picking his nose and he wasn't in the play and I thought I could get away with flattening him, I would. He has no right to pick his nose in a football game."

I have never meant to badly hurt any football player. I was very, very, very physical and if you didn't like it…too bad.

When the papers came out, you would have thought that World War II was on again. *The Victoria Colonist* headline was "Dirtiest Player Injures Star." In the *Vancouver Sun* there was a picture of me standing upright, with Willie Fleming lying on the ground and the headline, "Lions Blackjacked By Cat's Brutality."

Joe Skrein, the B.C. coach, had a personal column in one of the Vancouver papers

And he said we were hungrier than the Lions were because we'd lost so many times in the Grey Cup. He also said also we weren't as good in that game as we were when we beat them in Hamilton during the regular season.

And this is what else he wrote:

> "You can break it down all you want, but Fleming's injury was the most damaging thing that happened. I'm glad he wasn't hurt seriously. At first we planned to send him to hospital, but a brain surgeon on our medical staff examined him at halftime and thought he'd be all right. I can't comment on the play Angelo Mosca made on Willie. It happened across the field. But I can comment on another thing I saw, when he went after Joe Kapp. I've never seen a more deliberate attempt to injure a player. He rolled Joe and then brought the big elbow around. There's no reason for this in football. A man can play as rough and tough as he wants but that type of thing is not part of the game."

I don't recall much about the play Skrein was talking about. I know that I always used everything that was available to me, and the rules were such that we could head slap and spear. The only thing I remember concerning Joe Kapp is that I went to try to shake his hand after the game, he pushed me away and told me to fuck off. There was a picture in one of the papers of Joe looking away from me when I was trying to shake his hand.

I became instantly synonymous with the Willie Fleming hit. People had called me "dirty" long before that hit, but because I was the guy who put Fleming out, they really started speaking up about it. Now when Grey Cup time comes around, people who weren't even born will see me and go, "Oh, yeah, it's the guy who hit Fleming." Out in B.C. there are still some people who hate me all these years later. I find that amazing.

Aside from the Fleming incident, I had a really good year in 1963. I was even nominated for my first Schenley Award, which I used to call the Shitley Awards. They're called the Gibson's Finest CFL Player Awards now, but for a long time it was the Schenley Distillery, which made Black Velvet rye whiskey, that sponsored the awards.

There were fewer categories when I played then there are today, and in 1963 offensive and defensive linemen and line-backers were all lumped into the "Linemen of the Year" cate-gory. It was really hard for a lineman to actually win the award because the linebackers got more tackles and were more visible on TV coverage. Plus, there were four teams in the East, but five in the West, which gave them more voters: from 1958 to 1973, when they changed the awards, only two Eastern players won lineman of the year, and one of them was John Barrow, who was our representative eight years out of nine. He won it once, in 1962. I lost to Tom Brown of the Lions in 1963, but that week we won the bigger trophy.

Gene Ceppetelli tagged me with the nickname, "Big Nasty," and it really fit. Around that time, Gordie Walker of the *Globe and Mail* created a thing called Mosca's Meanies. He used me as kind of an antihero and I chose the so-called tough guys of the league every year. It continued long after I finished playing, too. I had earned a reputation, and the Fleming hit just amplified it.

Gordie Walker was a very humble, quiet man who just loved the CFL and for a long time acted as the league statistician. He and I played gin together in the dressing room for a long time too. I got to know Gordie's brother Hal, who wrote for the old *Toronto Telegram*. He left the Tely to go work in the west and I once lived with him for about a month when I was wrestling out of Calgary. One time, I came back from an out-of-town trip and Hal is sitting there with a bottle of whiskey, very drunk, and he's writing a column. The paper came out around noon the next day and I said, "I gotta read this column. I don't believe that you can write a column drunk." I read the column, and you'd never believe that this guy had had one ounce of liquor in him. The column was just unbelievable. He was a great writer. A lot of those newspaper guys in that era were like that, except for Milt Dunnell of the *Toronto Star*, who never drank.

After the season, the advertising agency for Schick, the razor blade company, approached me to do a TV commercial. It was the first commercial I ever did, although I've done dozens of them since then: in print, on radio and on television. The common thread was that all of them centred around my toughness, like the one I did in 1978 for Yamaha, which said, "Yamaha, One Tough Customer," and showed another tough customer, which was me.

I went to a studio in Toronto to shoot the Schick commercial, and they encouraged me to relax and act natural. They gave me the script, and in those days, you'd do the whole commercial all the way through and you'd have to repeat it if you made a mistake. We did take after take. Go ahead and say, "The new Schick Super Chromachrome Blades" 80 times and see if you don't' go fuckin' nuts. The ad concept was that I was a very threatening guy, but I was getting this really soft smooth shave. The ending line was that if you didn't believe that I was getting this tremendous close shave you could, "Come and tell me to my face." I paused between the "tell me" and the "to my face" parts for dramatic effect, and I'd really growl the "to my face" part slowly. That commercial became very popular, particularly because of the Fleming hit, and people often used that line in regular conversation.

One of the other things I was starting to enjoy was speaking at banquets, and I'm still doing it today. It started after the Grey Cup win in Vancouver because the Ticats were in demand all over Ontario. I had no trouble speaking, so I did it a lot. I would tell some jokes and talk about pro ball in general, and what it could do for kids. There were a lot of guys who did sports banquets in those days, and it didn't cost an arm and a leg for an organization to bring them in like it does today. The Montreal Canadiens were the star hockey team at the time and a lot of those guys were out doing banquets and we'd end up at the same head table together: Henri Richard, Maurice Richard, Dickie Moore. These were all guys from my era of Canadian sports and at any big banquet in any town in Ontario, a handful of us would be there. I've done banquets with Gordie Howe, Bobby Baun, Tim Horton, Johnny Bower, Jim Brown, Fergie Jenkins, Whitey Ford, Yogi Berra: big stars of the time. The hockey referee Red Storey, who also played for the Argos, was one of the best and funniest dinner speakers I ever heard. I worked dinners with Ted Williams, too, that was pretty amazing. All those years after I bombed out at selling hot dogs at Fenway because I was watching him in batting practice, I was sitting beside him at head tables.

Agencies started to come to me for commercials and a few years later, also for some movies and TV dramas. One time I walked into a casting room, and the director — I'll never forget it — looked at me and immediately sent everyone else home.

That's the way the movie business goes: he wanted my face. When people thought of Angelo Mosca in those days, they pictured my face and thought, "He's an animal. He's a tough sonuvabitch, he doesn't care." But I really do care. I'm not an animal; that was just my reputation. I'm okay with that, though. No problem. As long as I get paid.

In the spring of 1964 I was up for a new contract. I went into Ralph Sazio's office and before I could say a word he said, "I guess you're going to want a raise." I did. I deserved it after the year I had in 1963. Ralph then offered me the phone and dared me to call around to other teams to see if I could get a deal. I just took the phone, told him I knew he'd probably already called everyone else in the league and told them to keep their hands off me and I threw the phone at him. Then he threw the phone right back at me. It was hilarious. In the end, I got the raise.

I always liked Ralph, and I really respected how he could coach. But he and I had a million and one differences of opinions. One was about my wrestling. I was really starting to get a name in wrestling, and starting to travel across the continent and Ralph didn't like it. He wasn't worried about me getting hurt, it was that wrestling had a certain stigma attached to it. Like we used to say at the time, "Pro wrestling's an exhibition of strength and skill,' which was the answer you'd always give to the question about whether it was real or not. So I used to say to Sazio, "Ralph, my bank manager calls me 'Sir.' What's yours call you?"

I not only made more money in 1964, but I played less, technically. Sazio decided that I would only play one way, which, of course, was on defence. For my whole career, with the exception of Ottawa, I had played on both sides of the ball. A lot of guys were starting to play only one way right around that time, and it was a really nice change from two years before when Jim Trimble had me on the field for almost every play.

We had another good season in '64, although it didn't start that well. We lost our first two games, to Montreal and Ottawa, and were only 4–3–1 by mid-season. We won our last six games and nobody scored more than 16 points on us in any of the last eight games of the year; so playing only one way seemed to be paying off. At the end of the year Ralph Sazio was chosen as the coach of the year and Tommy Grant won the Schenley as most valuable Canadian. Tommy had 1,049 yards in receiving and he was the first Eastern receiver since Hal Patterson in 1960 to go over 1,000 yards. Remember, we played only 14 games in the East, while the West had 16.

We finished first in the East, which was becoming almost normal. Ottawa finished second and demolished Montreal in the Eastern semifinal. Ottawa shocked us by winning the first game of the two-game, total-point Conference final 30–13 at Lansdowne. The big play was Ottawa's Gene Gaines running back a kickoff for a 128-yard touchdown, which was a CFL playoff record.

We were in a corner heading back to Civic Stadium for the second game, down 17 points. Russ Jackson, Ottawa's QB, was having a really tremendous year and led the league in passing, but somehow he always had a rough time in Hamilton. We hadn't lost a game at Civic Stadium since mid-September, so we figured we'd play better than we did in Ottawa, but could we be 18 points better? It turns out that's exactly what we were. We won 26–8, and eliminated Ottawa, again.

That put us in the Grey Cup rematch with the B.C. Lions. They were having a spectacular year, even better than us, to tell you the truth. They went 11–2–3 in the regular season and only allowed about 12 or 13 points a game on defence, with Tom Brown having another great season at linebacker.

The Grey Cup Game was back at Exhibition Stadium, again. It was a wet day so the field and the ball got greasy really quickly. We had a pretty physical team with good running backs in Bobby Kuntz and Willie Bethea so the conditions weren't really against us, but the Lions might have been a little more used to it than we were, because the weather in Vancouver is like that a lot of the time. The Lions opened up a 19-point lead by halftime, and we just couldn't catch up. Their fullback Bob Swift scored their first touchdown on a one-yard plunge. Swift was a rookie that year and rushed for just over 1,000 yards and 11 touchdowns, but he got hurt later in the first half — this time a player injury didn't cost B.C. the Cup, I'd say it won it for them. One of their defensive backs, Bill Munsey, filled in for Swift at fullback, and he killed us. Just murdered us. I've always said that if Swift stayed in the game we would have won, but that didn't happen. Not only did Munsey fill in better than anyone expected, Munsey scored twice in the third quarter, once on offence on an 18-yard run, and once on defence, when he picked up a fumble by Johnny Counts and ran it back 71 yards. And he ate us up on the ball control game through the middle. He was the MVP of the game, and the Lions ended up winning 34–24. It probably made B.C. fans really happy, in a payback kind of way, that Fleming scored a touchdown for them on a 47-yard run. I'm sure the whole team was motivated by the previous year's loss, especially Fleming.

We got back to the Cup in 1965, which no one expected because we brought in nine new starters that year; but at 10–4 we were again the only team in the East with a winning record. Everyone knows, though, that in the CFL it's not how many you win it's when you win them, and through the '50s and '60s the Hamilton Tiger-Cats not only won a lot, they won at the right time. In 1965, we won the last three games of the schedule, then all three games in the post-season, including the Grey Cup. We lost only one game all year at home, and during the regular season we gave up only about 12 points a game on defence. That team wasn't quite as good as the 1967 team, which was easily the best team I ever played on, and it might not have been as good as the 1966 team which *didn't* make the Grey Cup. In 1966, though, Ottawa was unbelievable with Russ Jackson playing really well and Margene Atkins, Whit Tucker and Vic Washington having unbelievable years.

But in 1965, we knocked the Rough Riders out in the Eastern final by a combined score of 39–23, and went on to meet our old archrivals, the Winnipeg Blue Bombers, in the Grey Cup. Once again, the game was played at Exhibition Stadium, and once again, weather was a problem. This time, it was wind. It was like playing in a full gale, and it was blowing right into your teeth for two quarters: the second and fourth for us, the first and third for Winnipeg. The wind was so bad that an hour before the game, the two head coaches, Ralph Sazio and Bud Grant, got together with the commissioner, Sydney Halter, and made up a new punting rule. The problem was that with the wind as strong as it was, the team going into it would probably not be able to punt on third down because the kick would be blown back toward them and cause a "no-yards" penalty every time. The rule they created for the game was that when a ball was punted into the wind, it would be blown dead as soon as it hit a punt receiver, almost like a fair catch. The other strategy you could use was to concede a safety touch for two points if you were punting in your own end. In 1965 the rule was that by conceding the points you got to keep the ball on offence, with a new first down, on the 20-yard-line I think. That rule was changed right after the season — now you have to kick the ball away after a safety touch — and it was because of what happened in that Grey Cup, forever known as the Wind Bowl.

We were lucky to have Joe Zuger on our team and it was never more obvious than in that game. He was probably the greatest punter I've ever seen, even better than Dave Mann in the sense that he could kick the ball against the wind as well as he could with it.

The Wind Bowl was a tough, tough game; one of the most demanding I've ever played in. Most of the scoring was done with the wind, but it was what was done against it that really made the difference. The wind was absolutely howling, and three times — once in the first quarter and twice in the third quarter — Bud Grant decided to give up safety touches when they went to third down in their own end. I thought they were doing exactly the right thing, but we never gave up a safety all game. We didn't have to because we either had better field position, or we'd use Zuger and his incredible punting. But the real reason we didn't give up any safeties all game was that Ralph Sazio would never *give* you anything. That's the way Ralph coached, whether we were in a bad spot on the field or not. The wind was simply atrocious, you couldn't throw against it — Bernie Faloney hit Willie Bethea for a 67-yard touchdown with the wind — and we ran the shit out of ball. Zuger with his punting was the one who really saved us. One time, in our own end with the wind in the third quarter, the snap was really high, but Zuger managed to jump up, haul it down and kick it right over their receiver to get us out of trouble — it was a key, and often forgotten, play of the game. We won 22–16 and although I thought Bud Grant did the right thing, Winnipeg lost the Grey Cup by exactly those three safeties. People talked that one over for a long, long time.

We never got Grey Cup rings for that game. Teams didn't start presenting them until after the 1965 game and in fact, the only ring I'd got so far in my career was for the Cup I won with the Ottawa Rough Riders. But five years ago I raised $50,000 to buy the guys from the '65 team rings. About three-quarters of the guys came back to a presentation at Ivor Wynne, during a Cats' game.

That was the last game in an incredible Grey Cup rivalry: Hamilton and Winnipeg were in seven Grey Cups in 13 years and just about every one of them had something strange or historic to it. But like the Lions after they played us the year before, it would be 19 more years before the Bombers made it back to the Grey Cup. I still had a couple left in me, though.

The Best Team
There Ever Was

THE 1967 HAMILTON TIGER-CATS WERE the greatest football team I've ever seen assembled in Canada. I always
say it was because the core of the team all came of age at the
same time. Zuger, Barrow, Ceppetelli, Henley, myself, we were
all 28, 29, 30 years old and full of experience. Ceppetelli was
the centre, Jon Hohman and Bill Danychuk were the guards,
Charlie Turner and Ellison Kelly were the tackles. That was the
greatest offensive line I've ever seen. We had Tommy Joe Coffey
and Tommy Grant catching the football, and Dave Fleming
and Willie Bethea, running the ball. Those two weren't classic 1,000-yard rushers, but they did everything. They pounded
the ball, caught the ball and Bethea returned kicks, too. People
don't realize that Bethea played eight years and Fleming played
10 years. You never hear of that. You don't see many American
running backs play more than five years in this league. Those
two guys were big, strong and durable enough to last a long
time. In 1971, Fleming took a pass from Joe Zuger and went
108 yards with it; the longest pass and run in Hamilton history.

One of the things that really bothers me is that if you look at
the Wall of Fame in Ivor Wynne Stadium, there are no running

backs up there. After McDougall, Gilchrist and Bobby Kuntz, Hamilton didn't have many good running backs until these two guys came, and stayed. I'm trying to get both of them on the wall.

You can't have a successful team without team chemistry, and we had a great club for that. I had some really good roommates in my time and Dave Fleming was one of the best. He was a rugged sonuvabitch from a rough area of Pittsburgh and was with the Steelers for a couple of years before he came to the Tiger-Cats in 1965. I remember in his first year, I watched him reach into his pocket for a comb, but he pulled out a toothbrush instead, so he started combing his hair with it. Right away I thought, "This guy has to be a teammate of mine, he's a real character." Dave did a lot of crazy things in his time, but he sure has taken care of his family. His wife Sue is a great woman but she has been bedridden for more than 20 years with Multiple Sclerosis. She can't even talk now. I was at their daughter's wedding a few years ago and I saw Dave pick Sue right up and carry her over to her wheelchair. I couldn't believe my eyes. They live back in Pittsburgh, and at the age of 67 Dave set the Pennsylvania state record for the bench press in his age category. I asked Dave why he wanted to bench so much, and then I figured out for myself that he needed to stay strong so he could pick Sue up and carry her when he needed to.

In football you don't spend as much time on the road as you do in the other sports but it's important that when you do, you have the right roommate — you never have your own room. In 1967, Gene Ceppetelli was my roommate and he was great. We liked to talk about the game, we always discussed it in advance: what our plans were, how we planned to use everything the next day. We also played a lot of pranks on each other.

One day early in the '67 season a newspaper guy called up to our room and wanted to talk to me, so I went downstairs to the hotel lobby for the interview. I never ignored a press guy because I needed them just as much as they needed me. When I finished the interview I went to take a shower and when I pull back the curtain there are two great big turds sitting in the tub! Ceppetelli had crapped in the tub. What a great prank! I had to do something even better to get back at him. I decided not to say anything about the tub prank, I didn't mention it to him or to anyone. I'm sure my silence was eating away at him. Six weeks later, we're on the road again and Ceppetelli steps out. I then squat up on his bed and I crapped in the bed, right in the bottom of the sheets. That night, when he crawled into bed he stretched out his feet to the bottom, right into the stuff. He turned to me, stared at me for a long, long time and slowly said, "We're even." Now, that's a good roommate. I know it's gross and juvenile, but nobody ever said we were mature.

Ceppetelli was the victim of another one of my favourite road pranks. Hotels often have adjoining doors between rooms: one door opens into your room, the other opens into the room next door, and each one has a lock on its side. One night while I was lying in bed I could hear this thud that kept repeating. I had just seen the movie *Dr. No* on television and saw how James Bond listened through a wall, so I grabbed a glass and put the open end against the wall and the bottom against my ear to listen. I said to Gene, "Cep, I think they're screwing over there." I open our door, and the other door's unlocked. I could hear the heavy breathing, and I said, "Cep, c'mon over here and catch this." So Ceppetelli gets out of his bed, naked, and steps in front of me so that he could hear the couple next door. Suddenly, I take my foot and kick him right in the ass. Ceppetelli shoots through the door and into the adjoining room. I slammed our door right behind him and locked it. Imagine it: Ceppetelli all of the sudden appears, naked, in this couple's room. The guy in bed with the woman bolts straight out of bed. They don't have any idea what's going on. Ceppetelli has to run and unlock their main door and run out into the hotel hallway. But our main door is locked, too. Ceppetelli was naked, pounding on our door and screaming his head off! I'll never forget it.

We had some great characters on that 1967 team. Bill Reddell was a quarterback we got that year in a trade with Edmonton. He ended up coaching high school ball in California and he had Wayne Gretzky's son, and Joe Montana's son, too. Smokey Stover, who played fullback and linebacker, was only with us that one season, but what a year he had. In January, he won the Super Bowl with the Kansas City Chiefs and in December he won a Grey Cup with us. Another guy who played only that season with us was offensive end Ted Watkins, who had been with Ottawa before that. A few years later he was shot and killed in the States by the police. They were actually trying to get his brother, but they killed him by mistake. I'm not clear on the details, but I think they were robbing a bank.

The '67 team was a great bunch of guys and I still keep in touch with a lot of them. It was a team that was perfect for the city of Hamilton. Defence represents Hamilton. It epitomizes the city. We played it big, tough and dirty. Hamilton had always been a defensive town, but even more so with Ralph. He was a defensive guru and he never put a guy in a position they didn't belong.

In the CFL records, and the Ticat media guides, it shows that our 1967 team gave up 195 points in our 14 regular-season games. But if you actually add up the scores of the individual games, you find out that we only gave up 165 points that year. We gave up five fewer points the year before, but in 1967 we didn't give up a touchdown in the last six games we played, including the Grey Cup. I still can't believe that. It was phenomenal. Ralph used to say, "Give me eight points and I'll beat you 8–7."

It was Canada's Centennial Year and we wore special helmets all season that had the Centennial logo in the background behind the Tiger-Cat symbol. Ottawa was hosting the game, and I'm sure a lot of fans wanted Ottawa to be in the Grey Cup, given that Ottawa is Canada's capital. But there was no way Ottawa was going to beat us that year. In the East final we beat them 11–3 in Ottawa and then 26–0 back home. It was no contest. Saskatchewan won the West in a really close final against Calgary. They had stars like Ron Lancaster, Hughie Campbell and big George Reed, who rushed for more than 1,400 yards that year.

To show you what kind of football town it was, 25,000 Hamiltonians attended a downtown rally before the Grey Cup to send us off to Ottawa. It was great to see that the community really embrace our team.

We were practicing for the Grey Cup one afternoon in Ottawa and a guy named Jerry Selinger was watching us from the sidelines. Jerry was actually from Hamilton, but he played centre for Ottawa and we had just beaten them out. We didn't like each other and probably still don't. Whenever it was the Rough Riders against the Tiger-Cats, he played over top of me. You could do a lot of things to a centre in those days, because they had to keep their head down. Now, I understand, you can't even hit the centre at all. But in those days I used to take my head and aim right at the centre's chest and roll him just like a bowling ball. And then make fun of him. All during that practice at the Grey Cup Selinger kept on me and as we're walking off he's gesturing and saying, "Hey, tough guy!" So I said, "C'mere. I'll show you how fuckin' tough I am." And BA-BOOM. I cold-cocked him, knocked him out. I'm looking at him on the ground and saying to myself, "Wow. I've still got a punch." It hit the press and I had a lot of fun with it. During my time there was kind of an anti-fraternization rule. You would be fined if you fraternized with the other team.

The Centennial-year Grey Cup wasn't even close. In the first quarter, Joe Zuger scored on a short run, and that was all the scoring we needed. Alan Ford got Saskatchewan's only point of the game in the first quarter on an 87-yard quick kick, which you never, ever, see any more. It was the longest punt in Grey Cup history. Ted Watkins later scored on a 72-yard pass and run, Joe kicked three singles and Bill Ray Locklin ran back a fumble for a touchdown. We clobbered Saskatchewan 24–1, the biggest margin of a victory since the Cats beat Winnipeg 10 years earlier, 32–7. The Grey Cup was the sixth straight game that we didn't allow a touchdown, and in the three playoff games, including the Cup, we allowed all of four points. Nobody's ever going to convince me that our club wasn't the greatest team this country has ever seen. Four points against in three games at the most important time of the year? Forget about it.

CHAPTER EIGHT

My Last Game and the Year Hamilton Will Never Forget

BETWEEN 1968 AND 1972 THE Ticats were still mean, but those years were lean. Just a year after we had the best team ever, our 1968 team was a shadow of the 1967 championship squad. It was Ralph Sazio's last season as coach, and we kind of stunk up his farewell party; it was the only time in my 15 CFL seasons that my team had a losing record, we finished 6–7–1. It was also the only losing season Sazio had as Hamilton coach. Prior to that year he was the head coach for five seasons, went to the Grey Cup four times (winning three), and had a regular-season record of 49 wins, 20 losses and one tie. Phenomenal. But in 1968 the stingy defence we had the year before wasn't nearly as good and we gave up 292 points, 10 points per game more than we gave up in 1967. And we lost to the Argos in the semifinals, which never sits well with Hamilton fans.

I did, however, become a naturalized Canadian in 1968. That's a term that doesn't exist in the CFL anymore but it was good for the league at the time. The deal was that if you were an American and had played in the CFL with the same team for more than five years in a row, and you got your Canadian citizenship, you no longer counted against the import ratio.

That helped keep the core of a team together, which was good for the fans, and it also made Canadians out of a lot of guys who'd probably never heard of Canada, or at least thought of it, when they were growing up — like me. I was one year behind John Barrow in getting my Canadian citizenship and naturalized-Canadian status. We had about seven Americans on our team in the late '60s who became naturalized Canadians. Some people argued that it would eventually phase Canadians out of the game, but I didn't believe that. In any case, they ended the idea about 40 years ago and I think the immigration laws today would probably prevent it ever from coming back.

In the middle of October that year we went into Ottawa, where the fans always hated me. Two high school students had made a banner which they unfurled in front of the south stands at Lansdowne Stadium. I read the story in the paper later of how one night one of the kids said to the other, "That Angelo Mosca looks like a gorilla." So when they unrolled the banner it said, "Mosca Eats Bananas!" Our bench was on the other side of the field and so the sign was pointing right at us. The other guys were all laughing and grabbing my arm and pointing in that direction. I shook my fist at the other side of the field, and covered my eyes, pretending I didn't want to see it, but really I was peeking out from behind my fingers, hoping. I did the same thing in wrestling: fans would make fun of my King Kong ring name by yelling "Ping Pong" and I'd do the same kind of thing: cover my ears as if it really bothered me, but I'd be opening the fingers to listen and hope they were building up to a crescendo. At Lansdowne, the kids had turned around to show the south stands the banner and the place went completely crazy, and went even more nuts when I pretended to cover my eyes. It made papers all across Canada.

Twenty years later, when the 1988 Grey Cup was in Ottawa, I was down there making a speech at the Nepean Canadian Sports Club and the same two guys came and unfurled the same banner again. I told the audience, "I love this. It's what football needs." And two days later at the Grey Cup parade, with me on the review stand, they marched in the parade and unfurled the banner again. It was great.

I also met my second wife, Gwen Wotton, in 1968 — at 35,000 feet. She was the stewardess on the plane we had for a road game. One of the sports writers was trying to hustle her, but it was me who ended up getting her number, and we started dating after that. She was a lot of fun and we eventually got married in 1972. I never asked my daughter about this, but I think she never liked Gwen because she was taking the place of her mother. Jolene was 13 when Darlene and I divorced. I paid alimony and I saw the kids as much as I could, but I admit it wasn't that much. I have good kids. I really do. I always felt that I was a good provider but that I wasn't a great father. I wasn't there enough for their schooling, for their plays, for their games, and I didn't know how to raise kids. I didn't really even know how to treat a woman.

After the 1968 season I was away wrestling in Japan when Ralph Sazio moved up to General Manager and Joe Restic became head coach. Restic was the guy who recruited Paul Hornung for Notre Dame, and he was an assistant coach for us for six years. In my opinion he wasn't really head coaching material. He used to drive us nuts before the game. He'd walk around the dressing room in fear. I think the fear was that he was going to get beaten by the other team. The whole time he was coaching, six years as an assistant and three years as head coach, I think I saw him laugh maybe once. But Joe was an interesting guy. For example, during the Second World War, he was the guy they dropped way behind enemy lines because he spoke the language. But as a football coach, I had my doubts. He was a different kind of guy, especially following somebody as tough as Ralph. One time in 2010 I saw a receiver at Ticat practice drop three passes in a row. I said, "If Ralph Sazio was here right now, he'd pull the guts right out of that guy." But Restic wasn't that kind. He went to Harvard in 1971 and coached there for more than 20 years. It was exactly where he belonged: you don't have to recruit there.

After my only losing season, in 1968, we started winning again during the season, but couldn't win in the playoffs. We finished third again in 1969 and those two years were the only time in my career my team didn't finish first or second in the East. Toronto beat us again in the semifinal, 15–9, and that was really hard for Hamilton fans, back-to-back playoff losses to the Argos.

Restic said he was going to make me a captain the next year but I said, "Forget it, I've had enough of appointed captains. That's all we've ever had since I've been here. The only way I'd be a captain is if the team elected me." So Restic polled the team and I was made a captain. We finished first in 1970 at 8–5–1, and I had a really great year. I was the Eastern nominee for the lineman of the year but lost to Calgary's great linebacker Wayne Harris, who won the fourth of his five Schenleys. I was pushing 34 years of age and was one of the oldest linemen ever to be nominated for the Schenley. We didn't make the Grey Cup again because we lost in the Eastern final to Montreal Alouettes, who had a pile of rookies and Sonny Wade at quarterback. After beating us, they went on to win their first Grey Cup since the late 1940s.

Al Dorow became the coach in 1971 but lasted only one year. We finished 7–7, beat Ottawa in the semis but lost to Toronto in the Eastern final. The Argos headed to *their* first Cup since 1952 and had it won, but that's the year Leon McQuay fell — people joked that he tripped over the five-yard line — and fumbled, costing them the game against the Calgary Stampeders. I'm not going to sugar coat it. I had a horrible year in 1971. It was only a year after I was the finalist for the Schenley but I was starting to feel it, especially in the knees, after all those years of playing such rugged football and I was beginning to think about retirement.

In 1972, Jerry Williams was the new head coach and another of those connections between the Philadelphia Eagles and the Hamilton Tiger-Cats. He was head coach of Calgary for a few years in the mid-60s, then was head coach of the Eagles for two years before the Eagles did something you don't see that often: they fired him after the 1971 exhibition schedule. Ralph Sazio, now the GM, brought him in to be our head coach in January of 1972. Jack Silly was also a coach with us that year and he was a coach at Notre Dame when I was there. He was a really good-looking blond guy and acted in a lot of movies in the early '50s, including, *Twelve O'Clock High*. He and Jerry Williams played together on the Philadelphia Eagles when Jim Trimble was the coach. Football is a very small world.

The 1972 Grey Cup was going to be held in Hamilton for the first time since 1944; the city was excited. Civic Stadium had been renovated and renamed Ivor Wynne Stadium after the guy who ran all the parks in Hamilton. The renovations brought the capacity to over 34,000; and believe it or not, that was the largest stadium in the CFL for about five years.

We didn't have a great football team in 1972. We were a mish-mash of players: lots of veterans and a ton of young guys, too. But it was a good and interesting mix. There were only 33 guys on the team, and we were a pretty tight group of guys. We had veterans like Willie Bethea, Dave Fleming, Rick Shaw — I used to call him "The Chinaman," (rickshaw, get it?) — myself, Garney, Bob Krouse, Gary Inskeep, Gerry Sternberg and Mark Kosmos. There was also a guy named Al Brenner on the team who set a CFL record by intercepting the Argos' Joe Theismann four times. He picked off 15 in all that season. He went missing in 1983 and nobody, not even his wife and four kids in Burlington, heard from him for years. He simply disappeared before calling his family about eight years later. The CBC did a show on him and his disappearance.

Garney Henley was another veteran we had, and one of our elected captains. He had played mostly defence his entire career, but Jerry Williams switched him to offence early in the season. Henley was a gazelle and very sly. Garney and Hal Patterson were probably the two best all-round athletes I ever saw in the CFL. Like Hal, Garney was a good basketball player and he ended up coaching university ball in Ontario.

Chuck Ealey was one of the rookies, and he was backing up Wally Gabler at quarterback. Chuck came out of Toledo University where he started all three years and never lost a single game, a record for U.S. college football that still stands. Tony Gabriel was another rookie — he played receiver, and he was nice to watch. Tony grew up in Burlington right across the bay from Hamilton and went to Syracuse where he had a really good career. He is a really great guy but he could drive you nuts: yakkety, yakkety, yakkety. He didn't mean anything by it, he's a tremendous person, but that was just Tony. He was like that when he was 21, and he's still like that at 61. He had a really good team attitude

As the season began I realized I couldn't do it anymore, and I didn't *want* to do it anymore. I was 34 years old, I had been playing the game very physically since I was a teenager, and I guess it was all catching up to me. My legs really started to bother me, and I wasn't playing well at all; I knew that and no one had to remind me. I was late getting off the ball, I was going the wrong way and I just wasn't sharp. I had always been in good shape from wrestling but my conditioning seemed down. Early in training camp I told Williams that it would be my last season. I had thought about it a lot and was ready to retire and move on. He said that was fine and we went on with business.

We were training at McMaster and Bobby Taylor, Dave Fleming, Gary Inskeep and I are standing outside the dressing room and we say, "Let's not fuck with each other's rooms this year. No pranks on each other." We all agreed. But one day, I'm so tired all I want to do is go back to my room and doze off. I put the key in the door, open it up and it looks like the A-bomb had hit the fucking room. Those pricks had turned my room inside out and upside down and stuff was thrown all over the place. They had ransacked my room. Taylor and Fleming, two tough bastards, I called them. And they were laying all the heat on Tony Gabriel for doing it. I knew who really did it but figured I'd lay all the heat on the guy in the middle. So I took all of Tony's clothes and burned them up. He had to go home from training camp with no street clothes. I said to him, "You come to the dance you have to pay the fiddler." I finally got Bobby Taylor though. The bottom of the door to his room was a half-inch up from the floor and I got a fire extinguisher and sprayed all the foam under the door. I had Fleming with me and you could hear Taylor choking and gagging in bed. When he opened the door, he looked like Casper the Ghost. And we hit him with a pail of water just as he opened the door.

In training camp, I had no inkling that Chuck would end up as the No. 1 quarterback. Wally Gabler was the quarterback everybody expected to lead us and he started the season. We picked up Wally from Winnipeg when Joe Zuger got hurt in 1970. He was a drop-back passer, and a real nice guy. Chuck was the first black quarterback Hamilton had had for many, many years, maybe since Bernie Custis came up from Syracuse in 1951. Chuck had good speed, that's what I remember the best about him. When he played, Jerry Williams changed a lot of the formations to utilize his speed.

On the 1972 team Dave Fleming and Dave Buchanan were the halfbacks, we didn't call them tailbacks then. We didn't have a fullback, because the game was changing. But rushing was still a big part of the Canadian Football League. We didn't have slotbacks, we had what we called flankers, who played the wide receiver positions. When I first came to Canada, the formation with two receivers on the same side was called a twin forma-tion. Jim Trimble was the guy who used it most and he created a lot of formations to fit the Canadian rules. We used two backs all the time; very seldom did we use a single back. The first guy would fake into the line and the other would come around the other way and get the ball. We never used the quarterback in the shotgun; he was always under centre. Joe Theismann was using the shotgun in Toronto, though.

We won the first game of the 1972 season and then we lost three straight. I wasn't playing well, but the bigger problem was that we had no offence. Jerry worked on the offence and started Chuck at quarterback in our fifth game.

Benching Wally wasn't the only change the club decided to make. Jerry called me into his office and said, "Angelo, you've had a great career. You've got wrestling…" And I said, "What are you driving at here?" He said, "We're asking you to retire." And I said, "With full pay for the rest of the year?" And he said, "No."

I was really hurt when he said that. I had already told him I was going to retire at the end of the season and I wanted to finish the whole year out. I was going to be done not because the Grey Cup was in Hamilton, but because it was time for me to retire.

"Jerry," I said, "you don't have the balls to cut me. Public opinion will kill you in this town. I'm not trying to push you around but I think I know what I mean to this team. I even told you at the beginning that this was my last year. Gosh, do I have to beg? All I want to do is finish this season, is that too much to ask?"

I was really hurting that day when I left Jerry's office. It stung. Jerry never talked to me about my retirement again. I just kept on practicing and playing. Although I did switch out from time to time with Bob Steiner, I played regularly. I kind of acted for the rest of the year like it just never happened. I figured it wasn't Jerry's idea and that the whole thing came from Ralph Sazio. That's the way Ralph was.

Chuck started his first game in Montreal, the week after the Alouettes had beaten us by a couple of points at Ivor Wynne. The Als were playing at the Autostade in those days — God it was a terrible place to play. It was concrete, it was cold and the 55-yard line seemed like it was miles away. We beat the

Alouettes 25–12 and we began changing as a team. Jerry changed the offence to a roll-out offence: Chuck would fake to one of the backs then he would roll out behind the other back. They would make up running plays for Chuck, and we'd use the old quarterback option play. Chuck was good at that, really good. He was the right quarterback in the right situation for the right coach at the right time.

Once we beat Montreal, we got on an incredible roll and won the rest of our 14-game schedule — ten straight wins! I'd never had that, ever, in my entire career. I couldn't believe it. We just kept right on winning, and when you win like that, you're expecting to win. The people in the city went completely ga-ga over us. You couldn't get a ticket. I got caught up in all the hype and it elevated my play, my attitude, everything. I gave it all that I had.

After starting so badly and worrying everyone, we finished with the best record the Cats had had in a 14-game schedule, at 11–3. Ottawa had the same record, but we beat them both times we played them and finished first in the East to get a bye to the Conference final. That's what you used work for: that bye. We got a week off while the other teams slugged it out. Ottawa advanced to face us in the two-game, total-point series and we lost the first game 19–7. It was the first time anyone had beaten us since mid-August, and the first time Chuck Ealey had lost a game in his college or professional career. But Ottawa had to come back to Hamilton and they had a horrible record in Ivor Wynne. It could have been the last game of my career, but with the crowd going completely crazy, we beat them 23–8 to win the total-point final by three points. The difference was a 44-yard field goal by Ian Sunter, a kid from Burlington. It sounds close, but I felt we were in complete control. They had a last-ditch effort on the final series but a couple of us broke in on their quarterback, Rick Cassata, got our hands up in the air and the pass went nowhere. I can remember running off the field pointing to the sky and the place was just jumping. The first Grey Cup to be held in Hamilton in 28 years was the next Sunday, and the Tiger-Cats were going to be in it.

And it was going to be the last game of my career. You couldn't make that stuff up.

As you can imagine, it was a pretty crazy week in Hamilton leading up to the Grey Cup. We were going to play the Saskatchewan Roughriders, who had Ron Lancaster at QB and a great running back in George Reed, one of the toughest runners to tackle in CFL history. The city was out of its mind for us and it had become common knowledge that this would be my last game. It was my 15th and final season and my ninth and final Grey Cup. Nobody's ever played in more and I'm glad one of the guys I share the record with is Tommy Grant, whose last Cup was in '67, the last time the Cats had won. I was ending my career having missed only one regular season game — which came while they were trading me to Ottawa.

It was the end of an era and a lot of the writers were flocking around for the story of my last week. Ellison Kelly was also going to retire. In my day, the writers were always welcomed in the locker room. And Gordie Walker of *The Globe and Mail* always liked to come over to Hamilton to cover the team and to play gin rummy with me. We played for a dollar a game. We only played for probably 15 or 20 minutes every time, but we kept a running score on a piece of tape stuck up in the locker room. When we played, I'd sit above the bench that he was sitting on, and I could see every single card in his hand. We went on like this for eight or nine years, and I never told him anything. And all that I beat him for after all was said and done was $5.00. Gordie and I played one last game on Grey Cup weekend. I can still see his hand today: he had the seven of spades and the eight of spades and another nine. I had the nine of spades. So I sat back and I said, "I think you need this card, but I think I'll just keep it right here," and I held the card up against my forehead, face open to him, showing him the nine of spades. Gordie doesn't say a thing. He's trying to be innocent. He's still trying to pretend he doesn't have a pair of nines, or doesn't need a run. I'll never forget that as long as I live. And here's how things cross paths: Gordie's son Terry, a CBC producer, did a whole TV piece on me during the 1996 Grey Cup in Hamilton. Terry also finished the book his dad started. It was a labour of love called, "And That's Why I Love the Argos." Of course, I didn't love the Argos, and they never loved me.

Things really built up the closer we got to Grey Cup weekend. During one of the practices that week Angelo Paletta showed up and presented me with a 1,300-pound steer. Then, before the game, my childhood friend Harold Kelley came up from Waltham and presented me with a trophy that he said was from the City of Waltham in recognition of what I'd done in football. I didn't believe him — to this day I'm pretty sure the trophy was his idea, but he never admitted it.

The Grey Cup by then had been moved to Sunday as opposed to Saturday, and the night before the game the noise in downtown Hamilton was un-be-lieve-able. We had a rally in front of the Connaught Hotel and there were about 25,000 people there to support us. The city was pumped.

I'll never forget the day of the game. It December 3, 1972, the last time a Grey Cup game was scheduled for December. The day was cool, but good enough for football.

Even spaghetti advertisements played on my "mean" personality.

A sweet quintet: This was the still picture from the very first Tim Horton's Donuts television ad in the early 1970s. It features, from left, Gary Inskeep of the Tiger-Cats, Pat Quinn of the Toronto Maple Leafs, me, George Armstrong, captain of the Maple Leafs, and the legend and donut chain co-founder, Tim Horton.

The last few moments of my Ticat career in 1972. Governor-General Roland Michener presents Garney Henley and me, the two co-captains, with the Grey Cup. The '72 Ticats are one of only 2 teams to win a Cup on its home field since 1953. The 1994 BC Lions team was the other.

RIGHT: The iconic picture which appeared on the front page of the *Hamilton Spectator*, the day after my last game. The headline was "PURRRRR-FECT."

Team Love: Dave Fleming was one of the greatest teammates ever, and
here I'm showing him that I appreciate it.

Watching my first Tiger-Cat game as a spectator, after I retired.

Getting ready for a chain match with Maurice Vachon.

Two wrestlers, two Angelos. My son Ang. Jr. and I.

With former NFL player Wahoo McDaniel late in my career. Wahoo died in 2002.

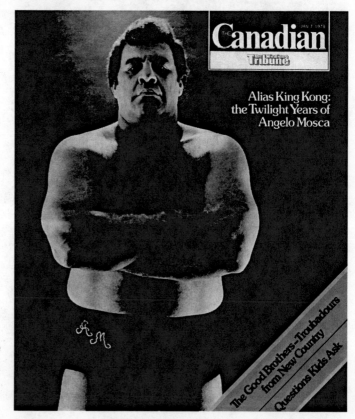

Alias King Kong: the Twilight Years of Angelo Mosca

In 1978, Earl McCrae wrote a poignant piece on the last few years of my wrestling career. Two of my favourite catch lines in that era was "From coast to coast I'm like honey and toast" and, "I'm going to give you so many lefts, you'll be begging for a right."

Carrying the star into a fund-raising banquet
at the Hamilton Convention Centre.

This is my sister Carol, a great girl.
She is the chaplain with the police
force in Port Hueneme, Calif.

After I retired I managed my son's wrestling career for a brief time.

My mother Agnes Mosca. She died in Waltham in 2007.

My wife Helen and I today. She is the most important part of my
life and it was Helen who encouraged me to write this book.

We started out really well. Al Brenner picked off a Lancaster pass in Saskatchewan's end and that set up Chuck Ealey's 16-yard touchdown pass to Dave Fleming down the sideline. TV replays showed he was out of bounds, but the officials missed it. Tom Shepherd, who was a big executive with Saskatchewan was really upset about that play, and every time I see him I hold out my Grey Cup ring, make a smacking sound and say, "kiss the ring." He always answers, "I'll kiss *you*, Mosca."

Ian Sunter kicked a field goal for us in the first quarter and we were up 10–0.

With a little less than two minutes to go and the game tied at 10, we had the ball on our own 15-yard line. Tony Gabriel hadn't caught a pass all game, but he sure picked a good time to start. Chuck hit him for 27 yards on first down, then hit him twice more and just like that we're at their 41-yard line. The crowd could taste it, and they were screaming as we ran off a couple of plays to move us closer.

On the final play of the game, we lined up to kick a field goal from Saskatchewan's 34-yard line. They were ready to kick it out of the end zone if it went wide. I played the right guard spot that year on the point-after team, which was also the field goal team, so I was on the field. Sunter was kicking from the left hash mark, and the hash marks were a few feet closer to the sidelines than they are today, so it was a harder kick than it would be now. After the ball was snapped and he stepped into it, I was leaning over to the side trying to follow the flight of the ball and I could see that it went right between the uprights! In the last 58 years a team has won the Grey Cup on its home field only three times, and one of those teams was us: the team that back in August no one, including us, thought would win anything that year. It was like some kind of novel: we had won the Grey Cup on the very last play of my career!

I had tears in my eyes and we all started rolling around on the turf, hugging each other. The crowd was going crazy, but on the field it was just us guys. I remember that it was about 45 minutes before we got off the field. The TV cameras were all over me and I was pretty emotional. I said on camera "I'm gonna leave a winner, along with these 32 other guys." I always wanted to be a good teammate.

It's funny how you remember certain things. I don't think it really hit me that this was the last time I'd be playing football until the moment I was walking off the field. As I headed into the archway that led to the dressing room, I looked up and saw a white sheet that some fans had painted with a message for me. It read, "Ang, Thanks and Goodbye." I started crying my eyes out. I started looking for my three kids. They were running around on the field and I just grabbed them and hugged them. Then I went into the dressing room, and it was just bedlam: players, coaches, families, friends, media — all celebrating. I got pictures of Dave Fleming and I kissing each other in the middle of it.

What it meant to not be playing football wouldn't really hit me until the next summer, when I didn't have to go to training camp. I still took a month off from wrestling where training camp would have fallen in my schedule had I been playing, and I did that for a few years. I'd go down to McMaster and watch the guys practice. I often said to myself, "What am I doing here? I don't belong." But the guys always made me feel welcome.

The day after the Grey Cup there was about a foot of snow on the ground and people couldn't get out of the city. It was Monday morning, the start of the workweek for other people. For me, it was the start of a new life. I was now an ex-football player.

SECTION
THREE

Wrestling
and
Beyond

CHAPTER NINE

Exhibitions of Strength and Skill

RIGHT AFTER I RETIRED, THERE were a couple of big dinners in Hamilton to honour my career with the Tiger-Cats. First, the Quarterback Club held a major banquet, and then Marty Martinello organized a huge roast at the Italo-Canadian Club. All the people I had met when I first came to Hamilton and didn't know a soul were there and I really appreciated that. It made me realize how much the city had become my home.

And after 13 years of wrestling part-time on the road and coming back to play football, I could finally get into wrestling fulltime. Most of the other guys were at it the full year, including the former football players because they retired long before I did.

Where I was born and how I grew up, my horizons could have been limited. But I made the most of my opportunities. Sure, I did some things I'm not proud of, but who hasn't? After 15 years in the CFL, I had created a persona: Angelo Mosca was, as my old teammate Gene Ceppetelli used to call me, "The Big Nasty." I was mean, physical and brash. With wrestling I had an opportunity to exploit this persona, and I did. Wrestling has paid me all sorts of money and taken me all over the world.

I've had matches in 35 different countries, including Japan. And it was all because I made the most of my opportunities.

An old wrestling guy named Joe Marconi told me early in my career that in wrestling, your face is your money. For the longest time I didn't have a wrestling nickname, and while a name is important, you can change it — but your face sticks with you, and you've got to make the most of it. I was becoming a heel, and my face became the identity of that role. People have told me that when they hear my name, they can immediately see my face. After Marconi gave me his advice, I started taking my helmet off as I was coming off the football field. Fans got to know my face that way. To this day, I always carry pictures that I can sign for any fan that wants an autograph. All the way through my wrestling career, as well as my acting career, my face was more important than any nickname. I tried different wrestling nicknames. The first one was, "The Mighty Hercules," which played on my physique; there was also the "Champion of Sicily," even though I had never wrestled in Europe. What I really wanted was to drop the "Angelo" part of my name because it was too nice for a heel. It was in the American Wrestling Association (AWA) that I got the nickname that stuck with me for the rest of my career, "King Kong Mosca." It was perfect. King Kong was big and ruthless, and so was I.

Wrestling really taught me about selling myself. I was already pretty good at telling stories and I liked speaking at public functions. You don't just have to project yourself visually when you wrestle; you have to do it verbally. One of the first things I learned was how to handle a microphone at ringside. You needed to be *on*. If you weren't, no one was going to pay attention to you. You need to know how to ad-lib, and how to read a crowd. It was a great education in show biz.

Eddie Quinn, who first got me into wrestling in Montreal in 1959, told me I was a natural for wrestling. When he said that to me I didn't think about it from an entertainment perspective. I understood how the athleticism from football would help me in the ring, but I failed to immediately understand how my street-guy attitude and lively persona also worked in my favour. Growing up on the streets of Waltham forced me to think on my feet and react very quickly — two things that were very important in wrestling. I could look right into the camera and do and say things instantaneously when that little red light came on. I found it very simple.

I think that's why I could always do commercials. I started them in the early '60s after the Willie Fleming hit, and I'm still doing them today. I've never had a real agent; I've always sold myself. One of the ads I remember liking the most was for Tim Horton's donuts in 1973. It was their very first TV commercial and in it they had hockey players Tim Horton, Pat Quinn and George Armstrong, as well as Gary Inskeep, who played with me on the Tiger-Cats, and me. We were sitting at the counter and the caption was, "You're liable to meet anybody at Tim Horton's." The original picture they took for the print version of the ad is still in the original Tim's at Dunsmure and Ottawa Street in Hamilton, which is one of the stores owned by Dave Sauve, who played defensive line for the Ticats in the mid-'80s.

When Eddie Quinn first suggested I get into the business, there were four or five guys from football already wrestling, and there came to be a lot more later as wrestling got bigger. There was Ernie Ladd from the Chargers and Chiefs; Black Jack Mulligan, who played with the Jets; Black Jack Lanza and Bobby Duncum, who both played college; Wahoo McDaniel from the Jets, and me. Before we were on the scene there was William Afflis from Green Bay and Bronko Nagurski Sr., from the Chicago Bears. Football players looked like athletes, and that was important because television was changing things dramatically and they wanted guys who were better at projecting themselves on TV They needed men that looked built, not just big. On television, you looked three inches taller and 30 to 40 pounds heavier than you looked in person. So, if you were already fat, you were going to look fatter. Some of the smaller, fatter guys who were wrestling when I joined the business couldn't make it today. They would look too horrible on TV

Ralph Sazio always referred to wrestling as "that phony business," and that got under my skin. I never liked the word "phony" very much. Wrestling was an exhibition of strength and skill. Everything was an exhibition. But in many ways our pride made it so that we played it like a real game. I could throw a punch that would look like it would knock your head off but I wouldn't even touch you.

It was very physical. Some of the contact was acted out but all of it took energy and timing. We were flying in that ring. A main event match lasts close to 30 minutes — there is a lot of work that goes into that match — and I was the kind of guy who liked to give people plenty of action, so you had to be in good shape.

I learned moves from watching other wrestlers, and from gaining experience in the ring — feeling it out. The best way to learn the business was to get away from the business at home and get out on the road, and that's exactly what I did. You're talking wrestling all the time, learning from everybody else. I was hardly ever at home through the '60s, which is why Darlene and I divorced.

Backdrops, slams, hip tosses and the facial aspects of the business are all pretty simple to learn if you have the feel and desire for it. It's all in the presentation, in selling it. Same as pulling a guy's hair: you just put your hand on his hair and he should act like it was killing him. There are all sorts of tricks to make wrestling look real — and they aren't secrets — I'm sure most wrestling fans today know them. When an opponent's head was on the mat, you'd didn't actually leg drop right on his head. You made it look like you were hitting him in the head, but really you're breaking your momentum with your other leg, which lands on the mat first. If you had a guy in a headlock and wanted to pop him a few, you made the punching motion while you used your foot to hit the mat and make it sound like you were whacking his head. If your opponent was down on his back and you wanted to do an elbow drop, you'd bring your elbow down lightly and let your hand and body make the big noise. One of my favourite moves, which played on my size and strength, was to clamp onto a guy's shoulders. You're not really clamping like a vice, but you sure look like you are. And you're working with the guy to make sure he sells what you're doing to him — that's the key to the whole match, if you want to get it over to the public. If he doesn't react, it ain't going to mean shit.

It's very easy to body slam a guy, although it looks like it should be really difficult. The person who is going to get slammed usually has momentum when they come toward you, and you use that. You grab him under the crotch, and then just pick him up. The person getting slammed will normally help you with a little jump, too.

Getting up on the ropes is trickier, because it's hard to maintain balance. When you're standing up on the top rope, your head is 11 feet or so above the mat. If you're going to come all the way down with an elbow on your opponent, there has to be trust. As the guy on the mat, all you can do is lie there and hope that the elbow isn't what actually makes the hardest contact — as the guy jumping, you absorb the impact with anything you can but your elbow. It's all about trust. Wrestlers need to trust each other with their bodies, and that can be tough to do when you have seem some guys do the vicious things I've seen. Some wrestlers just didn't give a damn about whether they dropped a guy, or landed an elbow.

I used to do some things right out of the blue and that's when people really believe the business. Sometimes, you actually don't have to build up to a crescendo, because if you do something that catches people napping, then you really leave an impression and they come away believing. One time in my fourth year of wrestling I did a goofy thing that I've never seen anyone else do. I only did it one time myself. It was one of those things that just occurred to me out of the blue and then, of course, I just had to do it. I had learned to walk the ropes and then I figured out how to have a guy wiggle the rope while I was up there, and I'd fly off it like a springboard to dive back into the ring. One, night I walked right across the top rope from corner to corner. As I was walking I had the guy I was wrestling against shake the rope and I slammed myself down like I had caught my nuts on the rope. Soon as I did that it shot me back up and then right down to the arena floor, a 15-foot drop. I didn't get hurt, luckily.

It was about six months after I started wrestling that I caught onto the "blade" business. There's a saying in the wrestling world: "red brings green." Which means that if you bleed, you make money. I didn't know what that meant at the time but like always in my life, I never acted like I didn't know what was going on. One night in the dressing room in Sherbrooke, Quebec, a wrestler said to me, "I'm going to have to give some juice tonight." Then I saw him in the dressing room making a blade and I made sure I paid close attention. Out on the mat, I didn't even see him cut himself, but all of a sudden his face is full of blood. Anybody who didn't believe it would say that it was tomato sauce or ketchup or something. Tomato sauce my ass, it was real blood and it was his. What you do is break a razor blade in half and then tape it all around so that just a point is sticking out. Then you hide it somewhere. I used to be able to hide mine in my mouth. When the time is right, about 10 minutes into the match when you're good and warm, you take the blade and hit yourself in the head where the blood is close to the surface. You plug your nose to apply pressure, and the blood just spurts out. Once I got onto it, I used to sit in the dressing room with the blade just sticking in my forehead — it used to drive the young guys nuts! Some of the guys who were a little queasy would go crazy on me. You can still see a lot of little marks in my head from the blade cuts.

As I mentioned earlier, my first match was against Angelo Savoldi at the Montreal Forum in the winter of 1960, after about 10 days of preparation time. Just a few years ago, I was speaking at a Pro Wrestling Hall of Fame dinner in New York and Angelo was right there in the audience. "I thought I killed him back then," I joked. That was 45 years after he was my first opponent. I remember that bout well but I don't remember my second one. I stayed in Quebec about a month, until the promoters got tired of me. We went out on the road to all the Quebec arenas; Laval, Victoriaville, Trois Rivieres, Verdun, all those places. Greg Oliver from *SLAM! Wrestling* wrote an article talking about how one of the other wrestlers on that tour named Gino Brito remembered working with me in Granby after we went for half an hour instead of the five or six minutes we were supposed to. "He was a big bastard," Brito told *SLAM!*, "You came out of the ring, you were drained out completely. You could tell the guy had been in sports before. He knew timing and playing to the crowd too."

I didn't have a contract with Eddie Quinn because it was a handshake business in those days, but he told me, "Don't worry we'll look after you financially." I didn't know what looking after me meant, exactly. But I made nearly $4,000 for my first month of wrestling in Quebec and I said to myself, "Holy Fuck, are you serious?" That was a lot of income in 1960. It was also how they hooked you on the business. They made sure you got paid so much you got really interested. I never even wrestled a Main Event in Quebec, until years later when I was an established name and they'd fly me in for a big card. The Main Event is for the wrestler, or for both wrestlers, on the card who can draw the people because he's either hated or loved in the area. In the business, there's really no name for the other bouts, other than the semifinal. And the semifinal winners don't go to the final like they do in other sports. It's just a name to make it the second-most important match on the card. And that's all about the pay scale. I learned as I went on that if another big-name wrestler was going to be on the same card I had to make sure it would be called a double main event because the Main Event pays the money: usually seven percent of the gate.

One of the guys I wrestled with in Quebec when I first started was Bulldog Brower, who was a huge name in the business. He was pretty short, but weighed 330 pounds. We became good friends and because he was a veteran he knew everyone in wrestling. He suggested that I call Stu Hart out in Calgary. At that time I'd never heard of Stu Hart, or anybody else really. Stu was a big promoter in Canada, running Stampede Wrestling and syndicating it as a TV show. He and his wife had 12 children, including six sons who wrestled (Owen was killed in his ring entry stunt at a 1999 WWF pay-per-view card). I called Stu and I'll always remember how he talked on the phone that day. "You come out here," he said in that funny voice of his, "and we'll make you a fuckin' champion." And, just like Stu said, in Calgary I shot up the ranks quickly.

We used to wrestle five days a week: Mondays in Lethbridge, Tuesdays in Edmonton, Wednesdays in Saskatoon, Thursdays in Regina and Fridays in Calgary. Every Friday night there was a huge crowd in Calgary: about 5,000 fans, which was a really large audience in those days. I was making $700 for the five-day week, which was still a lot of money but not near the $4,000 I made for my rookie month in the business.

I was learning quickly that wrestling was very different than playing for the Tiger-Cats. The first half of my wrestling career I was still playing football which is a team business. And wrestling is very much an individual business, and more than that it's a dog-eat-dog individual business. I often refer to it as a whore's business. You learn not to trust people and you sell yourself for money. When I broke in, a lot of wrestlers had never been athletes. They didn't have to be. Some wrestlers, all they did was tell stories about other guys, so eventually I learned to travel alone so that stories never got back to the promoter's office. That's why I was known as kind of a loner in the business.

When I started out, you got two cents a mile for gas, which sounds cheap today but wasn't then. You still wanted to save money by sharing rides, so in Calgary I rode with a guy named Wayne Coleman and we'd often be wrestling each other, too. He eventually wrestled under the name "Superstar Billy Graham" and became a one-time champion of the WWF. He was another football player who played in the American Football League, then had tryouts with Calgary and Montreal. The Alouettes stuck him in a hotel and gave him free rein while he was there. And, from what I heard, he scooped up all the hotel stuff and kept it. And this was a guy who was really religious, an evangelist. In fact, he took his wrestling name from the famous TV preacher. He also took steroids to build up his arms, which he later admitted. I think guys started to take steroids in wrestling in the late 70s, because they wanted to look good. Not me though, my answer was to go to the gym and work out. Nobody ever really suggested I do steroids and I would never have done them anyway. I was big enough from weight lifting. I never benched 500 pounds, but I squatted 1,100. I was a big freakin' squatter and I was doing it before it was even fashionable.

It's funny how the world works: I met Big John Quinn in Calgary while wrestling, not in Hamilton, where we both lived. At the time, Hamilton used to be called "The Factory" in the wrestling world. I'm not sure why the city was so good at producing wrestlers, but maybe it was because of the tough image the city had, or because "Whipper" Billy Watson, an idol in the sport, was from Toronto, just down the road. Hamilton produced John Quinn, Dewey Robertson, the Love Brothers, Billy Lyons and John Powers, to name just a few. There was a couple of wrestling schools in Hamilton, but I didn't go to them. Sometimes I worked out at the Hamilton Jewish Centre and met some wrestlers who showed me a few things, but they didn't train me. I was in business on my own.

Another guy I met in Calgary, and a guy I liked a lot more than Coleman, was Gene Kiniski. Gene grew up in Edmonton and his mother was an alderman there, one of the first female politicians in the country. His brother was a TV news guy, and Gene was a good enough football player to get a scholarship to the University of Arizona. He was at training camp with the Eskimos in the late 1940s, right around when Stu Hart was playing for the Eskimos. Kiniski started with the Eskimos on the offensive line in the early 1950s and played with Normie Kwong and Johnny Bright who I played against in the 1960 Grey Cup. But Gene blew out his kneecap and went back to Arizona to get into wrestling.

Gene became a star with Maple Leaf Wrestling in Toronto, and he billed himself as Canada's Greatest Athlete. He was one of the first football players, after Bronko Nagurski's father, to become a world champion. Like me, Kiniski was a heel, and didn't mind being one. Kiniski brought me out to Vancouver with him and we wrestled in the old Pacific National Exhibition as part of the National Wrestling Alliance's All-Star Wrestling. Later on, in the 1970s, Gene and I did this thing where we always argued on TV about which one of us was Canada's Greatest Athlete, and then we'd slap the shit out of each other right on air. We raised money for charity with a skating race, even though I couldn't skate worth a damn , and drew about 14,000 people. We did the same thing in Winnipeg, playing hockey with a tennis ball, and sold out six straight wrestling shows there. Of course, they already hated me in Winnipeg because of football.

Vancouver was part of the territory of the NWA, which was based out of St. Louis and was the No.1 outfit at the time. There was also the American Wrestling Association, which was run by

Vern Gagne out of Minneapolis. Then there was the Worldwide Wrestling Federation run by Vince McMahon Sr. out of Connecticut. He ran a lot of the eastern states. Boston was his big site. The NWA never touched him. They were almost everywhere else except the upper Midwest — Iowa, Minnesota and Nebraska — which was Vern's. Vern eventually got Alzheimer's disease and people might remember that in January of 2009 he body slammed and killed a 97-year-old resident in his retirement home who also had Alzheimer's. They didn't press charges because Vern didn't have the mental capacity to know what he was doing. It was a sad story. Vern was a great wrestler in his day, and I got to wrestle him one time in Denver. After the bout the referee said to me, "Boy, you sure made that old man look good." And I said, "That old man signs my pay checks."

I worked mostly under the umbrella of the NWA. We were lucky that at the time, with three organizations you could get up and leave any time you wanted. You weren't beholden to anyone, you'd give six-weeks notice and then move on. As I finished my wrestling career, there was really only one guy who ran it all: Vince McMahon Jr., and he told you what to do. I first came into contact with the McMahons in 1976 and they treated me really well. But for the most part I stayed independent, and wasn't fully tied to any organization. Promoters hate to hear that you're independent. They liked to make sure that the wrestlers didn't make too much money, because it kept them dependent. A lot of wrestlers would blow all their money — they treated whores better than they treated their wives — and spent all their dough. I was lucky to get into the business late enough in life to know to save my money.

I worked some Main Events in my early years, and in the final 15 years of my career I was lucky enough to work a Main Event pretty well every time I wrestled. You got seven percent of the gate for being in a Main Event, but when it came time to collect your money, it seemed that the gate figures were usually lower than they looked like. That's the way the business went. It was hard to tell a guy to stick a check up his ass when it was $2,000 for a night's work, even though it should have been $2,500. Because you were making good money you kept your mouth shut most of the time. But when I thought Stu Hart wasn't paying me enough I'd hold him up. I'd sit in the dressing room with my wrestling clothes on ready to go and he'd say, "Get ready, you're going to be on in about 10 minutes." I'd say right back, "Only if I get the extra money from the last show." One time I did that, he immediately gave me $300 and thought that was it. But I said, "And I want to be paid the same thing for tonight. Now." So that night I put over $1,000 in my trunks and went out and wrestled. There was a lot of cash involved in those days.

The money was good, and if you kept smart, you could transfer organizations to make sure you always maximized your worth. It was lucrative.

I started wrestling internationally around 1964, but my first tours weren't in the States, they were in Japan. I was recommended to Japanese promoters by Bulldog Brower. He got me into Asia. When we were in Quebec, even before we wrestled each other and got to know each other well, Bulldog had watched me in the ring and must have seen something he liked. Bulldog was a star on the world stage, and I think he knew I'd create a stir in Japan. I was one of those big guys with hair on my chest, and the Japanese aren't hairy people, so the people would say "Mosca-san," and then come up and pull the hair on my chest and imitate me like I was a big ape, or like I was a big Sumo wrestler. Four or five of us from North America would go over to Japan and we'd wrestle against Japanese guys, not each other.

It was the toughest place in the world to work; to get a reaction out of the audience was like pulling teeth sometimes. At a Japanese wrestling show the front row of spectators sat on the floor. In Japan they don't "boo" or "yay," they "hiss," and they hiss a lot. Some of the venues had 10,000 or 15,000 people in them, but it was cold, even in the springtime, because there was no heating in the arena. And the place would be full of big balls of cigarette smoke. It was awful.

There was a Hawaiian referee working with us and he just loved Sumo wrestlers. Sumo is like a religion over there, and four times a year — summer, fall, winter and spring — they have a big event. I told the Hawaiian ref that I could knock a Sumo down, and he decided to arrange a private bout. I squared off with a Sumo in front of four or five spectators. The first move a Sumo does is come at you with his arms cocked and palms facing toward you. That was perfect because we saw that all the time in football. When you're blocking somebody, you look right through them and then you *drive* right through them. I did that — hit him with a forearm shiver, grabbed his heel and I flipped him right on his ass. Then I laughed. That's a big insult in Japan and word got out to the public that I knocked a Sumo wrestler on his ass, and laughed. Now they think I'm a mean sonuvabitch, plus I've fooled with their tradition and caused shame. One of the promoters embellished the whole story and then people really came to the arena to see me wrestle. They even had pictures of me hung up in the market places.

I'd go over to Japan for six or seven weeks and make really good money. I've made close to 25 trips over there in my lifetime. I stopped going in 1982, when I started my own wrestling promotion business. Obviously, when we were in Japan they were the good guys and we were the bad guys, and vice versa on this side of the ocean.

I was already fighting in Japan for a few years before I finally started getting booked in the U.S. It was natural to go from Vancouver down to Portland, Oregon. It was part of the territory that included Washington and California and the promoter for the area was a guy named Roy Shire, out of San Francisco. I probably learned more about wrestling from Roy than from anybody else I ever met. Roy used to give you payments like this: $525.15. Not, $500, not even $525. It'd have to be $525.15. He wanted to make sure he was giving you the "true percentage." Who did he think he was kidding? He was probably screwing you, but he thought the 15 cents made it sound real. "You want to fuck up my books?" he'd say. That was Roy Shire, what a great promoter.

Roy's the guy who got me going in the States. I was his property in that area and if anybody wanted to have me they had to go through him. He was almost like an agent for me but, as I've mentioned, I was an independent. Roy booked me into the South Pacific during the winters off from football. I wrestled in Fiji, Tahiti, Samoa, everywhere. Then, I started booking myself over there: I lived in Hawaii in the off-season, right on Waikiki Beach, and I'd work my way from there back to Japan. I met a few girls there... and missed a few planes because of it. One time I joined the Mile High Club with a woman I met on the plane coming back from the South Pacific to Vancouver, and there were a few other incidents. I know that sounds like bragging or something, but I'm just telling you the way it was in those days. There's nothing to brag about…I played the situation. But I do admit there have been some women.

Pat Patterson was Roy's booker, and he took me under his wing. He liked my style of work. Roy, Pat and Ray Stevens, who was known as "The Crippler" in the ring, those are the guys who taught me the psychology of wrestling.

It's all about how you play with the minds of the people who pay to come watch. It offends some people, but I have always described it like Hitler, how he controlled people. He was a tremendous manipulator of people, and could make them go "Yay!" or "Boo!" anytime he wanted, and you'd manipulate the audience the same way in wrestling, to a far lesser degree of course. Imagine, for instance, a guy has me locked in a headlock, but I'm reaching up to grab his hair from behind his head. But I'm going slowly and I over-emphasize what I'm doing. It seems to the audience that the guy doesn't know I'm doing this and the crowd is going completely fucking crazy. They are mad at me and they are trying to warn him. In the end, I'm not grabbing his hair at all, I just put my hand on his scalp. It's all part of the illusion, and both of us have to sell it hard. But it works. I learned so much about that kind of stuff and other crowd psychology from Roy. He'd tell you how great he was, of course, and I'd always mimic him. He'd run his finger against his thumb all the time, like a nervous tic, and I'd imitate that and it used to drive him nuts.

First of all, I was a pretty good talker on my own but Roy taught me *how* to talk, how to coordinate things, how to put stories together. He taught me how to do "ever-y-thing-in-se-quen-ce-and-not-real-fast" and how to pace myself, not to give everyone everything all at once — give them a little bit at a time. We have an expression in wrestling, "Let's jerk but don't let 'em come." Very crude, but it's very true. And Roy taught me that. The only time he bothered me was when he tried to lay out my entire interview for me. It sounded like he was talking, rather than me. I would sit in the room and listen: he was like a teacher. But I also used to hate it because I had my own style — let me do it, don't you do it for me — and finally he realized that I was doing the right thing, and he let me talk on my own. But his lessons were important to me.

You have to have an imagination in the wrestling. It is your job to create an image. That's why there were a lot of stereotypes, a lot of them racial. Once you have an image you needed to nurture it. A good way to do that was to keep using the same line, the same verbiage, over and over again until people knew what you might say at any given moment. I used to say, "I walk and I talk and do exactly what I want to do." And when I was in trouble in the ring the people would start shouting, "Hey Mosca, you walkin' and talkin' now? You're getting the shit kicked out of you!"

King Kong Mosca

DURING MY ERA, BEFORE THE WWF — now called the WWE — took over completely, there were a lot of different champions in professional wrestling. A lot of them were regional. For instance you could be NWA United States Heavyweight Champion in San Francisco, which I was once, but there would be another U.S. Champion in another area at the same time. Champions add importance and a higher gate to a card, and so does a "title" fight. A title belt looks really important and it has prestige associated with it.

If you look it up on the Internet, you'll see I had a number of championships to my name at various times: AWA British Empire Heavyweight Champion, NWA Florida Global Tag Team Champion, The NWA Florida Bahamian title, the NWA Columbus Champion, the NWA Canadian Champion (five times), NWA Champion in Columbus and Macon, World Wrestling Council Caribbean Champion. And lots more. Sometimes when I wrestled, I was even billed as the Champion of Sicily, and I never wrestled in Europe! Although I didn't wrestle in Canada that much after I got my feet wet, my first real big belt was the Canadian Championship in 1966. It was in Toronto at Maple Leaf Gardens and came against the Iron Sheik. I won the belt and never actually lost it: it was taken away from me later for not defending it. Getting a chance to become a champion depends on how the people have taken to you. You aren't going to have a chance to be a champion if the people aren't really interested in you. It's what the business calls "getting over." Getting over can come from crowds loving you, or hating you. Either way, if you are causing an emotional reaction that puts butts in the seats, that's good. When you help a guy get that emotional reaction from a crowd it's called, "putting him over."

When it looks like you're going to become a champion, the promoter calls you into the room the day of the match. You know it's coming, so you figure out how to get it done. It was a general principle that we didn't really practice it. Later, under Vince McMahon Jr. and the WWF, they'd actually practice the endings of fights. You could get fired in my time for that. But then and now, when you're going to be champion you work the match so it looks like you're going to lose. I was the so-called good guy — the white hat — in the match against the Iron Sheik in Toronto. It was a tough spot for me to be in, not only because I was usually a heel, and was better at it, but because of where it was. The people in Toronto hated me from football, especially around then because the Argos weren't winning and the Tiger-Cats were. They didn't buy it that I was a good guy and had a hard time cheering for me. It was tough for them not to boo me, and it felt weird even for me in the ring. But the Iron Sheik was really good at being a heel, and nobody could ever cheer for him.

When I wrestled, and especially back when I won that belt over the Iron Sheik, I was a big guy and looked the part of a champion. But I had a philosophy about championships. The belt's not the most important thing. I'd rather go out and not get the belt, but lose it and win it at the same time. What I mean is this: lose, "1–2–3," and while the guy celebrates and the crowd goes wild, get up and kick the shit out of the guy. Now, what part is the crowd going to be talking about when they leave the arena? And who will they come back to see next time?

Bobby "The Brain" Heenan became a good friend of mine while I was wrestling in the AWA. One night when I was half-bombed (which was rare), I went up to see Bobby at his hotel, but Bobby was single at the time and had a woman in his room and wouldn't open the door. So, because I was half-bombed I broke the door right off the hinges and threw it to the side while I was roaring "Aaaarghh!" as loud as I could. I stood right in the door-way and Bobby jumped up and growled at me, "You look just like fuckin' King Kong." And that's where it started. I went up to his room as Angelo Mosca and came back down as King Kong Mosca. I wasn't the first guy to use that name, Bruiser Brody also was known as King Kong Brody; there was King Kong Bundy, plain King Kong, who was a guy named Emile Czaja, as well as King Kong Kirk in England. But nobody was using that name with any oomph in the U.S. at that time, so it stuck.

After tearing off the door, and getting a new nickname, I went back to my own hotel and about 30 minutes later a cop shows up at my room and takes me back to the hotel where I busted the door off the hinge. With the cop there, the guy man-aging the hotel starts complaining about how much it's going to cost him to have it fixed and I finally reach into my pocket and said, "I'll give you 300 dollars, that's all I have." But I had lots more money in the other pocket. It was a cheap price for a nickname that I used most of the rest of my career.

With the King Kong nickname I used the spiel on TV: "I walk and I talk and I do exactly what I want. Ha Ha Ha Ha," and I'd look directly into the camera with a dark menacing face and I'd lean in and make it fill the whole screen. That expression was part of my shtick, including the laughing part, and I'd been saying that since I was a kid on the street corners in Waltham. I'm not sure where I got it but I think it came from the *Howdy Doody Show*. When you repeat a line like that, or have a catchy nickname, and you're a heel, the audience picks up on it. People at the arenas would start yelling "Ping Pong" instead of "King Kong." To keep it going, I'd use reverse psychology by putting my hands over my ears like I couldn't stand it. But, really, I wanted them to yell it louder. And they did. Late in my career, I was walking across the parking lot after a match in the Midwest with the writer Earl McRae and a bunch of kids outside the arena start yelling "Ping Pong, Ping Pong" as we walked. I can't count the number of times that the good guy was beating the hell out of me in the ring and the people are yelling at the top of their lungs, really happy, "You're really walkin' and talkin' now aren't ya, Mosca?" I never minded that at all, for the same reason that I never really minded losing. The fans would remember me because of the nickname and the way they turned it around on me, just like they would remember me, not the champion when I'd kick the shit out of him after the count.

While I was wrestling in the NWA and the AWA, my wife Gwen was back home in Caledon, north of Toronto. We had been living in an apartment together and then got married in 1972, my final year with the Tiger-Cats. We were living in Mississauga and we decided to build a home in Caledon because of access to the airport. We both had to go there all the time. She was still working for the airlines and I was basically living on airplanes.

Was it a good marriage? I'd say it was fair. My wife, God rest her soul, was an alcoholic. And I didn't know. I swear I did not know about her drinking when we got married, or for the first little while afterward. Gwen was always fun and she could drink more than a lot of the guys I knew, but I never thought much about it, and probably should have seen some signs. One of the first was that she retired, and she didn't have to. She had worked for the airlines for about 23 years and had a pension but I said, "What are you going to do with your time?" I discovered how deep her problem was when I'd be on the road eight months of the year. She'd come and stay with me if I was in Florida or Hawaii, the nice places, but the rest of the time I worried about her back at home drinking.

Her drinking became very sad. I'd have some guys over to the house, cooking and eating, and I'd open a wine bottle and find that it had water in it. She was hiding her drinks. I never was a big drinker, myself, and to this day I hardly drink much alcohol at all. For a guy who has led my kind of life, I could have been a drunk. But I could count on fewer than 10 fingers the times I've been loaded in my entire life. I saw so much alcohol during my childhood that there was no way I was going to become an alcoholic or a heavy drinker. Those times I'd rip a door off a hotel room or something like that, I wasn't really hammered, I was a little happy-high. I kibitzed. Alcohol was not to blame for anything I've ever done. I always wanted to be in control. I take responsibility for all of my own actions, everything I've done in my life. I might have been pushed into some things, but I don't blame anyone for anything. I handle things. I had a brother who went to jail for nearly 20 years because he didn't know how to handle things. I'm a different kind of individual and, I'll say it once again, sports saved my life.

As I realized Gwen was drinking far more than socially, I thought I would try to understand alcoholism. I had never understood it when my parents were drinking, so I thought I would try to understand it with my wife. I went to the local Al-Anon meeting and was the only guy in a room of seven women. As I listened to them, it seemed like it was all about how they hated men — the drinkers in their lives. When it came to my turn to tell my story, I was feeling funny and wasn't ready to talk about. Really, all I wanted was to get out of there as fast as I could because of the hatred of men I heard in their stories. One of the women then said, "Hey, aren't you Angelo Mosca?" and I said, "I thought this was a first-name-only basis." I ended up just leaving and they never heard my story, and I never got to understand Al-Anon, or alcoholism. I tried to carry on my life with Gwen. Possibly it was a mistake and I probably should have had a professional help me along the way. But, I had been an asshole with Darlene, my first wife, even though I didn't realize it at the time. She gave me those three great kids but I didn't respect her enough, because I didn't know how to treat women. With Gwen, I was far better. I'd learned not to be an asshole, but her addiction hit me like a truck. I just didn't understand it. Being on the road caused me a lot of worry. To be fair, she worried, too. I hadn't completely changed, and she was always worried about how many women I was taking care of. Her worry was understandable, especially considering my past. I did have my moments here and there, I'll admit — it was hard to change completely — but I was much more concerned with her health. We were married 20 years before Gwen died in 1992.

Just before Canadian Thanksgiving in 1975, Gwen and I were on vacation in Hawaii when I got a phone call from George Scott, the NWA booker in Charlotte, North Carolina. He said, "I'd like you to come to Charlotte and work." I told him I'd call him when I got back to the mainland after my vacation. At the time, I was considering getting out of wrestling and staying at home for once and sticking with my banquet hall called the End Zone that I operated in Burlington with former teammate Bill Danychuk — one of the many different businesses I dabbled in. But two days later, George Scott called me again. Same thing, "we'd really like you to come in here." I wondered to myself, "Since when does a promoter need you that much that they keep calling you?" So I called him back and found out that the reason they needed me so badly was that a small plane had crashed on a really short hop from Charlotte to Wilmington, carrying four wrestlers and the promoter David Crockett, the son of Jimmy Crockett, who essentially ran the NWA in the south. Nobody was killed on the day of the crash but the pilot eventually died two months later from severe injuries. People still call it the plane crash that changed wrestling. Johnny Valentine, the NWA's U.S. Heavyweight Champion was sitting next to the pilot and was also injured badly. He ended up paralyzed and had to retire from wrestling. Ric Flair was on the plane, he was only 24 then and just getting going on his career. The Crockett family had him slated to be a future champion. He broke his back in two places in the crash, and at first the doctors told him he'd never wrestle again. But he worked hard at getting back and continued to build his fame. The two other wrestlers were Bobby Bruggers and Tim Woods. The authorities blamed the crash on pilot error because he didn't distribute the weight evenly, which you always have to do when you have heavyweight wrestlers on a small plane.

The plane was flying to Wilmington because Woods, the white hat, was supposed to wrestle Valentine, the heel, that night. Wrestling fans weren't as hip back then as they are now, and they would have questioned things if they knew a heel and a white hat were flying together on the same plane. They were supposed to be mortal enemies. So, George Scott and the NWA did what's known in the business as a "kayfabe." When you kayfabe you're making up certain things to make it look like everything's legit. They pretended Woods wasn't on the plane at all. When they cancelled the match in Wilmington that night they announced all the guys who were on the plane, except for Woods. They said he got lost on the way to the match.

Valentine and Flair were the huge stars for the Crocketts, and they really needed two guys to fill their places, and they had to be two big guys. So they asked Black Jack Mulligan and myself to go down there. It was the biggest break of my career. Black Jack and I went to Charlotte and we blew the territory wide open. All of a sudden, instead of drawing 10,000 fans we're drawing 15,000, and we were only there three weeks. In Richmond, Virginia, we were drawing 20,000. I was making big money: an average of $4,000 a week. And a room in the Marriot Hotel was costing me only $24 a night. In 1975–76 the average Cadillac cost $7,500, and that's what I bought. I bought it in New Orleans and drove it back to Canada when I finished for the season, and nobody said anything at the border. Things were different then. I was making all this money, and I never looked back, and I worked the south a lot after that. And I was always aware of the irony.

I might have been called King Kong, suggesting I was the biggest thing in the jungle, but I was small compared to Andre the Giant. He had an over-active pituitary gland and was 7-foot-4. His real name was Andre Roussimoff, and he was from France although his family history was Russian. Andre was a great guy and he and I wrestled a lot in the Midwest. I had another wrestling friend who had a trailer in a rural area outside Milwaukee and I'd go up there to see him before matches. I found out that Andre was coming into Milwaukee to wrestle in about six weeks, when I'd also be there, so I decided to set up a little fun. One day, I went out to my friend's trailer and sat there having a beer with him, looking out the window. Then I suddenly sat up straight and said, "I think I see a Sasquatch." I kept saying it over and over again, "Sasquatch! Sasquatch!" and he didn't believe me of course. Six weeks later, I was with Andre and said "Want to have some fun? I've been telling this guy that a Sasquatch is around his place." Andre was a fun guy and he said, "Okay Boss," in his deep accent. When we went out to my friend's place, I dropped Andre off at the end of the long driveway, but I didn't know what he was going to do. I went into the trailer and sat down, placing myself beside the window. Meanwhile, Andre had taken mud and smeared it all over his face. And he's got that great big Afro. His head was huge, like a great big monster's. He snuck up to the trailer and put his head right in front of the window. And I start acting like I can't talk, because I'm so scared. "Aah, Aah, Sas, Sasq, SAS-quatch!" My friend turns around to see what I'm talking about and Andre's

head is completely filling the window. He screamed so loud —
I'm sure he almost shit himself! Andre was one of a kind.

We had a lot of fun in the business but there were guys you
couldn't get along with. For some reason Wahoo McDaniel and
I were always at logger-heads. I don't know what it was but he
and I just didn't get along. I think he might have been jealous
of me, whether it was for how I got into the business so quickly,
or whatever. Wahoo would get pissed off at me and I would get
pissed off at him. He became a booker as well as a wrestler and
one night in Charlotte, North Carolina, he sent "the finish" over
to the dressing room. The finish is the way the match is going
to end and at the time they'd do it through the referee, who'd
go from locker room to locker room. Wahoo wanted to put this
guy over, which means he wins on a "1-2-3" pin. I sent the finish
back with the referee and said, "You tell Wahoo to go fuck himself." Wahoo sent it back and changed it to "disqualification,"
so the other guy can still get his arm raised as the winner. There
are a million ways that the other guy can get his arm raised, but
I was not going to let him pin me. It didn't happen in that case,
but we had a philosophy that when you leave the territory you
"put a guy over." In other words, you let him beat you if he was
still going to stay in the territory. If I didn't particularly like the
guy, I'd do eight false finishes and then have him beat me. I'd
call all kinds of false finishes: "1-2, kick out", which means lifting your shoulders off the mat. You know how weak that makes
a guy look: he can't close me off in one shot? There's *so* much
psychology to the business.

One time, Wahoo and I and these other two guys are having
a double Main Event. Wahoo was a full-blooded Choctaw and
his big thing was a hand chop which was supposed to be a
native hatchet chop. Kind of like the fans of the Atlanta Braves

do when they're rallying the team. The understanding in the wrestling business is that you don't use another guy's signature finishing move. Wahoo and I are mad at each other so what I did was tell the kid I was wrestling against to chop me, because I knew Wahoo was in the other Main Event and was watching us. Wahoo went nuts when he saw what I was doing: it's his finishing move and I kicked out of it, and I'm doing all this other stuff in return. By then I had all the tricks of the trade in my hip pocket and that night I saw that the reaction from the crowd was so strong about the way the kid and I were working together that I pulled the him over on top of me. And "1-2-3." Wahoo went crazy because it was supposed to be a disqualification, plus the kid had used his move. Then I got up and kicked the shit out of the kid, now that the match was over, because I know that's what the crowd will remember.

The crowd not only remembers, they are serious about it. If you're a heel and can make them believe, they really take it to heart. Once I signed a piece of cardboard for a kid and then he lit a match and burned the cardboard up right in front of me. A kid! Another time in Conway, South Carolina, there was a pretty good crowd in the arena and they were pretty hot. I jumped out of the ring onto the floor and immediately, I felt something cold in my side. A cop had stuck his gun into my ribs and said, "Jump right back in that ring." He was worried about a riot starting. I said, "Go ahead and shoot me. I've got a big audience here." Always playing to the crowd. I finish the match and I get in the car with a wrestler named Gene Anderson. As I'm going down the road, I look in the rearview mirror and a cop is on my tail. He pulls me over and he wants to arrest me for inciting a fuckin' riot. So they take me to jail and book me. I could have posted my own bond for a hundred bucks so I don't know why he was such a prick about it. It's two in the morning and I'm with all these guys and they've got a little TV in the cell. They know who I am because they watched wrestling. I said to these eight guys "Don't fuck around, don't make too much noise, or they'll blame me and I want to get out." I did get out an hour or two later.

Fans take all kinds of liberties when you're a heel. I've had cigarettes thrown at me, where they stick on your back because of the sweat. You could smoke in the arenas back then and lot of the arenas had lower ceilings. I didn't notice it then, but looking back I realize how smoky it would be in there. Now, if you even smell a wisp of smoke you're aware of it and think there's a fire, but it was really thick in there in those days.

In the 1980s body builders became the new norm for wrestling. Athletes like myself weren't getting recruited as much. The body builder phenomenon really took off when Sylvester Stallone used Hulk Hogan in Rocky III, but it was starting well before that. It was the body builders that brought steroids into the ring. I'll never forget John Studd. He was 6-foot-7, 320 pounds, and often wrestled Andre the Giant. I used to tell him, "John, there is only one giant, and it ain't you." I used to watch him juice, and he took too much. I would go into the gym and kiss my arms and say, "N.S." The guys would ask what it meant and I'd say, "No Steroids!"

Costuming started to come in at this time as well. Some guys always used them as part of their persona but most of us just used wrestling trunks with the straps over the shoulders. The Mexicans were the big costume people. Everyone in Mexico uses a mask. I wrestled in Mexico City two or three times in the mid-'70s when I was at the peak of my career. I didn't wear a mask, instead I'd point to my face and say,

"This is my mask, what you see is what you get." Wrestling in a mask is one of the toughest things you can do. I tried it one time. I used to wrestle a guy out of Georgia and he had to wear a mask because he was only 5-foot-10 and the recognition factor was in the hood. We did a little angle during a match where I took his hood off and I put it on my own head. I thought I was going to die. I don't know how the hell they ever worked in there: they were made of cloth and it was hot and very claustrophobic.

The biggest change that hit wrestling in the late '70s and early '80s came out of Connecticut. As I mentioned, the country was loosely split up into territories. The NWA worked the south all the way to St. Louis. And the AWA with Vern Gagne controlled Midwest. California took whatever wrestlers they wanted and worked with them. Vince McMahon Sr. was an independent working his WWF out of Connecticut. He was a great guy, one of the greatest in the business and had worked with the NWA for a long time before he withdrew. He worked Maine, New Jersey, Rhode Island and Massachusetts. It was still the car era in American wrestling, so you had to be able to drive to the venues. Vince McMahon's son Vince Jr. encouraged his father to expand, and by the early '80's Vince Jr. had taken over the WWF and started showing its stars on TV in regions traditionally belonging to other federations. Eventually the WWF controlled the majority of the industry.

I'd met the McMahons in the mid-1970s, and always liked the father. I'd jokingly call him the lesser of all the evils, because he was a great promoter. When the WWF started to make their move at the end of the '70s, I was working in Minneapolis and

I sent word out to Pat Patterson, who occasionally booked for Vince. He put the word in Vince's ear that I was a good heel, and in 1980 I went to work for the McMahons. It was Senior who hired me. He was a big Irishman and a real nice man. I'll tell you what kind of guy Vince Sr. was: he would call you in, bring you into the territory and he would tell you exactly how long you were going to be there and tell you exactly how much you were going to make. When you'd come into their territory, you had to get established and they'd put you in certain matches in certain strategic towns and you build up your following. If fans reacted to you then you'd eventually be in a Main Event. I spent three or four months working Boston and Pittsburgh and those cities before I got a chance to wrestle in New York. I was a "semifinals" guy at the start. I didn't appear in any Main Events.

All the wrestlers would go to Allenstown, Pennsylvania for a day-and-a-half and we would do interviews in all the towns we were going to be wrestling in for the next three weeks. Your job was to sell the live wrestling because you were soon going to visit those towns. We'd do all the interviews, then they'd drop an interview for each separate town into the TV fight, which was also taped in Allenstown, and then send it to that town, where it would be shown on TV. You might do a hundred interviews and appearances, so it was a lot of talking. Vince Junior used to do all the interviews. He was a body-building type of guy and he'd wear these suits with the big wide lapels and the shoulder pads. He'd interview me and during the interview I'd grab him by the shoulders and swing the padding under the material shaking it loose and say, "How you doing today, Vince?" Right on air. It drove him nuts. After the camera was off, he'd say, "Mosca, I'm gonna kill you!"

In the WWF I wrestled as King Kong Mosca. And in the early 1980s, I was given two fights against the WWF Champion, Bob Backlund. Both fights were at Madison Square Garden. I didn't know that they put your name on the marquee when you were appearing there, and when I drove by, there's my name up there in lights. It actually made me kind of nervous when I got into the ring. I started thinking about all the great shows that had been staged in the middle of this arena, and how I was suddenly part of one of the great entertainment capitals of the world.

There were 21,000 people there. It was big-time, and I got about $10,000 for the night's work. Not bad for 1980.

Backlund was the baby face (good guy) and I was the heel. I was really playing it up and I got the crowd to a crescendo — a fever pitch where you can't go any higher. So I said to Bob, "Grab a hold Bob, I think I'm going to come." Using the old wrestling line. He looked shocked and said, "WHAT?" and I said, "Aw, forget about it, you wouldn't understand."

Some guys took the business so seriously. I never got serious enough, I guess, because I was too busy entertaining the people out there. I used to drive promoters crazy. Sometimes I'd say, "Oh, I guess I'll go out there and fake it for about 15 minutes." If you believed in this shit you were in trouble. We had to make them, the audience, believe it. That's what I used to tell guys. "Don't make me believe, make believers out of them out there."

When Bob and I had the crowd to that pitch where they couldn't go any higher, I said "C'mon Bob it's time to go home." He said, "Huh?" I said, "It's time to finish, let's satisfy the people right now." So he pinned me 1–2–3, stayed champion and the people were all happy. He knocked off King Kong Mosca. The second time I fought Bob I got myself disqualified. Vince was the kind of guy who only used you twice for a Main Event in New York, so that was it.

The WWF was really taking off at that time, and they booked me in the States and for a few shows in Japan. But I wasn't exclusive with them so I could also book myself. I sent out some tapes and a promoter from Africa wanted King Kong Mosca to go to Rhodesia. It was April of 1980.

I flew to South Africa, where I was also going to wrestle, and the plan was to go from there to Rhodesia. The flight to South Africa was a marathon, 18 hours long. We stopped at an island where the Russians were refueling their plane and this was still the Cold War, so that was something you didn't see every day. Then we had to fly around Angola because their civil war was still on.

By the time I got to my hotel, I was bagged, but the promoter's son finds me and tells me that I have to show them a few holds and counter-holds so that I can get my license to wrestle. I do a couple of moves and then I lean over the ropes and said to the promoter, whose name was Bull Heffer, "If you don't like what you see, then send me home right now because my ass is dead fuckin' tired." Bull Heffer said, "Boy, Ahn-gelo's kind of nah-sty isn't he? We better give him his license."

Fighting in South Africa was hard. It was three rounds, unlike American wrestling where you perform by time. In our business you build a story in a match, but when you're doing something by rounds that story gets cut off and you have to build it back up again the next round. That's a lot of work. I was wrestling the South African Champion — I can't remember what his name was — and I suggested we do something a little bit different. We were wrestling in Johannesburg, 45 miles down the road, the very next night and I was thinking we could set it up really good for the last night, but he had only one objective, to beat me. But you don't make money just by beating me. I've always said I've made more money on my back than I did with my hand raised, because it's all in the way you do it. Anyway, I said to him, "Let's get some juice." He just looked at me, and Bull Heffer says, "This guy don't blade himself." I said, "He will tonight!" And Bull said, "You gotta be fuckin' kiddin' me," because he knew exactly what I was going to do. We get in the ring that night and it was a helluva match. I wanted to do a double pull-apart, with blood. A double pull-apart is where the ref pulls the two wrestlers apart and declares that there's no winner. We're coming back with a rematch down the road the next night and that would have been a perfect set-up. But this South African champion didn't get it.

Bull Heffer is sitting ringside with his pipe in his mouth, and it's my turn to go at the champ. I take my blade out of my mouth and quickly stick it in his forehead. You don't have to make it deep. I zapped him so quickly that he wasn't sure if I did or not. Then the red started to show and I said, "Sell the shit out of this, kid." The blood was really spewing. Bull Heffer saw that blood coming out of his head and I think he swallowed his fuckin' pipe.

I still had the blade and I cut myself a bit later. It turned out to be a disqualification, with no pin. I had to keep the champ happy, but I wasn't going to let him pin me because he wasn't a businessman. I *was* going to do a number for him before I left the country, like we'd do at home before leaving a territory: put the guy over by letting him pin me. But, in the ring during the second fight in Johannesburg, I told the referee to get ready to disqualify me for possessing a foreign object. I wasn't going to get pinned: the other guy wasn't a businessman and I didn't want to do business with him.

We headed to Rhodesia after that, but when I got there they asked me to not to wrestle because the country was going through a huge change. They had had elections and in a few days the country was going to be called the Republic of Zimbabwe, after it had been called Zimbabwe Rhodesia for a few months. They didn't want any promotions to distract from the start of the new independent country. So we went back and wrestled in Durban and stayed six more weeks in South Africa.

And yes, I know, South Africa had Apartheid then. My birth certificate said "White" under race, but of course I didn't tell anyone about my heritage. Even if you're one-quarter black, even one-tenth, that doesn't matter. Not in Georgia and certainly not in South Africa. I have black blood and the irony certainly did occur to me at the time. But once again, I pulled the wool right over their bigoted fuckin' eyes.

As the 1980s went on, the WWF was getting really big, basically controlling the world of wrestling. In 1983, Hulk Hogan crossed over from the AWA, which made them even more popular. He'd been a big star for the NWA too, and he very quickly became WWF Champion. I only was around him for about six months, before I left the WWF.

With my shoulders and knees hurting a lot, I was starting to taper down my ring appearances. It was the tail end of my wrestling career and the NWA came up with the idea of changing me to a white hat. Suddenly I wasn't the villain anymore and people loved me. Part of the psychology of the business is that when you're a bad guy people believe everything they see about you because it's so obvious, and way out there. But now you do it as a good guy and they *really* believe you, because you've seen the light and made the switch. Plus they know you have the ability.

I had become a baby face and I hated the term. I used to tell that to my son Angelo all the time and it drove him nuts. Angelo played football at Concordia in Montreal and was drafted by the B.C. Lions. They cut him, and they were dopes for that. Think of the promotion they could have had: another Angelo Mosca in B.C. When Angelo graduated, there weren't many jobs around, so he came down to Tampa and lived with me for a while.

"Are you eyeing the business?" I asked him. He kind of hemmed and hawed and admitted that he was. I had him train with Gene Anderson, and Ang caught on just like that. He had a great body and was very strong. But he wasn't really cut out for wrestling. I always said that if he had his sister Jolene's personality, he would have been a huge star. Ang is a quiet guy, and wasn't all that natural on the mic. My son is too honest, and only in wrestling would that be considered a shortcoming.

I used to make Angelo nuts, making him sign autographs. One time, some female fans were trying to get him to sign and he was trying to get the door of our car open to climb in and get away. So I locked the door on him, and I could see his hands trying to open the door, but he had to stay and sign those autographs.

Someone said to me at the time that it wouldn't work if I went baby face with my son Ang and did a tag team. But we made it work. Ang and I wrestled as Mosca and Mosca. We wrestled as good guys in tag matches and usually he'd tag me and I'd make the "save" against the other guys. But my son never would have got as far as he did if I kept saving him all the time. I didn't want them to beat him down: I was well established, and I wanted him established too. So we ended up reversing the routine. I had them kick the shit out of me while he was battling to get into the ring to help out. The opponents would keep pushing him back and then finally I'd barely make the big tag and the place would simply erupt. He'd rescue me and kick the shit out of everyone.

There were two other guys named Mark Lewin and Kevin Sullivan who had a pretty good shtick going. They were both really good performers. Actually, a lot of the guys were good performers because you had to be, to survive. You had to keep coming up with innovative ideas. Sullivan had a Devil worship thing going on in the ring, with all the rituals and tortures and things. He was supposed to be in one-on-one matches but Sullivan and Lewin were actually a team. Everyone knew the other guy was coming into the ring, they just weren't sure when it was going to happen.

I came up with an idea that would involve Angelo with them. I told them, "I want you to stab my son."

It was set up that Angelo would be at the TV interview stand when Sullivan (and Lewin) were going against a promising young white hat and doing their nasty things to him. Before the match, I took blood out of my own arm and filled a condom with it. I didn't want anyone else involved because as soon as that happens, they all want a piece of the action, so I wanted to use my own blood. Ang hid the condom in his mouth and ran down to the ring to try and help the good guy. One of the Devil worshippers had a pointed object, and would pretend to stab Ang in the throat. Angelo was supposed to fall, bite the condom and the blood would come spurting out everywhere. But the first time, he went down so hard that the condom popped out of his mouth without breaking and landed on the floor of the arena. He had to think quickly and pull it back under himself so he could hide it.

We had a good thing going with that and decided to change territories and try it in Carolina on a fresh audience. But in wrestling, when you have something good going, often people will get jealous. Someone back at the head office, Paul Jones I think, started calling all the churches in Carolina about the Devil worship. It got the locals all riled up, and suddenly there's a lot of heat. Devil Worship in the south? We had to cut it back, and then stop it entirely, which was too bad because it was a very hot item.

By then I was winding down my career in the ring and leaning more toward promoting matches and doing television commentary. The WWF hired me briefly in the mid-80s to do some TV, but Jesse "The Body" Ventura soon replaced me. I was pushing 50, and my body was hurting so I stopped accepting bookings in the ring.

In 1989 Vince McMahon Jr. asked me to come out one more time, and I agreed. But the schedule looked something like this: first night, Dallas, Texas; the next night, Los Angeles, California; the night after that back to San Antonio, Texas; and it went on like that. I did a handful of fights, and when we got to Chicago, which was the second or third last stop on this tour, I decided to retire for good after the match. I took my wrestling boots and threw them as far as I could into Lake Michigan. And just like that, 30 years after Eddie Quinn called me into his office and after more than 7,000 matches, I was retired from wrestling.

Life After Pro Sports

EVEN THOUGH MY WRESTLING BOOTS were somewhere on the bottom of Lake Michigan, that didn't mean I was through with the business. I was still going to the gym to work out, I was doing wrestling promotions and I had a few TV and radio commercials going on. I was taking advantage of what was presented to me. I used to keep a tape recorder beside the bed, and when I'd come up with ideas for promotions, I'd talk into the recording. Gwen and I were living at the big home in Caledon and even though it was the first time I was spending an entire year in one place since the first year came to Canada, I was a pretty busy guy.

In 1985 I decided to run some shows myself, they were billed as "Mosca Manias," and both were at Hamilton's Copps Coliseum, which opened in late 1985 and was built to get the city an NHL team. (You may have noticed that Hamilton still doesn't have that team.)

I was selling myself and my history as much as the wrestling, but the Mosca Manias had pretty good cards. I used NWA wrestlers: the Main Event was Ric Flair vs. Dusty Rhodes, and we had Abdullah the Butcher against Jimmy "The Boogie Woogie

Man" Valiant; Sergeant Slaughter vs. Hamilton's Dan Johnson:
The Road Warriors (Animal and Hawk) against The Russians,
Nikita Kolov and Krusher Kruschev; and my son Ang Mosca
Jr. and Vic Rossettani against the Kelly Twins — we had midgets, too. It was a big deal. I paid the guys well, I made some good
money and we gave a buck per ticket to spinal chord research.

At the time Amstel Brewery was located in Hamilton. A few
months before the first Mosca Mania, which was scheduled for
February 2, 1986, I went down there and said to the president,
a guy from Holland, "I'm running a wrestling show and I'd like
you to advertise with me." He asked me how much it would
cost, and that's where my background as a hustler came in. I
had no idea how much to charge, so I took a number right off
the top of my head: "$25,000." He asked what he got for that
dough and I told him he'd get advertising on the ring apron and
the backdrop behind the wrestlers during their TV interviews.
I didn't have any money to buy TV time, but I figured if he gave
me the money then I would. "What else do I get?" he asked.
And I looked him in the eye and said, "Me!" I swear to God I
said exactly that.

He told me to come back in a couple of days, and I got a check
for $15,000 — the other $10,000 would come at the completion of the show. The Amstel president went back to Europe a
long time ago but early in 2011 he called me up out of the blue
to remind me of the time I said, "Me!" He loved that confidence
and said "I had to call you because I never forgot what you did."

For about eight years, beginning in 1985, I also had my
own wrestling TV show out of CKCO in Kitchener called, *Pro
Wrestling Canada*. I had an announcer, Milt Avruskin, and I
did the colour commentary myself. I was working under the
NWA and I supported the television show with live shows out

of Kitchener and Brantford; we did our taping for *Pro Wrestling Canada* out of Brantford. I'd use the NWA compilation tapes that they shot out of Charlotte, North Carolina, and use their guys like Ric Flair, Dusty Rhodes and Sergeant Slaughter, and mix them in with the stuff that we shot in Ontario. *Pro Wrestling Canada* was aired in the Vancouver, Edmonton and Calgary as well as Ontario.

Once, Dusty Rhodes and Ric Flair didn't show up for a TV taping in front of a live audience in Brantford. It's the worst thing a wrestling promoter can experience. In retaliation, I didn't pay any of the American wrestlers. I only paid the Canadian kids. I got a lot of angry letters and death threats: "I'm going to blow up your fuckin' house." There were no names on the letters but they were from wrestlers. I do have an idea of who sent them, though, and I know that a lot of those guys are broke today.

With my television and live events I was crossing over into WWF territory. Vince McMahon Jr. had the Tunney family booking for him in Toronto, and I was stirring things up. Vince wanted me gone. I made the mistake of not pursuing a partnership with him. I could tell they were squeezing me out of the fold even before I ran the Mosca Manias. When I was still working with the WWF, doing colour commentary, they brought in Jesse "The Body" Ventura to join me and he eventually replaced me. Ventura was a heel when he helped the WWF get big, and he became their signature colour commentator. He had been a Navy frogman and was gassed by Agent Orange when he was serving in Vietnam, and later became governor of Minnesota, but for some reason Ventura was scared to death of me. I knew what was going on when they put him on the broadcasts with me — I saw the writing on the wall because you don't have two heels working together on a broadcast.

I ran another show in Hamilton as a promoter and I choked to death. The WWF deliberately ran a show in Toronto at roughly the same time and stacked it with all their big wheels, billing it as Roddy Piper's last time in Toronto. I lost about 20,000 bucks on that one and figured I'd better jump off the ship. The other shows made me money but Vince was too powerful. I knew enough to get out. I sold my wrestling business to Vince in the early 1990's.

I still see Vince when he comes to Hamilton to do shows at Copps Coliseum. He gives me passes and I take a bunch of the Tiger-Cats with me.

Wrestling really played on the tough guy image that I first gained playing football, and that image helped me get some acting roles on TV and in commercials. I was in the TVO series *Goosebumps*, and one time and I had a principal role in two episodes of CTV's *Night Heat*. When you have a principal role you get your own trailer, so I thought I was some kind of big wheel. I used to drive the director Mario Azzopardi nuts. I'd say to him, like I was some kind of star actor: "Don't bother me, I'm putting my feet up."

My part in *Night Heat* was to be an organizer of meat heists. I did another show where I played myself in a spoof of the 6/49 Lottery, and they paid me a good chunk of dough for that. I'm a member of ACTRA and still get residual checks from the reruns of some of those shows. When I was still playing I did a General Motors commercial which demonstrated the ruggedness of their trucks which played on the ruggedness of my character. Even in my 60s and 70s I have been doing stuff on TV and radio.

Sometimes you'd get asked to do things that were a little more off the beaten track. In 1990 Charlie Jurvavinski invited me to a celebrity race at Flamboro Downs, the track he owned near Hamilton. I had never been on a sulky, or anything like it before. As the horse was running down the track it kept turning its head as if to say, "Let that freakin' rein go." Eddie Shack, John Ferguson and George Plimpton were also in the race. Ferguson owned and trained horses and was the only one of us who knew anything about them. My horse finished third and Plimpton's horse won. He had just written *Paper Lion*, a book where he documented his process of trying out to be quarterback of the Detroit Lions. Ferguson finished last because his horse stopped right in the middle of the track and turned right around the other way! We really busted his chops about that one.

The Four Seasons Nature Resort near Freelton, which is near Hamilton, brought the TV and radio commentator Gordon Sinclair and I out to their resort to judge the Miss Nude World contest. The place is a nudist resort so not only were the contestants nude, so was everyone in the audience. The winner got a trip for two to Florida, a pantsuit, a bikini and a live monkey — don't ask me, I didn't come up with the prizes.

Anyway somebody, probably from Europe, took a picture of it. I'm wearing a suit, and they show the women from the back. That picture appeared the next day in the newspapers in Europe and a friend of my wife comes back from Sweden with the paper and shows it to Gwen. I didn't tell her I was doing this, and she gave me hell. To prove it was legitimate I made her come to the finals with me. She didn't want to come, but did, and she just looked straight ahead the entire time we were there.

By the mid-'90s I was out of wrestling after more than 30 years in the business. It was wrestling that gave me my pure financial independence and allowed me to see the world, and I'm thankful for that. And while I didn't need football for my wrestling career, I probably would never have got into the ring in the first place without playing in the CFL.

Around February 1987, I found out that I was going to be elected to the Canadian Football Hall of Fame. They made the official announcement on May 2, and we had the induction dinner during the CFL season at the Hamilton Convention Centre, which is basically right across the road from the CFL Hall of Fame.

I was inducted with two other players and two builders. The other players were Tom Wilkinson, the Edmonton quarterback who won five Grey Cups, and Dick Huffman, a two-way lineman for the Stampeders and Bombers who retired the year before I came to Canada. The builders were Bob Kramer, who ran the Saskatchewan Roughriders in the '50s and '60s, and Harold Ballard, who owned the Toronto Maple Leafs for years and the Tiger-Cats from 1978 to 1989. I didn't agree with Ballard going to the Hall of Fame. In fact, I think it was the biggest joke ever. He didn't deserve to get in just because he was an owner. He didn't care about Hamilton, he left the city high and dry in 1989 with no football team. That's why I had no respect for him. David Braley had to step in a take over the team, and he's done it twice more since then with Vancouver and Toronto. He's made this league survive, and he's been around it for some 20-odd years. He should be in the Hall in Ballard's place.

When I was inducted it was 15 years after we won the 1972 Grey Cup; I had been out of the league just about as long as I played in it. I was lucky to be nominated because I think I was coming to the end of my eligibility. I have to admit that I expected to get into the Hall, and each year when I wasn't announced, I was disappointed. I played on five teams that won the Grey Cup and I went to the Grey Cup nine times — nobody's played in it more. I missed only one game in my entire career, made the Eastern All-Star team five times and was twice up for Lineman of the Year. You'd think I might have been eligible to go in. But nobody really helped me, nobody backed me, and you need that. Ralph Sazio didn't back me. Doug Mitchell was the commissioner at the time and I think that's how I got in. But it had been so long it almost felt like a slight. I was kind of bitter at first and I said I wasn't even going to go down there and accept the nomination because it took them so long. About 20 years later, TSN did a poll which chose the top 50 players in the history of the CFL, voted on by 60 former players, coaches and veteran media. I finished 37th. A lot of people thought that was too low, but even at 37th, you'd think that I'd get in the Hall of Fame a little earlier.

But it was still a huge honour, and I swallowed my ego and came around to that. The induction dinner was one of the biggest the Hall of Fame ever had up to then, with over 1,000 people. My first grandchild Nathan, Gino's son, was born in the same year and all the kids were there when they unveiled our busts. The organizers had us walk up one-by-one. It was an emotional experience.

I'm not sure what it was with the CFL and me over the years, but I've never had an opportunity to get back into the league. I'm not bitter about it. I couldn't have coached, but I always saw myself as more of a management-type, or an ideas person. I had ideas for selling the game. I could have been the best thing for the CFL when it was struggling in the late '80s and '90s. It seems, though, like no one ever fully trusted me. Ron Foxcroft brought me in for the 1996 Grey Cup, and Scott Mitchell brought me in as an ambassador for the Ticats when he became president of the team a few years ago. But I still don't know why I didn't have more opportunity. Am I a bit rough around the edges? Yes. Do I say what's on my mind? Yes, I'm very direct. But that's what a lot of people want me for. I'm a good door opener. I don't know if the league wanted me out of the way because I was very outspoken, but, it's too late now.

Still, I've been a lucky guy because of football and I've done a few things for this league, even though they didn't want me around. I did TV and radio, dozens of interviews over the years, just talking about how great Canadian football is. In the mid-'80s I went out to Regina to help the Roughriders, who almost went broke. Steve Ruddick, the guy who does sports and weather on CHCH in Hamilton, was working in Regina then and we did two full nights of TV in Saskatoon and Regina raising money for the team. I would not have thought in a million years that the Roughriders would get to where they are today, with $20 million in the bank. I came down to Ottawa to help with marketing the team when Jo-Anne Polak was the general manager for three years, starting in 1989. Jo-Anne was only about 30 and was the first female general manager of any professional sports team in North America. Everybody laughed at her, but she was good. She was pretty sharp and she worked really hard. Ottawa was in trouble financially too, so I came down there and did a telethon. I don't think Russ Jackson was there at the time, but I was.

When David Braley owned the team in Hamilton, we did a telethon at City Hall in 1990. We locked up City Hall for the day, and the city gave us all their phones. We scooped all the ad time on CHCH-TV for a day and a half, and instead of ads, I would do interviews with ex-players and business people in the city. I learned all of my interview skills from wrestling, and when Braley saw that I could do it, he just let me go at it.

Braley offered me a deal to come work with the Tiger-Cats and afterwards the only reason that I could figure out why he did was so that I would keep my mouth shut. Don Crump was the commissioner at the time, and he had been one of Harold Ballard's sidekicks with the Tiger-Cats and Maple Leafs. The press interviewed me and the headlines on the stories the next day were "Mosca's on a 'Dump Crump' campaign." It was right after that that Braley hired me. Maybe because I wasn't going to criticize the CFL when I was working for a team. I did keep my mouth shut but the team never had anything for me to do. The whole charade lasted six months.

Braley was controlling this league pretty good at the time, and he still is. But we're very fortunate to have him. I don't think he's got that great of a personality, but he's invested a lot of money in this league. He believes in it like I do. He better have a lot of belief in Toronto though because Toronto is in big trouble as a live market. I could never see why they weren't able to amalgamate with the soccer team and play at their stadium. They don't belong in that bloody dome. But they're in good hands with Braley. He's done a great job for this league, and if he has an ego about it, that's great, and if his ego is his pocketbook, that's even greater.

Anyway, they kept me quiet for a while about Crump, and I'm usually not quiet about commissioners. I've been asked a lot about CFL commissioners over the years and I always gave my opinions, which weren't always popular. Especially with the league. I thought Sydney Halter, who was the commissioner when I came to Canada, didn't know what day of the week it was. Any guy who calls a football game off with nine minutes to go, like he did with the Fog Bowl, had a whole different attitude. Jake Gaudaur was very smooth and came along at the right time. Jake was a lucky guy with his timing: it was the 1960s and the CFL was hard-core in Canada. You didn't need any promotion and two people could run the office. I thought Doug Mitchell was one of the better commissioners I've seen. And you now know how I felt about Donald Crump. It was a joke. The other joke was Larry Smith, who took over as commissioner in 1992. He started the American "experiment." I personally believe he almost ruined this league. I made a statement to him one day: "Let's you and I walk down any street in Canada, and people will say 'Who's that asshole with Mosca?'" He laughed, he thought it was a joke, but I never trusted him at all. He became president of the Alouettes and I called him "All-Wet." Larry was getting bonuses for finding new teams and bringing them into the league, but the CFL should never have been in the U.S. On Friday night in the U.S. they've got high school ball, on Saturday college and on Sunday the NFL. Where the heck were we going to fit in? How we ever survived that, I still don't know. This must be the most resilient league on record. The current guy, Mark Cohon, I'm not sure what he does to sell the game, although I'm told he does a lot behind the scenes. You turn on the TV 365 days a year in the U.S. and you're going to find an NFL commercial of some kind. What about us? We're not promoting this game enough in this country. I also once told Mark he shouldn't wear those brown shoes with a blue suit. I just think that we don't sell the CFL game enough. This is a really great game. But I guess Mosca says too much some times for some people's sakes. But I don't do it for my ego, I'm sincere about what I want for this league. And I'm honest. So you don't like me, it's your bad luck. I see that Cohon, though, has been suspending players for different things and I think that's good. We haven't been hard enough on players in the past who bring disrespect to the game.

The guy who has done as much for this league as most commissioners, without the fans knowing about it, is Ron Foxcroft. Ron owns Fluke Transport in Hamilton and also co-invented the Fox40 whistle and markets it. He works for the NBA, grading their officials, and was a top international and NCAA basketball referee himself. He was on the floor when Bobby Knight threw that chair across the court.

I met Ron in 1996 when Hamilton was host to the Grey Cup. Immediately I couldn't believe that anyone in the world was as nice as Ron was. I kept thinking that it was all an act, but it wasn't. Ron has the biggest heart of anyone I've ever met, and when he says he is going to do something, he does it. In 1996 he was the co-chairman of the Grey Cup Committee, along with Marnie Paikin. He called me up and asked if would come aboard, and he paid me a pretty good salary. I asked him what he wanted me to do, and he told me to promote this game anyway I knew how. I knocked on a lot of doors, sold a lot of ideas, sold the game itself. My first big encounter was when the City of Hamilton wasn't bonded to put extra seats in Ivor Wynne Stadium. I told the guy who was the manager of the stadium, "If I were the mayor, I would have fired your ass in seconds." He didn't like me after that because I told him the truth. Here we have the Grey Cup game back in Hamilton after almost a quarter century, and we almost lost the game because we couldn't add more seats. We eventually got the seats in, but I expressed my opinion. Ron appreciated my work and he's been in my corner ever since. He's a terrific guy. Ron has also had a lot to do with keeping the Tiger-Cats alive. Working behind the scenes, Ron helped find stable ownership.

I work for the Cats as an ambassador, now, selling the Canadian game however I can — to the fans and to the players alike. I'm happy with the way the franchise is going. Bob Young realized that he had the wrong people at the helm. Good teams don't start on the field; they start upstairs. First and foremost you have a good owner and president, after that you need a good general manager and then you need a good coach — a guy that can handle the men and the Xs and Os. Right now the Tiger-Cats have all three, and I'm looking forward to the future.

After I stopped wrestling and playing football, I had to make sure I kept working out or I would have ended up fat and soft in a really hurry. One morning in April of 1992, I got up around 5 a.m. to go the gym. I was sneaking around quietly because I didn't want to wake Gwen, who was still sleeping. I went to the gym in Orangeville about 20 minutes away and did my routine. When I came back to the house in Caledon around 10:30 in the morning I could sense that something was wrong. We had a dog, a lhasa apso, and it was acting strange. He wasn't really my dog, he was Gwen's, but he was jumping up all over me. I started upstairs because I was worried about Gwen, given her drinking problem. We had already had an incident in the past year. She was drinking and driving about eight months earlier and had a car accident. I got a good lawyer, which was maybe the worst thing I ever did because we beat the charge, and things didn't change.

When I got upstairs Gwen was lying in bed, and she looked like death. She was pale, unconscious and had been incontinent. I called 911 and they took her to hospital, but she had had an aneurysm in her brain and two days later she was dead. She was only 57 years old. In the two days she was unconscious her hair went from blond to completely white. I made sure we had a closed casket.

She had been taking a combination of pain pills and alcohol, and it was tough for me to understand why. There were times when I wondered if it might have actually been suicide, but the doctors assured me it wasn't. I've survived a lot of things in my life, but I felt horribly guilty about Gwen and at first I tried to blame myself. Because I didn't understand alcoholism I had always tried to cover for her. I'd always make an excuse for her in social situations. "My wife is not feeling well," I'd say. When she retired from Air Canada it was the biggest mistake of her life. With her seniority she only had to work six or seven days a month and we could fly everywhere for free on Air Canada. Working kept her from drinking all the time, and without it, she spiraled out of control.

I began to think "Why me? Why me?" Gwen had a girlfriend named Barb Lacey and she helped me through that, and is still a good friend today. She told me that it wasn't my fault, that it was really no one's fault. That it was the booze that did it. When I was first with Gwen I used to laugh because she could drink a case of beer in about six hours. I'm talking a case of 24, not 12. I thought it was funny but, you know, those things aren't funny. I didn't realize what was happening.

I've survived quite a bit of stuff in my life, but when Gwen died I was completely devastated. I was between a few things professionally, but I was still appearing at a lot of banquets, raising lots of money for charity (I was the spokesperson for Muscular Dystrophy for five years) and I still had the wrestling promotions. Vince McMahon had made me an offer for my television interests because he wanted the market. When Gwen asked if I was going to take it I said, "Naw, the best thing to do is not to jump at the first offer." A few weeks later I took that offer, right after she died. I decided to sell the house as well. There were a lot of memories with that house that hurt and I didn't want the daily reminder.

My bright idea was penthouse living. So I got a penthouse in downtown Hamilton, right by City Hall, 25 storeys up, 25 storeys down. It didn't take me long to ask myself what the hell I was doing in the elevator all the time. It was a nice place, but what a pain. I hated every minute of living there, actually.

In 1995 the new Ticat owners George Grant and David Macdonald — I didn't like Grant, and didn't know Macdonald that well — asked me to do an autograph signing on the field after one of the Ticat games. A redheaded woman, her son and his girlfriend approached me to get a picture with me. I'm still thinking I'm the cock of the walk and I told her to call me sometime. She said, "I don't phone men," and I thought, "Whoa, boy, I'm in trouble now." She said we'd met once before, but I didn't really remember. Then she slipped her business card in my pocket. Her name was Helen Cherney and she was in real estate.

I phoned Helen about a month later and we went out for dinner at the Oban Inn in Niagara-on-the-Lake. She lived in Virgil, which is part of Niagara-on-the-Lake. Then I brought three of my grand-kids and a bag of groceries along on the next "date" or the one after. I don't remember what we cooked, but we cooked it together. I don't know why I showed up with the grandchildren. I guess I'd been around them a lot at the time and they were a big part of my life. Helen didn't mind, she's very family-oriented anyway. So those were our big dates.

Her son Mark, the one who was there at the game, jokes now, "Yeah mom, you put 50 business cards in 50 different guys' pockets and he's the only one who called." She has four great guys as sons. I love those kids and they treat me like I'm their father.

I finally, after all those years, had come to a stage in my life when I didn't want to be involved with different women. Helen and I became a couple pretty quickly, but it wasn't really talked about. We just grew into the whole situation, sort of eased into and I never even thought too much about it. I didn't say 'love' much. Is it necessary to say it? I think I showed her. But I'm not one of those guys who say, "I love you, do you love me?" Of course, I love her. We went down to South Carolina for a few trips and we went down to Las Vegas, where she met my brother Mike. And eventually I moved into her place in Virgil. Later we bought a condo from the development that Helen was selling and Nathan, the youngest of her boys, came with us.

Then we decided to get married. Despite how my first two marriages went, I didn't have any anxiety or worries about getting married to Helen. We felt very comfortable together. It felt right and I have never felt more comfortable in my entire life. I have the greatest woman in the world: She tells me, "If you want to take off for a week, then just go ahead." She's slightly religious and she's very kind. She wants everything to be just right for everyone. She's the greatest gift in the world.

I told Bernie Faloney that we were getting married and he was very happy for me. Then he said, "I'd like to be your best man."

Bernie and I were always good acquaintances when we were playing, but I really got to know him later, away from football. After Bernie died, I moved to have a street around the football stadium named after him. Now the segment of Cannon Street just south of Ivor Wynne is called Bernie Faloney Way. Bernie was the quarterback and leader of the team, and some people put him on such a pedestal that nobody could touch him while we were playing. But Bernie was not that kind of guy. He was a great person, but some of the players on the Ticats — I don't really want to mention their names — they put him on a pedestal and kissed Bernie's ass. But Bernie didn't want anybody kissing his ass, *because* he was a good person. I was honoured to have him as my best man.

Helen and I were planning on getting married in either the spring or early summer of 1998 but Bernie said, "Can you push it up a little bit, and make it happen in 1997?" I asked him why and he told me that he had colon cancer, and I think he knew he didn't have long to live. So we pushed the date up to September 11, 1997, and Bernie was my best man. On June 14, 1998, Bernie died. It was very sad, and I was thankful he was around for my wedding.

We got married at the Little Wedding Chapel in Niagara Falls and had the reception at Casa Mia, a well-known restaurant in Niagara Falls. We still go back there for dinner sometimes. It was a small wedding, just family mostly because we have a big enough family now. All Helen's kids and my kids were there for the wedding. My sons Angelo and Gino, and my daughter Jolene, Helen's sons Nathan, Mark, Aaron, and Ryan; Angelo's girlfriend at the time, Gino's wife Gill and their four kids, Jolene's husband Bernie and their three kids, Ryan's and Aaron's girlfriends at the time, and Mark's girlfriend

Carrie, who is now his wife. Plus Bernie and Jan, and Helen's best friend since their days at Niagara District High School, Kris Peters, who stood up for her and another friend from high school, Gina Williams.

My daughter Jolene, God love her, is a chip right off the old block and took one look at the entire family at the wedding and said, "This is The Brady Bunch of the '90s."

Helen and I have settled into a fairly simple life together. I think Helen is the first person I've ever told with my own mouth about my family background. Jolene had already leaked it out to her, but it was still hard for me to voice it because I had hidden it for so long. Jolene had sort of figured it out over time. She and Angelo actually went down to Waltham to see my mother a few years ago. I have never talked to Jolene about that visit. I knew they went down, so I just left it at that.

With Helen, I have finally found out what a good marriage is supposed to be like. My first marriage, I thought I was in love, but I was so young. Darlene was a good woman but I had trouble seeing that. I was seeing other things. And Gwen was a good person, but we had problems because of the alcohol and because she didn't trust me. And I don't blame her, actually.

Helen probably had every reason not to trust me, either. But you know something? I ain't lookin' for anything anymore. She's the one I want to be with. She never pressures me, never asks me if, or when, I'm coming home, but I *want* to be home, I don't want to show up late. I'm right here. I'm at a different stage of life.

The Last Voice You Hear

I'VE HAD SOME BEAUTIFUL HOUSES since I moved to Canada more than a half-century ago, and I sure didn't grow up in one. In 2000, Helen and I moved into a great house in a great location, but more important, it's also a beautiful *home*.

It's in a development where Helen was selling condos and early in 2000 she suggested I come out and take a look, even though I always told her I was never moving again because I'd already moved too many times in my life. We picked up some Kentucky Fried Chicken and a bottle of wine and sat in the two chairs in front of the model unit, which is right next door to the end unit we eventually purchased. It sits right on Lake Ontario, not even half a football field from the water. We sat out there, ate dinner and watched the waves and I finally said, "I could live here." And now we do.

It's near Port Weller, which is part of St. Catharines. Looking out my front window I can see Toronto 55 miles away. There's green space everywhere. Just to the west of us there's a park with trails, and not far away is a park dedicated to 9/11. You have to have pretty good eyes, but you can see where the big ships come out of the Welland Canal and the lighthouse on the other side of the canal. It's a very relaxing place and it's got a gorgeous view in all four seasons. Even in the winter it's beautiful. We've got a 1,200 square-foot deck to take advantage of the view.

The house itself is about 3,000 squre feet, it's very bright and I love the kitchen. It's a very family-oriented place and each kid on both sides of the family has a key. I tell them if they don't come here, it's their own fault. My kids are in Hamilton and Helen's are in the area we live, and it really works well.

I'm living on the right side of the tracks now, a long way from Waltham. But, of course, just before we moved here I had one last kick at the old can. In July of 1999, we had just come back from Hawaii and I found out I had been busted while I was away. We were lying in bed watching TV and suddenly there's a picture of me. I was running card games in a small building on Main Street in downtown Hamilton. I gave 'em lots of coffee, lots of food, and no booze. I had a partner, so the card games were going on when I wasn't there and the police raided it. There were 29 found-ins but I was the only guy charged.

Poor Helen. She wasn't ready for all that. CHCH-TV brought their truck down and parked outside our house in Virgil, but they never saw me, I stayed in the house. Helen knew I was play-ing the games, but she didn't know that I was actually running them. I didn't tell her the whole truth. She was really good about it, but she just couldn't believe it. "My husband is a crook," she said. I laughed, but she was worried. It was all over the front page of *The Hamilton Spectator*. Some people wrote the editor asking why they were raking me over the coals when I'd done so much for the community. I was eventually fined $500, but didn't get a criminal record. I haven't run a game since, not so much because of the arrest, but because I finally realized I don't need to anymore. You get tired of it after a while, it's a pain in the ass.

I'd been around card games for more than 60 years; since I was selling those sandwiches at my dad's games. I enjoy playing and I was running games mostly to make a living or for extra dough. When I was very young I wanted to be totally independent, and I got to be. I didn't want to ask anybody for anything, not a fucking dime. I stole, I ran craps and cards, but I had my own money. Now, I play cards occasionally. I go across the river to the casino in Niagara Falls, New York. I don't go to Niagara Falls, Canada, because I'm well-known in the area and don't want people to make a big deal of it. And I only go for three hours now, where I used to be able to sit there for three days.

There are a lot of things that most of us did when we were younger that we can't do now. I'm walking around with a lot of injuries, but that's the price you pay. Your body reacts differently as you get older. A 20-year-old guy can cope with injuries, a guy over 70, like me, can't cope with any more injuries. I was in two sports that are very hard on the body. And there's a lot of discussion in the papers about football head injuries. But the head shots in our game are not as bad as they are in the NFL. The CFL field is 65 yards wide as opposed to the NFL, which is 53 1/3 yards wide. There's nearly 5,500 extra square feet on a CFL field, not counting the end zones, so guys can get outside and don't get hit as much as the guys in the NFL do. But we were taught to hit with our heads. I seem okay for now, but who knows, maybe I'll end up punch drunk.

While my head feels fine, I've got some other issues. Diabetes is the main one, but I also have a permanently crooked finger on my left hand and my right hand doesn't straighten properly from all those years of doing the head slap. I have two replacement knees, one is seven years old, the other is four. Unfortunately when they were doing my second knee, the left knee, they hit a nerve in my back that left me numb from my butt to my toes on my left side, which is why I walk with a cane. I've had both my shoulders replaced, too!

So none of the shoulders and knees I have now are the ones I was born with. When we go through airport security I often set off the alarm and the security guy has me stand there with my arms out as he waves his x-ray prod over my body. It is usually pretty active and invariably the officer will ask me what's going on. I'll then whisper in his ear, "Can you call my wife over? Tell her I'm getting an erection, and she'd better get over here." I do that almost every time we go through security. Some of them take it well, some of them don't. Big fuckin' deal. If you can't laugh at that, you can't laugh at all.

The Hamilton Spectator wrote an article about me a few years ago that started, "It's hard to know where Hamilton stops and Angelo Mosca begins." And that's true, I love the city, it's part of me. I came here in 1958 and have never really left. Even though I've often lived in other towns, they're not far from Hamilton and I feels like I'm in the city more often than I'm not. Coming to the city was one of the best things that ever happened to me.

There are a few things in my life I regret, although I'm not one to dwell on them. I regret what I put Darlene through. I didn't know how to create a family. I really wanted to be a good father, but I was never shown how. Not in any way. I also feel bad about the word "stealing." Once I received my first pro contract in 1958 — after I had dealt with the fallout of the typewriter stealing in Wyoming — I realized that I didn't need to steal any more. It took time for that reality to set in, though. One other thing, and it's not a regret really: I never really showed anybody in the U.S.

what I was really capable of. I think I've done that in Canada, but I didn't in the United States. If I had, I don't think I ever would have been in this country, I probably would have been in the NFL instead. But I don't have any problem with that. I love the CFL and I'm probably the best salesman this league has ever had.

When Julius Tucker arranged for me to play football in Canada I'm not sure he knew just how well it would turn out for me. I was lucky that it was Hamilton he contacted, just one of the many things I feel fortunate about; like still being alive. So many guys that I played with have gone. When we were writing this book I was looking at the 1958 Ticat team, my first one, and I kept saying, "He's dead, *he's* dead, *he's* dead." Every time one of my old teammates or an old wrestling crony dies — and it's happening a lot lately — I think I must be right around the corner from it myself. But you know something? I'm not scared of that at all.

The one that hit me really hard, though, was Bronko Nagurski. I cried and cried the day he died. It was March 8, 2011 and I'd talked with him about two weeks earlier. I was going on holidays with Helen and told him I'd fly up to Minnesota to see him on the 28th of March once we returned. He was sicker with cancer than I knew, and it took him almost a year to the day after he was told he had about a year left to live. We were friends for 55 years after that accidental meeting in the Chicago airport — he the country bumpkin and me the city slicker. He wasn't a really rugged player but he had excellent technique, which made him very effective. Most importantly, he was a good friend and I really miss him.

I've also been fortunate in that I'm still a well-known face. I can go anywhere in this country and usually get recognized. And I enjoy it when people recognize me. I try my best to give them my time. Back in the late 1960s, *The Globe and Mail* ran a story about the best-known faces in the country. The top two were Pierre Elliott Trudeau and me, in that order. I give people my time, I know when and how to cut it off, and I know what to say and I know when to go. And I never have to curse when I'm doing it. If you want someone to tell you to go fuck yourself, though, I'll help you along.

I also feel most fortunate to have Helen and our big family as an integral part of my life. I told one of the papers a couple of years ago, "There aren't the words to describe how much I enjoy being with my grandchildren. Maybe it's a little guilt, or making up for lost time when I was on the road and away a lot and didn't find enough quality time to spend with my own kids. Now the grandkids come first, that's all there is to it." And I'm fortunate that Helen not only understood my need to write this book, but that she was the first to encourage it. I know some of the rougher parts in it will be hard for her to read. It's the first time I've opened up, at all, to outsiders. I never even told my best friends some of this stuff. I feel good about it.

I'm often asked what else I want to do in life, but I never really thought much about that because what I do is what I want to do. Right now I'm enjoying travelling to warm locales. Helen and I love going to Hawaii; it's very low-key.

If I can, I want to keep working banquets and fundraisers. You can make some cash at it, that's for sure, but the real reasons I like them are that you get to see and mingle with a lot of people. Ted Williams was my hero when I was a kid and I ended up on the banquet circuit with him and all the other great athletes of that time. But no banquet has surprised me as much as the one in the Niagara Peninsula in October 2010. It was a "dinner of champions" and Steven T. Smith, a Mohawk potter presented me with an original piece of pottery. The notes that went with the presentation explained the meaning of the gift and the design:

> "In the ancient culture, they used abstract symbol-
> ism or pictographs based on nature to tell a story
> or convey an idea. Attributes found in nature were
> used as an analogy to reflect on a person's quali-
> ties. This piece symbolizes people looking toward
> Angelo, in awe of his powerful presence. The
> eagle headdress is symbolic of strength, vision
> and courage. The feathers symbolize respect and
> friendship. The wild woodland floral design sym-
> bolizes life, health, growth and fertility. The heron
> symbolizes patience, determination and perse-
> verance. The screaming eagle symbolizes power
> and mighty personality. The turtle symbolizes
> longevity. The various circles symbolize sacred
> and continuous life cycles of renewal. The blend-
> ing of the circular (female) with the linear (male)
> designs symbolizes the harmonious and prolific
> order of the laws and forces of nature."

You can see how I'd be deeply touched by that gift and, more, its explanation. But above all I love that when you are at a banquet you're usually raising money for charity, and usually kids. Since I've come to Canada, I figure I've spoken at more than 1,000 banquets, from very big ones to very small ones, and helped raise millions of dollars for various causes.

At almost every banquet, I use this as a tag line, and I'll sign off with it now: "May you live a hundred years...and may the last voice you hear be mine."

CFL Career of Angelo Mosca

1972: Played on the defensive line in his twelfth season with the Tiger-Cats...won the Grey Cup when Hamilton defeated the Saskatchewan Rough Riders 13–10

1971: Played on the defensive line in his eleventh season with the Tiger-Cats

1970: Played on the defensive line in his tenth season with the Tiger-Cats...named an East Division All-Star for the fifth time...named a CFL All-Star for the second time

1969: Played on the defensive line in his ninth season with the Tiger-Cats

1968: Played on the defensive line in his eighth season with the Tiger-Cats

1967: Played at defensive tackle in his seventh season with the Tiger-Cats...won his fourth Grey Cup when Hamilton defeated the Saskatchewan Rough Riders 24–1

1966: Played at defensive tackle in his sixth season with the Tiger-Cats...named an East Division All-Star for the fourth time

1965: Played at defensive tackle in his fifth season with the Tiger-Cats...named an East Division All-Star for the third time...won the Grey Cup after defeating the Winnipeg Blue Bombers 22–16

1964: Played at defensive tackle in his fourth season with the Tiger-Cats

1963: Signed with the Hamilton Tiger-Cats...Named an East Division All-Star for the second time...named a CFL All-Star for the first time...won the Grey Cup after defeating the B.C. Lions 21–10

1962: Signed as a free agent with the Montreal Alouettes

1961: Played defensive tackle in his second season with the Rough Riders

1960: Traded to the Ottawa Rough Riders for Hardiman Cureton on August 15, 1960...named CFL East Division All-Star for the first time...won the Grey Cup after defeating the Edmonton Eskimos 16–6

1959: Played all season at defensive tackle in his second season with the Tiger-Cats

1958: Signed as a free agent with the Hamilton Tiger-Cats after being drafted by the NFL's Philadelphia Eagles in the 30th round.

College: Played three seasons at Notre Dame University and one at Wyoming

Personal: Wrestled under the names King Kong Mosca and The Mighty Hercules during the offseason and following his playing career.

Wrestling Career of Angelo "King Kong" Mosca

NWA Canadian Heavyweight title reigns (Toronto-based title)

Angelo Mosca beat Great Hossein Arab (The Iron Sheik) on July 20, 1980 in Toronto, ON
Great Hossein Arab beat Angelo Mosca on August 10, 1980 in Toronto, ON
Angelo Mosca beat Great Hossein Arab on December 28, 1980 in Toronto, ON
Mr. Fuji beat Angelo Mosca on July 12, 1981 in Toronto, ON
Angelo Mosca beat Mr. Fuji on July 26, 1981 in Toronto, ON
Big John Studd beat Angelo Mosca on September 20, 1981 in Toronto, ON
Angelo Mosca beat Big John Studd on January 17, 1982 in Toronto, ON
Sgt. Slaughter beat Angelo Mosca on July 24, 1983 in Toronto, ON
Angelo Mosca beat Sgt. Slaughter on January 22, 1984 in Toronto, ON
Title deactivated, March 1984

Titles Held:
Stampede North American 1969
NWA U.S. (San Francisco) title 1975
Mid-Atlantic Television title 1976
British Empire Heavyweight 1978
NWA Georgia title 1978
Mid-South Brass Knuckles title 1979
NWA Canadian Heavyweight title 1980-84 (5x)
WWC Caribbean title 1982
Bahamas Heavyweight title 1983
Global (Florida) tag team 1983
NWA Southern (Florida) title 1984

Results:
1969
02/21 Calgary, AB beat Gil Hayes
02/28 Calgary, AB beat Bud Osborne
03/07 Calgary, AB beat Bud Jones
03/14 Calgary, AB beat Newton Tattrie
03/21 Calgary, AB beat Fred Sweetan
03/31 Vancouver, BC w/. Bob Brown & Bad Boy Shields, beat Earl Maynard, Eric Froelich, & Bud Rattal
04/11 Calgary, AB lost to Jerry Gouldie by DQ
04/18 Calgary, AB no contest vs. Archie Gouldie
04/25 Calgary, AB beat Archie Gouldie
*Won the Stampede North American title
05/02 Calgary, AB lost to Archie Gouldie by count out
05/09 Calgary, AB drew Archie Gouldie
05/16 Calgary, AB lost to Archie Gouldie
*Lost the Stampede North American title
05/20 Edmonton, AB w/. Dave Ruhl, vs. Jack Kris & Clem St. Louis
05/26 Vancouver, BC w/. Gene Kiniski, beat John Tolos & Johnny Kostas

06/02 Vancouver, BC lost to Don Leo Jonathan
06/03 Seattle, WA lost to Don Leo Jonathan by DQ
06/03 Seattle, WA lost in a Battle royal
06/04 Tacoma, WA beat Jerry London
09/19 Greensburg, PA w/. Ivan Koloff, drew Bruno Sammartino & Battman
11/30 Toronto, ON beat Porky the Pig
12/14 Toronto, ON beat Eric the Red
12/28 Toronto, ON beat Porky the Pig

1970
01/09 Calgary, AB beat Dan Kroffat
01/15 Regina, SK beat Dan Kroffat
01/17 Beaver Falls, PA w/. Ivan Koloff, lost to Bruno Sammartino & Battman
01/18 Edmonton, AB vs. Ray Osborne
01/22 Regina, SK beat Gordon Ivey
01/23 Calgary, AB beat Jose Quintero
01/26 Vancouver, BC w/. Gene Kiniski, drew Dean Higuchi & Steve Bolus
01/29 Regina, SK drew Bobby Christy
01/30 Calgary, AB beat Alex The Butcher
02/05 Regina, SK lost to Bobby Christy by DQ
02/06 Calgary, AB lost to Bob Lueck by DQ
02/12 Regina, SK beat Alex the Butcher
02/13 Calgary, AB double count out vs. Bob Lueck
02/20 Calgary, AB beat Buck Jones
02/22 Edmonton, AB vs. Alex the Butcher
02/26 Regina, SK lost to Jerry Christy by DQ
02/27 Calgary, AB w/. Wayne Coleman, lost to Stu Hart & Bob Lueck
03/05 Regina, SK beat Bob Lueck
03/06 Calgary, AB lost to Gordon Ivey by DQ
03/08 Edmonton, AB w/. Wayne Coleman, vs. Stu Hart & Bob Lueck
03/11 Regina, SK no contest vs. Bob Lueck
03/19 Regina, SK w/. Wayne Coleman, lost to Mighty Ursus & Bob Lueck
03/20 Calgary, AB w/. Wayne Coleman, beat Dan Kroffat & Bob Lueck
03/24 Red Deer, AB w/. Wayne Coleman, vs. Bobby & Jerry Christy
03/27 Calgary, AB lost to Mighty Ursus
03/28 Edmonton, AB vs. Dan Kroffat
04/02 Regina, SK w/. Wayne Coleman, lost to Bobby & Jerry Christy
04/03 Calgary, AB w/. Wayne Coleman, drew Mighty Ursus & Bobby Christy
04/04 Edmonton, AB w/. Wayne Coleman, vs. Mighty Ursus & Bobby Christy
04/08 Regina, SK lost to Gordon Ivey by DQ
04/09 Regina, SK w/. Wayne Coleman, lost to Bobby & Jerry Christy
04/10 Calgary, AB w/. Wayne Coleman, lost to Mighty Ursus & Bobby Christy
04/11 Edmonton, AB w/. Wayne Coleman, vs. Mighty Ursus & Bobby Christy

04/16 Regina, SK w/. Gorilla Marconi, beat Dave
Ruhl & Gordon Ivey
04/17 Calgary, AB w/. Wayne Coleman, vs. Bobby
Christy & Gordon Ivey
04/18 Edmonton, AB w/. Gorilla Marconi, vs. Dan
Kroffat & Bob Lueck
04/20 Vancouver, BC beat Moose Morowski
04/24 Calgary, AB beat Johnny Valentine Jr. (Greg
Valentine)
04/25 Edmonton, AB w/. Gorilla Marconi, vs. Dan
Kroffat & Dave Ruhl
05/01 Calgary, AB w/. Gorilla Marconi, beat Dan
Kroffat & Bobby Christy
05/08 Calgary, AB w/. Gorilla Marconi, beat Dan
Kroffat & Bob Lueck
05/09 Edmonton, AB w/. Wayne Coleman, vs. Carlos
Belafonte & Bob Lueck
05/16 Edmonton, AB vs. Dan Kroffat
05/18 Vancouver, BC w/. Bob Brown, beat Tex
McKenzie & Duncan McTavish
05/22 Calgary, AB beat Abdullah the Butcher by DQ
05/25 Vancouver, BC lost to Dean Higuchi
05/29 Calgary, AB lost to Abdullah the Butcher

1971
01/11 Vancouver, BC beat Dan Kroffat
01/18 Vancouver, BC beat Duncan McTavish
01/25 Vancouver, BC w/. Moose Morowski, beat
Duncan McTavish & Les Thornton
02/01 Vancouver, BC w/. Dutch Savage, beat Duncan
McTavish & Les Thornton
02/08 Vancouver, BC drew Les Thornton
02/08 Vancouver, BC w/. Dutch Savage & John
Quinn, lost to Don Leo Jonathan, Steven Little
Bear & Les Thornton
02/15 Vancouver, BC beat Butts Giraud
02/22 Vancouver, BC w/. Soldat Gorky, beat Duncan
McTavish & Bobby Nichols
03/01 Vancouver, BC lost to Dean Higuchi
03/08 Vancouver, BC w/. Dutch Savage, drew Dean
Higuchi & Duncan McTavish
03/15 Vancouver, BC lost to Duncan McTavish by DQ
03/22 Vancouver, BC beat Danny Babich
05/29 Honolulu, HI lost to Billy Robinson
05/31 Vancouver, BC beat Duncan McTavish
06/07 Vancouver, BC w/. John Tolos, lost to Dean
Higuchi & Steven Little Bear
06/21 Toronto, ON lost to The Sheik
12/16 Winnipeg, MB lost to Bob Lueck by DQ

1972
02/02 Quebec City, QC beat Dino Bravo
02/11 Pittsburgh, PA w/. Domenic Denucci, beat
Luke Graham & Mikel Scicluna
03/01 Quebec City, QC beat Pat Blake
03/03 Pittsburgh, PA w/. Domenic Denucci, beat
Blackjack Mulligan & Bobby Heenan
03/13 Montreal, QC beat Mike Loren
03/18 Ottawa, ON lost to Carlos Rocha
03/24 Pittsburgh, PA w/. Domenic Denucci, lost to
Luke Graham & George Steele

04/14 Pittsburgh, PA double DQ vs. Domenic
Denucci
05/05 Pittsburgh, PA w/. Luke Graham lost to Bruno
Sammartino & Domenic Denucci
06/02 Pittsburgh, PA lost to Bruno Sammartino by
count out
12/14 Winnipeg, MB beat Dick Murdoch by DQ
12/27 Ottawa, ON w/. Gilles Poisson, beat Billy Two
Rivers & Johnny War Eagle

1973
02/02 Quebec City, QC beat Dino Bravo
04/26 Winnipeg, MB lost to Billy Graham
05/08 Halifax, NS vs. The Beast
05/24 Winnipeg, MB w/. Wahoo McDaniel, lost to
Billy Graham & Ivan Koloff
06/12 Scarborough, ON vs. Bulldog Brower
08/30 Scarborough, ON w/. Pat & Mike Kelly, vs.
Canadian Wildman, Bruce Swayze & Wolfman

1974
01/27 London, ON double DQ vs. Waldo Von Erich
02/27 London, ON double DQ vs. Waldo Von Erich
03/10 London, ON w/. Vic Rossetani, drew Al
Costello & Don Kent
04/15 London, ON beat Mitsu Arakawa by DQ
04/16 Chatham, ON double count out vs. Baron Von
Raschke
04/16 Chatham, ON lost in a Battle royal
05/07 Thorold, ON lost to Mongolian Stomper by
DQ
05/08 Guelph, ON lost to Mongolian Stomper by DQ
05/09 St. Thomas, ON lost to Mongolian Stomper
by DQ
05/12 Sarnia, ON w/. Vic Rossetani, no contest vs.
Jimmy Valiant & Cowboy Parker
05/13 Chatham, ON w/. Vic Rossetani, no contest vs.
Jimmy Valiant & Cowboy Parker
05/14 Leamington, ON beat Canadian Wolfman
05/16 Windsor, ON beat Cowboy Parker by DQ
05/28 Leamington, ON w/. Bob Ellis, beat Jimmy
Valiant & Baron Von Raschke by DQ
05/29 Wallaceburg, ON lost to Bulldog Brower Texas
Death match
06/01 Barrie, ON lost to Mongolian Stomper
06/08 Barrie, ON no contest vs. Mongolian Stomper
06/16 Whitby, ON double DQ vs. Mongolian
Stomper
10/09 San Antonio, TX lost to Red Bastein
10/10 Corpus Christi, TX lost to Red Bastein by DQ
10/11 Houston, TX lost to Red Bastein by DQ
12/27 Calgary, AB vs. John Quinn

1975
01/29 Los Angeles, CA lost to Edouard Carpentier
01/31 Los Angeles, CA lost to Dennis Stamp
02/05 Sacramento, CA beat Reno Tufuli
02/15 San Francisco, CA beat Dennis Stamp
02/15 San Francisco, CA lost in a Battle royal
02/19 Sacramento, CA beat Manny Cruz
03/05 Sacramento, CA beat George Wells

03/15 San Francisco, CA beat Mr. Wrestling
03/19 Sacramento, CA w/. Lonnie Mayne, beat Peter
    Maivia & Raul Mata
04/02 Sacramento, CA w/. Lonnie Mayne, beat Peter
    Maivia & Pat Patterson
04/05 San Francisco, CA w/. Lonnie Mayne, beat
    Peter Maivia & Raul Mata
04/16 Sacramento, CA w/. Lonnie Mayne & Karl
    Von Brauner, beat Pat Patterson, Pedro Morales
    & Raul Mata
04/26 San Francisco, CA beat Raul Mata
04/30 Sacramento, CA w/. Lonnie Mayne, lost to
    Pedro Morales & Pat Patterson
05/14 Sacramento, CA w/. Kurt Von Brauner, beat
    Pepper Martin & Manny Cruz
05/17 San Francisco, CA beat Pat Patterson
05/28 Sacramento, CA beat Pepper Martin
06/07 San Francisco, CA w/. Lonnie Mayne, beat
    Manny Cruz & Raul Mata
06/11 Sacramento, CA lost to Pat Patterson
06/21 San Francisco, CA w/. The Brute, lost to Pedro
    Morales & Don Muraco
06/25 Sacramento, CA w/. Lonnie Mayne, beat
    Pepper Martin & Raul Mata
07/07 San Jose, CA beat Pat Patterson
*Won the NWA United States (San Francisco) title
07/09 Sacramento, CA beat Pat Patterson
07/12 San Francisco, CA lost to Lonnie Mayne
07/23 Sacramento, CA lost to Pat Patterson
07/26 San Francisco, CA beat Peter Maivia
08/09 San Francisco, CA w/. Rock Riddle & Karl
    Von Brauner, beat Pedro Morales, Peter Maivia &
    Don Muraco
08/13 Sacramento, CA w/. Gerhardt Kaiser, beat
    Pepper Martin & Raul Mata
08/22 Sacramento, CA w/. Dutch Savage & Invader
    #2, lost to Pat Patterson, Don Muraco, & Lonnie
    Mayne
08/22 Sacramento, CA lost in a Battle royal
08/23 San Francisco, CA beat Rocky Johnson
09/03 Sacramento, CA lost to Pat Patterson
*Lost the NWA United States (San Francisco) title
09/17 Sacramento, CA w/. Gerhardt Kaiser, lost to
    Peter Maivia & Don Muraco
09/20 San Francisco, CA w/. Gerhardt Kaiser &
    Invader #2, lost to Pedro Morales, Lonnie Mayne
    & Don Muraco
10/19 Toronto, ON beat Lou Klein
11/10 Cahrlotte, NC beat Klondike Bill
11/17 Charlotte, NC beat Swede Hanson
12/01 Charlotte, NC beat Pepe Lopez
12/19 Calgary, AB vs. Frankie Laine

1976
01/06 Raleigh, NC w/. Boris Malenko, beat Paul
    Jones & Wahoo McDaniel
01/19 Charlotte, NC double DQ vs. Wahoo
    McDaniel
01/20 Raleigh, NC lost to Paul Jones
01/26 Charlotte, NC w/. Blackjack Mulligan, lost to
    Wahoo McDaniel & Tim Woods

03/16 Raleigh, NC w/. Blackjack Mulligan & Ric
    Flair, lost to Rufus Jones, Tim Woods, & Tiger
    Conway Jr.
03/22 Charlotte, NC w/. Blackjack Mulligan, lost to
    Rufus Jones & Tim Woods
03/23 Raleigh, NC lost to Tim Woods
03/30 Raleigh, NC w/. Blackjack Mulligan, lost to
    Rufus Jones & Tim Woods
04/06 Raleigh, NC lost to Tim Woods Death match
04/19 Greenville, SC beat Bill Dromo
04/26 Charlotte, NC lost to Tim Woods
04/27 Raleigh, NC w/. Blackjack Mulligan & Jacques
    Goulet, lost to Andre the Giant, Tim Woods &
    Paul Jones
05/03 Charlotte, NC beat Tim Woods
*Won the Mid-Atlantic Television title
05/04 Raleigh, NC lost to Paul Jones
05/11 Raleigh, NC double DQ vs. Wahoo McDaniel
05/24 Charlotte, NC lost to Paul Jones
06/22 Raleigh, NC lost to Paul Jones
06/29 Raleigh, NC lost to Rufus Jones Death match
07/04 Charlotte, NC w/. Blackjack Mulligan, lost to
    Andre the Giant & Paul Jones
07/06 Raleigh, NC lost to Mr. Wrestling by DQ
07/20 Raleigh, NC lost to Paul Jones
*Lost the Mid-Atlantic Television title
08/17 Raleigh, NC beat Mr. Wrestling by DQ
08/26 Raleigh, NC beat Paul Jones by DQ
08/30 Charlotte, NC beat Paul Jones by DQ
08/31 Raleigh, NC lost to Paul Jones
09/06 Charlotte, NC beat Tiger Conway Jr.
09/13 Charlotte, NC lost to Paul Jones
09/28 Raleigh, NC lost to Rufus Jones by DQ
11/08 Charlotte, NC beat Tony Atlas
12/26 Toronto, ON lost to Andre the Giant by
    count out

1977
01/13 Winnipeg, MB beat Peter Maivia
01/16 Minneapolis, MN beat Vito Martino
01/19 Omaha, NE lost to Jim Brunzell by DQ
01/21 Denver, CO beat Jim Brunzell
01/22 Milwaukee, WI beat Billy Francis
02/03 Winnipeg, MB lost to Peter Maivia
02/10 Davenport, IA beat Billy Francis
02/20 St. Paul, MN beat Billy Francis
02/24 Winnipeg, MB beat Peter Maivia
03/16 Davenport, IA w/. Super Destroyer, lost to
    Peter Maivia & Billy Francis
03/17 Winnipeg, MB beat Peter Maivia
04/02 Rockford, IL beat Peter Maivia by DQ
04/07 Winnipeg, MB w/. Bobby Duncum, beat Peter
    Maivia & Billy Francis
04/12 Omaha, NE beat Larry Hennig
04/17 Minneapolis, MN w/. Moose Morowski, lost to
    Pedro Morales & Billy Francis
04/23 Chicago, IL drew Peter Maivia
04/28 Winnipeg, MB w/. Bobby Duncum, lost to
    Billy & Russ Francis
05/01 Minneapolis, MN w/. Bobby Duncum, beat
    Billy & Russ Francis by DQ

05/18 Davenport, IA w/. Bobby Duncum & Blackjack Lanza, lost to Billy Robinson, Jim Brunzell & Greg Gagne
05/19 Winnipeg, MB lost to Peter Maivia
05/21 Chicago, IL beat Peter Maivia
06/05 Green Bay, WI w/. Roger Kirby, lost to Jim Brunzell & Greg Gagne
06/09 Winnipeg, MB beat Billy Francis
06/18 Chicago, IL beat Peter Maivia
06/24 Minneapolis, MN no contest vs. Larry Hennig
07/07 Winnipeg, MB w/. Super Destroyer, beat Pedro Morales & Ray Stevens
07/16 Milwaukee, WI no contest vs. Pedro Morales
07/19 Davenport, IA w/. Super Destroyer & Roger Kirby, lost to Billy Robinson, Larry Hennig & Bob Backlund
07/23 Chicago, IL w/. Super Destroyer, beat Pedro Morales & Dick the Bruiser
08/05 St. Paul, MN w/. Super Destroyer, beat Ray Stevens & The Crusher
08/18 Winnipeg, MB no contest vs. Gene Kiniski
08/28 Chicago, IL beat Pedro Morales
08/31 Davenport, IA vs. Larry Hennig & Steve Olsonoski Handicap match
09/10 Chicago, IL w/. Super Destroyer, beat Dick the Bruiser & ?
09/15 Winnipeg, MB beat Gene Kiniski
09/17 Milwaukee, WI w/. Super Destroyer, beat The Crusher & Dr. X
10/01 Rockford, IL beat Larry Hennig
10/06 Winnipeg, MB w/. Super Destroyer, lost to Gene Kiniski & The Crusher
10/16 Toronto, ON beat Steve Bolus
10/27 Winnipeg, MB lost to Larry Hennig
11/05 Chicago, IL w/. Super Destroyer, beat Larry Hennig & Dick the Bruiser
11/09 Davenport, IA lost to Larry Hennig
11/17 Winnipeg, MB beat Larry Hennig
11/26 Milwaukee, WI beat Larry Hennig
11/30 Toronto, ON beat Ed Psota
12/03 Chicago, IL w/. Super Destroyer, beat Dick the Bruiser & The Crusher
12/08 Winnipeg, MB beat Larry Hennig
12/11 Toronto, ON beat Nick DeCarlo
12/17 Milwaukee, WI beat Jan Nelson

1978
01/08 Toronto, ON double DQ vs. Peter Maivia
01/12 Winnipeg, MB w/. Super Destroyer, lost to Larry Hennig & The Crusher
01/13 St. Paul, MN no contest vs. Billy Robinson
01/14 Chicago, IL beat Larry Hennig
01/22 Minneapolis, MN w/. Super Destroyer, beat Greg Gagne & Bob Orton Jr.
01/25 Davenport, IA lost to Rufus Jones by DQ
02/02 Winnipeg, MB beat Billy Robinson
02/05 Toronto, ON beat Peter Maivia by DQ
02/11 Milwaukee, WI lost to Rufus Jones
02/12 Denver, CO lost to Rufus Jones
02/14 Davenport, IA w/. Super Destroyer, beat Larry Hennig & Billy Robinson

02/17 St. Paul, MN w/. Super Destroyer, beat Larry Hennig & Billy Robinson
02/19 Toronto, ON beat Peter Maivia by count out
02/23 Winnipeg, MB w/. Super Destroyer, lost to Jim Brunzell & Greg Gagne
02/26 Minneapolis, MN w/. Super Destroyer, lost to Jim Brunzell & Greg Gagne
03/01 Stevens Point, WI w/. Super Destroyer, lost to Jim Brunzell & Greg Gagne
03/04 Milwaukee, WI w/. Super Destroyer & Nick Bockwinkel, lost to Billy Robinson, Rufus Jones & The Crusher
03/05 Toronto, ON lost to Billy Robinson
03/11 Chicago, IL beat Wilbur Snyder by count out
03/16 Winnipeg, MB beat Billy Robinson
*Won the British Empire title
03/17 Omaha, NE lost to The Crusher
03/19 Toronto, ON lost to Peter Maivia
03/31 Knoxville, IL w/. Alfred Hayes, lost to Verne Gagne & The Crusher
04/01 Milwaukee, WI lost to The Crusher Cage match
04/05 Winnipeg, MB w/. Super Destroyer II, lost to Billy Robinson & Verne Gagne
04/07 Minneapolis, MN no contest vs. Billy Robinson
04/10 Toronto, ON w/. Super Destroyer II, lost to Billy Robinson & Peter Maivia by DQ
04/22 Milwaukee, WI lost to Billy Robinson
04/27 Winnipeg, MB lost to Billy Robinson Non-Title
04/30 Green Bay, WI beat Rufus Jones
05/10 Davenport, IA lost to The Crusher
05/12 Minneapolis, MN lost to Rufus Jones
05/13 Milwaukee, WI lost to The Crusher Cage match
05/15 Toronto, On lost to Billy Robinson by DQ
05/18 Winnipeg, MB lost to Billy Robinson
*Lost the British Empire title
05/20 Chicago, IL beat Dick the Bruiser by DQ
05/25 Minneapolis, MN lost to Rufus Jones
05/26 Denver, CO w/. Nick Bockwinkel, lost to Verne & Greg Gagne
06/02 Atlanta, GA beat Adrian Adonis
06/03 Atlanta, GA beat Ted Allen
06/05 Augusta, GA beat Adrian Adonis
06/06 Macon, GA beat Adrian Adonis
06/07 Columbus, GA vs. Adrian Adonis
06/09 Atlanta, GA Won tournament
*Won the NWA Georgia title
06/10 Atlanta, GA beat Ted Allen
06/10 Atlanta, GA beat Bill Irwon
06/12 Augusta, GA beat Len Denton
06/13 Warner Robbins, GA vs. Steve Regal
06/16 Atlanta, GA beat Mr. Wrestling
06/17 Atlanta, GA beat Jose Medina
06/17 Chicago, IL beat Dick the Bruiser Chain match
06/18 Columbus, GA lost to Bob Armstrong by DQ
06/19 Augusta, GA lost to Thunderbolt Patterson
06/20 Macon, GA vs. Rick Martel
06/21 Columbus, GA vs. Dick Slater

06/23 Atlanta, GA beat Bill Irwin & Klondike Bill
   Handicap match
06/24 Atlanta, GA beat Jose Vasquez
06/24 Atlanta, GA beat Steve Regal
06/26 Augusta, GA beat Thunderbolt Patterson by
   DQ
06/27 Macon, GA lost to Rick Martel by DQ
06/28 Columbus, GA vs. Dick Slater
06/29 Rome, GA vs. Mr. Wrestling II
06/30 Atlanta, GA beat Stan Hansen
07/01 Atlanta, GA lost to Dick Slater by DQ
07/01 Atlanta, GA beat Billy Starr
07/03 Augusta, GA vs. Thunderbolt Patterson
07/04 Macon, GA vs. Thunderbolt Patterson
07/05 Columbus, GA vs. Mr. Wrestling II
07/06 Winnipeg, MB lost to Nick Bockwinkel (AWA
   World champion)
07/07 Atlanta, GA lost to Stan Hansen by DQ
07/08 Atlanta, GA beat Pete Austin
07/10 Augusta, GA lost to Thunderbolt Patterson
   by DQ
07/11 Warner Robbins, GA vs. Thunderbolt Patterson
07/12 Columbus, GA vs. Mr. Wrestling II
07/13 Rome, GA vs. Stan Hansen
07/14 Atlanta, GA lost to Stan Hansen by count out
07/15 Atlanta, GA beat Steve Regal
07/15 Chicago, IL lost to Dick the Bruiser Cage
   match
07/16 Toronto, ON lost to Nick Bockwinkel (AWA
   World)
07/17 Augusta, GA lost to Thunderbolt Patterson
   by DQ
07/18 Macon, GA Tournament - No other information available
07/19 Columbus, GA Tournament - No other information available
07/20 Rome, GA vs. Stan Hansen
07/21 Atlanta, GA lost to Stan Hansen Cage match
07/22 Atlanta, GA beat Steve Regal
07/24 Augusta, GA vs. Rick Martel
07/25 Macon, GA vs. Thunderbolt Patterson
07/26 Columbus, GA vs. Pez Whatley
07/27 Winnipeg, MB lost to Nick Bockwinkel (AWA
   World) by DQ
07/29 Atlanta, GA beat Dennis Johnson
07/31 Augusta, GA lost to Thunderbolt Patterson
   Texas Death match
08/01 Macon, GA vs. Thunderbolt Patterson
08/02 Columbus, GA vs. Mr. Wrestling II
08/03 Rome, GA vs. Thunderbolt Patterson
08/04 Atlanta, GA lost to Mr. Mystery
08/05 Atlanta, GA beat Sandy Ellis
08/07 Augusta, GA lost to Mr. Mystery
08/09 Columbus, OH vs. Mr. Wrestling II No DQ
   match
08/10 Rome, GA vs. Thunderbolt Patterson
08/17 Rome, GA vs. Thunderbolt Patterson
08/20 Marietta, GA lost to Thunderbolt Patterson
08/26 Atlanta, GA beat Billy Starr
08/27 Marietta, GA lost to Thunderbolt Patterson
08/31 Rome, GA vs. Rick Martel

09/07 Rome, GA vs. Mr. Wrestling II
09/10 Toronto, ON beat Nick Bockwinkel (AWA
   World) by count out
09/11 Augusta, GA lost to Thunderbolt Patterson
   by DQ
09/14 Rome, GA vs. Mr. Wrestling II
09/17 Atlanta, GA beat Dick Slater by DQ
09/18 Augusta, GA lost to Thunderbolt Patterson by
   count out
09/22 Atlanta, GA lost to Dick Slater by count out
   No DQ match
09/23 Atlanta, GA beat Dennis Hall
09/25 Augusta, GA lost to Thunderbolt Patterson
09/29 Atlanta, GA beat Dick Slater Lumberjack
   match
09/30 Atlanta, GA w/. Hartford Love, beat Ted Allen
   & Rick McGraw
10/02 Augusta, GA lost to Dick Slater
10/05 Rome, GA vs. Dick Slater
10/06 Atlanta, GA lost to Mr. Wrestling II by DQ
10/07 Atlanta, GA beat Ted Allen
10/09 Augusta, GA beat Dick Slater Street fight match
10/13 Atlanta, GA lost to Mr. Wrestling II by DQ No
   DQ match
*Mosca is stripped of the NWA Georgia title
10/14 Atlanta, GA beat Dennis Hall
10/20 Atlanta, GA beat Mr. Wrestling II by DQ
10/21 Atlanta, GA w/. Hartford Love, beat Dennis
   Hall & Pierre Lefebvre
10/23 Augusta, GA beat Mr. Wrestling II by DQ
10/26 Rome, GA vs. Mr. Wrestling II
10/27 Atlanta, GA lost to Mr. Wrestling
10/28 Atlanta, GA beat Chick Donovan
10/30 Atlanta, GA lost to Mr. Wrestling by DQ
11/02 Rome, GA vs. Pez Whatley
11/03 Atlanta, GA lost to Mr. Wrestling by count out
   No DQ match
11/10 Atlanta, GA w/. Bounty Hunter, lost to Rick
   Martel & Bugsy McGraw
11/11 Atlanta, GA beat Ron Moates
11/13 Augusta, GA w/. Ole Anderson, beat Tommy
   Rich & Bugsy McGraw by DQ
11/14 Macon, GA w/. Hartford Love, lost to Rick
   Martel & Bugsy McGraw
11/15 Columbus, GA vs. Tommy Rich
11/23 Atlanta, GA w/. Pak Song, lost to Jack & Jerry
   Brisco
11/27 Augusta, GA lost to Mr. Wrestling
11/29 Columbus, GA vs. Bugsy McGraw
12/01 Atlanta, GA w/. Stan Hansen, beat Rick Martel
   & Bugsy McGraw
12/04 Augusta, GA w/. The Spoiler, vs. Rick Martel
   & Tommy Rich
12/07 Rome, GA vs. Tommy Rich
12/08 Atlanta, GA w/. Kurt Von Hess, lost to Rick
   Martel & Tommy Rich
12/11 Augusta, GA lost to Bugsy McGraw
12/12 Macon, GA w/. Ole Anderson, vs. Jack Brisco
   & Bugsy McGraw
12/13 Columbus, GA w/. Stan Hansen, vs. Bugsy
   McGraw & Mr. Wrestling II

12/14 Rome, GA vs. Bugsy McGraw

12/15 Atlanta, GA w/. Stan Hansen, beat Rick Martel & Tommy Rich

12/17 Columbus, GA w/. Kurt Von Hess, vs. Rufus Jones & Bugsy McGraw

12/25 Augusta, GA beat Pierre Lefebvre

12/25 Augusta, GA beat Mr. Wrestling

12/25 Augusta, GA lost to Rufus Jones

12/30 Augusta, GA vs. Tommy Rich

12/31 Macon, GA Battle royal

1979

01/01 Columbus, GA vs. Tommy Rich

01/01 Atlanta, GA lost to Wahoo McDaniel

01/06 Atlanta, GA beat Frank Dusek

01/08 Augusta, GA w/. Luke Graham, lost to Rufus Jones & Wahoo McDaniel

01/12 Atlanta, GA beat Bugsy McGraw

01/13 Augusta, GA w/. Ole Anderson, vs. Rufus Jones & Wahoo McDaniel

01/14 Macon, GA w/. Ole & Gene Anderson vs. Jack Brisco, Wahoo McDaniel & Thunderbolt Patterson

01/15 Augusta, GA w/. Stan Hansen, lost to Tommy Rich & Wahoo McDaniel

01/19 Atlanta, GA drew Dusty Rhodes

01/20 Atlanta, GA w/. Stan Hansen, lost to Marvin Turner & Mike Stansel by DQ

01/22 Augusta, GA w/. Stan Hansen, lost to Tommy Rich & Wahoo McDaniel

01/23 Warner Robbins, GA vs. Wahoo McDaniel

01/25 Rome, GA w/. Stan Hansen, vs. Tommy Rich & Mr Wrestling II

01/26 Atlanta, GA w/. Stan Hansen, lost to Tommy Rich & Wahoo McDaniel

01/29 Augusta, GA vs. Wahoo McDaniel

01/30 Macon, GA vs. Wahoo McDaniel

02/01 Rome, GA w/. Luke Graham, vs. Andre the Giant & Tommy Rich

02/02 Atlanta, GA w/. Stan Hansen, beat Jack Brisco & Mr. Wrestling II

02/04 Macon, GA vs. Thunderbolt Patterson

02/07 Columbus, GA vs. Mr. Wrestling II

02/08 Rome, GA w/. Masked Superstar, vs. Andre the Giant & Wahoo McDaniel

04/01 Macon, GA vs. Tommy Rich

04/04 Columbus, GA w/. Ron Bass, vs. Tommy Rich & Thunderbolt Patterson

04/06 Atlanta, GA w/. Blackjack Lanza, beat Tommy Rich & Bob Armstrong

04/13 Atlanta, GA beat Joe Soto

04/16 Augusta, GA vs. Mike Stallings

04/18 Columbus, GA w/. Ron Bass, vs. Mike Stallings & Mr. Wrestling

04/20 McDonogh, GA beat Bill Dromo

04/22 Macon, GA Battle royal

04/23 Augusta, GA beat Bob Armstrong

04/25 Columbus, GA vs. Mike Stallings

04/26 Rome, GA vs. Wahoo McDaniel

04/27 Atlanta, GA w/. Blackjack Lanza, lost to Tony Atlas & Norvell Austin

04/28 Chicago, IL lost to Billy Robinson

04/29 Macon, GA vs. Wahoo McDaniel

04/30 Augusta, GA lost to Wahoo McDaniel

05/02 Columbus, GA vs. Wahoo McDaniel Bounty Match

05/03 Rome, GA no contest vs. Wahoo McDaniel

05/04 Atlanta, GA w/. Blackjack Lanza, lost to Bill Dromo & Bob Armstrong

05/05 Atlanta, GA beat Ron Moates

05/07 Augusta, GA vs. Wahoo McDaniel Indian Strap match

05/09 Columbus, GA vs. Wahoo McDaniel Indian Strap match

05/10 Rome, GA vs. Wahoo McDaniel

05/11 Atlanta, GA lost to Bob Armstrong

05/13 Toronto, ON beat Jacques Goulet

06/20 Baton Rouge, LA lost to Mike Sharpe (Jr.) by DQ

06/24 Tulsa, OK lost to Mike Sharpe by count out

06/25 Oklahoma City, OK w/. Luke Graham, beat Mike Sharpe & Jerry Oates

07/01 Baton Rouge, LA w/. Luke Graham, lost to Mike Sharpe & Tony Atlas

07/05 New Orleans, LA w/. Luke Graham, beat Mike Sharpe & Jerry Oates

07/06 Shreveport, LA lost to Jerry Oates by DQ

07/09 Tulsa, OK beat Mike Sharpe

*Won the Mid-South Brass Knuckles title

07/15 Marietta, GA w/. Blackjack Lanza, lost to Bob Armstrong & Mr. Wrestling

07/18 Baton Rouge, LA w/. Luke Graham, lost to Mike Sharpe & Buck Robley by DQ

07/21 New Orleans, LA beat Paul Orndorff

07/25 New Orleans, LA w/. Luke Graham, lost to Mike Sharpe & Charlie Cook

08/01 Baton Rouge, LA beat Bob Sweetan

08/06 Tulsa, OK beat Charlie Cook

08/08 Baton Rouge, LA no contest vs. Mr. Wrestling

08/16 New Orleans, LA w/. Luke Graham, lost to Bill Watts & Buck Robley

08/23 New Orleans, LA w/. Ernie Ladd, lost to Bill Watts & Mr. Wrestling II by DQ

08/30 New Orleans, LA w/. Ernie Ladd, lost to Bill Watts & Dusty Rhodes

09/03 Tulsa, OK lost to Mike Sharpe

09/09 Toronto, ON lost to Jimmy Snuka by DQ

10/12 Shreveport, LA w/. Bob Sweetan & Tank Patton, lost to Bill Watts, Dick Murdoch, & Buck Robley

10/19 Atlanta, GA lost to Mr. Wrestling II

10/25 Winnipeg, MB lost to Super Destroyer Mark III by DQ

10/25 Winnipeg, MB lost in a Battle royal

11/04 Baton Rouge, LA lost to Charlie Cook

12/06 Winnipeg, MB w/. Steve Olsonoski, lost to Jesse Ventura & Adrian Adonis by DQ

1980

01/05 Winnipeg, MB w/. Steve Olsonoski, lost to Jesse Ventura & Adrian Adonis

02/16 Atlanta, GA beat Marvin Turner

03/30 Toronto, ON beat Jimmy Snuka by DQ

04/13 Toronto, ON beat Jimmy Snuka & Gene
    Anderson Handicap match
05/25 Toronto, ON beat Masked Superstar by DQ
06/15 Toronto, ON beat Ray Stevens by DQ
07/06 Toronto, ON lost to Great Hossein by DQ
07/20 Toronto, ON beat Great Hossein
*Won the Canadian Heavyweight title
08/10 Toronto, ON lost to Great Hossein
*Lost the Canadian Heavyweight title
08/14 Winnipeg, MB w/. Mad Dog Vachon, beat
    Jesse Ventura & Adrian Adonis
08/24 Toronto, ON beat Gene Anderson
08/25 Guelph, ON w/. Ricky Steamboat & Jay
    Youngblood, beat Jimmy Snuka, Gene Anderson
    & Ray Stevens
09/05 Winnipeg, MB w/. Mad Dog Vachon, lost to
    Jesse Ventura & Adrian Adonis
09/06 Toronto, ON w/. Ric Flair, beat Greg Valentine
    & Hossein Arab
09/07 Minneapolis, MN lost to Jerry Blackwell
10/18 Buffalo, NY beat Frankie Laine
10/19 Toronto, ON beat Bobby Duncum
10/22 Winnipeg, MB beat Adrian Adonis
10/22 Winnipeg, MB lost in a Battle royal
11/03 Greenville, NC w/. Don Kernodle, beat Swede
    Hanson & Genichiro Tenryu
11/06 Winnipeg, MB w/. Andre the Giant, beat John
    Studd & Jerry Blackwell
11/16 Toronto, ON beat Greg Valentine by DQ
12/06 Buffalo, NY beat Jimmy Snuka by DQ
12/07 Toronto, ON beat Great Hossein by count out
12/28 Toronto, ON beat Great Hossein Cage match
*Won the Canadian Heavyweight title (2)

1981
01/08 Winnipeg, MB w/. Mad Dog Vachon, beat John
    Studd & Jerry Blackwell Cage
01/10 Kitchener, ON w/. Blackjack Mulligan, beat
    Bobby Duncum & Great Hossein
01/11 Toronto, ON lost to Ivan Koloff by DQ
01/13 Niagara Falls, ON beat Brian Mackney &
    Charlie Fulton Handicap match
01/13 Niagara Falls, ON w/. Ric Flair, beat Ivan
    Koloff & Roddy Piper by DQ
02/01 Toronto, ON beat Ivan Koloff No DQ match
02/05 Winnipeg, MB double DQ vs. John Studd
02/22 Toronto, ON beat Great Hossein
02/26 Kingston, ON beat Great Hossein
03/08 Toronto, ON lost to Jimmy Snuka by count out
03/29 Toronto, ON beat Jimmy Snuka by count out
03/30 Brantford, ON drew Swede Hanson
03/30 Brantford, ON beat Great Hossein Lumberjack
    match
03/30 London, ON beat Bobby Duncum
04/01 Ottawa, ON beat Great Hossein
04/02 Niagara Falls, ON w/. Tony Parisi, beat Jimmy
    Snuka & Great Hossein
04/12 Toronto, ON double count out vs. Harley Race
    (NWA World)
04/13 Brantford, ON w/. Ric Flair, beat Frankie
    Laine & Charlie Fulton

04/13 Brantford, ON beat Charlie Fulton
04/13 Brantford, ON w/. Ric Flair, lost to Roddy
    Piper & Jimmy Snuka by DQ
05/01 Richmond, VA lost to Ric Flair
05/02 Roanoke, VA lost to Blackjack Mulligan Lights
    Out match
05/03 Toronto, ON beat Jimmy Snuka Lumberjack
    match
05/05 Ottawa, ON beat Jimmy Snuka
05/06 Kingston, ON w/. Dewey Robertson, beat
    Jimmy Snuka & Ray Stevens
05/07 Oshawa, ON w/. George Wells, beat Jimmy
    Snuka & Ray Stevens
05/24 Toronto, ON beat Roddy Piper by DQ
06/14 Toronto, ON beat Mr. Fuji by DQ
06/15 Dundas, ON w/. Ric Flair, beat Ivan Koloff &
    Mr. Fuji
06/16 Oshawa, ON w/. Ric Flair, drew Ivan Koloff
    & Mr. Fuji
06/28 Toronto, ON beat Mr. Fuji
06/29 St. Catherines, ON w/. Ric Flair, beat Roddy
    Piper & Mr. Fuji
07/04 Atlanta, GA beat Ken Timbs
07/05 Atlanta, GA drew Steve Olsonoski
07/06 Augusta, GA lost to Ken Patera
07/12 Toronto, ON lost to Mr. Fuji Texas Death
    match
*Lost the Canadian Heavyweight title
07/26 Toronto, ON beat Mr. Fuji Street Fight match
*Won the Canadian Heavyweight title (3)
07/28 Oshawa, ON double count out vs. Ray Stevens
08/09 Toronto, ON beat Ray Stevens
08/30 Toronto, ON beat Greg Valentine
09/20 Toronto, ON lost to John Studd
*Lost the Canadian Heavyweight title
10/16 Toronto, ON beat John Studd by DQ
10/20 Kingsport drew Bruiser
11/01 Toronto, ON lost to John Studd
11/15 Toronto, ON beat John Studd by count out

1982
01/17 Toronto, ON beat John Studd Cage match
*Won the Canadian Heavyweight title (4)
02/20 Bayamon, Puerto Rico beat Pierre Martel
*Won the WWC Caribbean title
Leaves the territory still recognized as the Caribbean
    champion in March.
04/04 Toronto, ON beat Tarzan Tyler
04/12 Greenville, SC w/. Sgt. Slaughter, double DQ
    vs. Paul Jones & Jack Brisco
04/18 Asheville, NC w/. Roddy Piper, double DQ vs.
    Jack Brisco & Wahoo McDaniel
04/18 Charlotte, NC w/. Sgt. Slaughter, double DQ
    vs. Ric Flair & Wahoo McDaniel
04/19 Greenville, SC beat Paul Jones
04/22 Sumter, SC double DQ vs. Blackjack Mulligan Jr.
04/25 Toronto, ON beat Nick Bockwinkel (AWA
    World) by DQ
04/26 Ottawa, ON double count out vs. John Studd
05/09 Charlotte, NC w/. Killer Khan, lost to Jack &
    Jerry Brisco by DQ

05/16 Toronto, ON w/. Jake Roberts, beat John Studd & Nick Bockwinkel
05/17 Guelph, ON beat Tito Senza
05/17 Guelph, ON beat John Studd by count out
05/18 Oshawa, ON beat John Studd by count out
05/19 Niagara Falls, ON w/. Tony Parisi, beat Don Kernodle & Jan Nelson
05/25 Buffalo, NY beat John Studd by DQ
06/05 Charlotte, NC lost to Paul Jones
06/06 Toronto, ON beat Gene Kiniski
06/10 Sumter, SC lost to Paul Jones
06/13 Roanoke, VA beat Ron Ritchie
06/22 Sumter, SC lost to Jay Youngblood
06/27 Toronto, ON beat Gene Kiniski Texas Death match
07/04 Roanoke, VA lost to Jack Brisco
07/04 Roanoke, VA w/. Gene Anderson & Don Kernodle, lost to Johnny Weaver, Jake Roberts & Jay Youngblood
07/05 Greenville, SC lost to Ricky Steamboat by DQ
07/06 Columbia, SC w/. Gene Anderson, lost to Paul Jones & Jay Youngblood
07/12 Greenville, SC lost to Ricky Steamboat
07/17 Greensboro, NC lost to Paul Jones
07/19 Greenville, SC w/. Ivan Koloff & Masked Superstar, beat Jimmy Valiant, Jack Brisco, & Ricky Steamboat
07/20 Columbia, SC w/. Gene Anderson, lost to Ricky Steamboat & Jack Brisco
07/25 Toronto, ON beat Gene Kiniski Lumberjack match
07/27 Ottawa, ON beat John Studd Lumberjack match
08/02 Greenville, SC w/. Gene Anderson, beat Johnny Weaver & Jay Youngblood
08/02 Columbia, SC lost to Jake Roberts by DQ
08/06 Charleston, SC lost to Johnny Weaver
08/07 Greensboro, NC w/. Gene Anderson, beat Johnny Weaver & Jay Youngblood
08/08 Toronto, ON beat Sgt. Slaughter by DQ
08/09 Greenville, SC lost to Jake Roberts
08/10 Raleigh, NC lost to Jack Brisco
09/29 Miami, FL w/. Jake Roberts & The Outlaw, lost to Barry Windham, Butch Reed & Ron Bass
10/05 Tampa, FL w/. Jake Roberts, beat Dick Murdoch & Ron Bass
10/12 Tampa, FL beat Ron Bass by DQ
10/26 Tampa, FL w/. Jake Roberts & John Studd, beat Barry Windham, Butch Reed & Dusty Rhodes
10/27 Miami, FL w/. Jake Roberts & John Studd, lost to Barry Windham, Butch Reed & Ron Bass
11/02 Tampa, FL beat Ron Bass
11/03 Miami, FL lost to Terry Allen by DQ
11/09 Tampa, FL lost to Ron Bass Texas Death match
11/16 Tampa, FL lost to Ron Bass Bullrope match
11/20 Miami, FL lost to Ron Bass Brass Knuckles match
11/21 Orlando, FL w/. Ernie Ladd, lost to Rufus Jones & Charlie Cook
11/23 Tampa, FL w/. Ernie Ladd, drew Rufus Jones & Dusty Rhodes

11/27 St. Petersburg, FL w/. Kendo Nagasaki, beat Barry Windham & Ron Bass
11/30 Tampa, FL w/. Kendo Nagasaki & J.J. Dillon, lost to Dusty Rhodes, Rufus Jones, & Bruce Walkup
12/01 Miami, FL w/. Kendo Nagasaki, lost to Barry Windham & Ron Bass by DQ
12/15 St. Petersburg, FL w/. Jimmy Garvin, beat Ernie Ladd & Rufus Jones
12/22 St. Petersburg, FL lost to Ernie Ladd
12/26 Toronto, ON lost to Leroy Brown by DQ
12/28 Tampa, FL w/. Jimmy Garvin, lost to Ernie Ladd & Rufus Jones
12/29 Miami, FL w/. J.J. Dillon, lost to Ernie Ladd & Rufus Jones

1983
01/02 Orlando, FL beat Brian Blair
01/04 Tampa, FL w/. Jimmy Garvin & Jake Roberts, lost to Ron Bass, Rufus Jones, & Mike Graham
01/09 Toronto, ON beat Leroy Brown
01/15 Tampa, FL lost to Rufus Jones by DQ
01/18 Tampa, FL lost to Rufus Jones by DQ
01/25 Tampa, FL beat Barry Windham Texas Death match
02/01 Tampa, FL beat Ron Bass Cage match
02/02 Miami, FL lost to Ron Bass Texas Death match
02/06 Orlando, FL w/. Leroy Brown, lost to Andre the Giant & Ron Bass
02/07 West Palm Beach, FL lost to Ron Bass by count out
02/09 Miami, FL w/. Leroy Brown, lost to Ron Bass & Rufus Jones by DQ
02/13 Orlando, FL lost to Ron Bass
02/14 West Palm Beach, FL w/. Jake Roberts & Roddy Piper, beat Ron Bass, Rufus Jones & Charlie Cook
02/17 Ocalla, FL w/. The Texan, lost to Ron Bass & Charlie Cook
02/20 Orlando, FL lost to Barry Windham Taped Fist match
02/22 Tampa, FL w/. Kevin Sullivan, beat Barry Windham & Ron Bass
03/01 Tampa, FL w/. Kevin Sullivan, beat Barry Windham & Ron Bass
03/02 Miami, FL lost to Barry Windham by DQ
03/08 Tampa, FL w/. Kevin Sullivan & Leroy Brown, lost to Dusty Rhodes, Barry Windham & Ron Bass by DQ
03/09 Miami, FL lost to Barry Windham
03/12 Jacksonville, FL beat Ron Bass
03/13 Orlando, FL lost to Charlie Cook by DQ
03/13 Orlando, FL lost in a Battle royal
03/15 Tampa, FL w/. Leroy Brown, lost to Barry Windham & Dick Murdoch
03/16 Miami, FL beat Scott McGhee
03/20 Orlando, FL beat Ron Bass Lights Out match
03/27 Orlando, FL w/. Frank Dusek, lost to Dusty Rhodes & Blackjack Mulligan
03/29 Tampa, FL w/. Frank Dusek & Kevin Sullivan, lost to Dusty Rhodes, Blackjack Mulligan & Barry Windham

03/31 Miami, FL w/. Frank Dusek, lost to Dusty
Rhodes & Blackjack Mulligan
04/05 Tampa, FL w/. Kevin Sullivan, lost to Barry
Windham & Blackjack Mulligan
04/06 Miami, FL w/. Purple Haze, drew Dusty
Rhodes & Blackjack Mulligan
04/10 Orlando, FL w/. Kevin Sullivan & Purple
Haze, beat Dusty Rhodes, Blackjack Mulligan &
Barry Windham by DQ
04/12 Tampa, FL w/. Purple Haze, drew Dusty
Rhodes & Blackjack Mulligan
04/13 Miami, FL w/. Kevin Sullivan & Purple Haze, lost
to Dusty Rhodes, Blackjack Mulligan & Big Daddy
04/16 St. Petersburg, FL w/. Frank Dusek, lost to
Barry Windham & Blackjack Mulligan
04/17 Orlando, FL lost to Blackjack Mulligan
04/?? Tampa, FL beat Rufus Jones
*Won the Bahamas Heavyweight title
04/20 Miami, FL lost to Blackjack Mulligan by DQ
04/26 Tampa, FL w/. Bobby Duncum, lost to Barry
Windham & Ron Bass
04/27 Miami, FL lost to Barry Windham by DQ
05/01 Greensboro, NC w/. Gene Anderson, lost to
Jack & Jerry Brisco
05/08 Orlando, FL w/. Bobby Duncum, beat Terry
Allen & Brad Armstrong
*Won the Global tag team titles
05/09 West Palm Beach, FL w/. Bobby Duncum, beat
Terry Allen & Brad Armstrong
05/11 Miami, FL lost to Ron Bass by DQ
05/15 Toronto, ON beat Bob Orton Jr.
05/18 Miami, FL w/. Bobby Duncum, lost to Ron
Bass & Big Daddy
05/24 Orlando, FL w/. Bobby Duncum, drew Ron
Bass & Dick Murdoch
06/05 Orlando, FL w/. Bobby Duncum, beat Ron
Bass & Barry Windham
06/12 Toronto, ON lost to Don Muraco by DQ
06/14 St. Louis, MO w/. Lanny Poffo, beat Moose
Cholak Handicap match
06/22 Miami, FL lost to Blackjack Mulligan
06/25 Orlando, FL lost to Blackjack Mulligan by DQ
07/01 Miami, FL w/. Bobby Duncum & Kevin
Sullivan, lost to Barry Windham, Brad Armstrong
& Mike Graham
07/02 Key West, FL w/. Ron Bass, lost to Barry
Windham & Blackjack Mulligan by DQ
07/05 Tampa, FL w/. Bobby Duncum, lost to Mike
Graham & Scott McGhee
*Lost the Global tag team titles
07/10 Toronto, ON beat One Man Gang
07/13 Miami, FL beat Kevin Sullivan & Purple Haze
by count out
07/19 Orlando, FL beat Purple Haze
07/20 Miami, FL w/. Blackjack Mulligan, beat Kevin
Sullivan & Purple Haze
07/24 Toronto, ON lost to Sgt. Slaughter
*Lost the Canadian Heavyweight title
07/26 Tampa, FL w/. Barry Windham & Blackjack
Mulligan, double count out vs. Purple Haze,
Leroy Brown & Ray Candy

07/27 Miami, FL beat Kevin Sullivan
07/31 Orlando, FL w/. Blackjack Mulligan & Angelo
Mosca Jr., beat Kevin Sullivan, Ron Bass & Purple
Haze
08/03 Miami, FL beat Purple Haze
08/07 Toronto, ON double DQ vs. Sgt. Slaughter
08/10 Miami, FL w/. Blackjack Mulligan, lost to
Leroy Brown & Ray Candy
08/28 Toronto, ON lost to Sgt. Slaughter by count
out No DQ match
09/18 Toronto, ON beat Sgt. Slaughter by count out
10/16 Toronto, ON beat Sgt. Slaughter Lumberjack
match
11/13 Toronto, ON w/. Jimmy Valiant, beat Leo
Burke & Intelligent Destroyer
11/20 Kitchener, ON w/. Ric Flair, beat Dick Slater &
Bob Orton Jr. by DQ
12/04 Toronto, ON w/. Blackjack Mulligan, beat Sgt.
Slaughter & Don Kernodle

1984
01/08 Toronto, ON beat Sgt. Slaughter by count out
01/22 Toronto, ON beat Sgt. Slaughter Cage match
*Won the Canadian Heavyweight title (5)
02/12 Roanoke, VA beat Ivan Koloff by DQ
02/13 Fayetteville, NC lost to Ivan Koloff
02/16 Sumter, SC w/. Angelo Mosca Jr., lost to Bob
Orton Jr. & Don Kernodle
02/19 Charlotte, NC w/. Angelo Mosca Jr., beat Ivan
Koloff & Ernie Ladd
02/21 Raleigh, NC w/. Angelo Mosca Jr., lost to Bob
Orton Jr. & Don Kernodle
02/24 Richmond, VA w/. Dusty Rhodes & Jimmy
Valiant, beat Paul Jones & The Assassins
02/26 Asheville, NC w/. Wahoo McDaniel, no contest vs. Animal & Hawk
02/27 Fayetteville, NC w/. Angelo Mosca Jr., beat
Ivan Koloff & Great Kabuki
03/01 Norfolk, VA beat Great Kabuki
03/04 Charlotte, NC w/. Angelo Mosca Jr., beat Ivan
Koloff & Great Kabuki
03/06 Raleigh, NC beat Ivan Koloff
03/09 Charleston, SC w/. Angelo Mosca Jr., beat Ivan
Koloff & Great Kabuki
03/11 Sumter, SC w/. Jimmy Valiant & Rufus Jones,
beat Paul Jones & Assassins
03/13 Columbia, SC w/. Angelo Mosca Jr., lost to
Ivan Koloff & Great Kabuki
03/15 Norfolk, VA beat Ivan Koloff
03/18 Columbia, SC w/. Angelo Mosca Jr. & Junk Yard
Dog, beat Ivan Koloff, Great Kabuki & Gary Hart
03/18 Charlotte, NC beat Great Kabuki
03/20 Raleigh, NC w/. Angelo Mosca Jr., lost to Ivan
Koloff & Great Kabuki
03/23 Charleston, SC w/. Angelo Mosca Jr. & Dory
Funk Jr., beat Ivan Koloff, Great Kabuki & Gary
Hart
03/24 Richmond, VA lost to Ivan Koloff Chain match
03/25 Roanoke, VA w/. Angelo Mosca Jr. & Junk Yard
Dog, beat Ivan Koloff, Great Kabuki & Gary Hart
03/25 Greensboro, NC beat Ivan Koloff

03/26 Fayetteville, NC lost to Ivan Koloff
03/27 Raleigh, NC w/. Angelo Mosca Jr., beat Ivan Koloff & Great Kabuki
03/31 Hickory, NC w/. Angelo Mosca Jr. & Junk Yard Dog, beat Ivan Koloff, Great Kabuki & Gary Hart
04/01 Fayetteville, NC w/. Angelo Mosca Jr., beat Ivan Koloff & Gary Hart
04/01 Greensboro, NC w/. Angelo Mosca Jr., beat Ivan Koloff & Gary Hart
04/03 Raleigh, NC lost to Ivan Koloff Chain match
04/06 Norfolk, VA w/. Angelo Mosca Jr., beat Ivan Koloff & Great Kabuki
04/08 Savannah w/. Angelo Mosca Jr., beat Ivan Koloff & Great Kabuki
04/09 Greenville, SC beat Great Kabuki by DQ
04/10 Raleigh, NC w/. Angelo Mosca Jr., beat Ivan Koloff & Gary Hart Chain match
04/13 Richmond, VA w/. Angelo Mosca Jr., beat Ivan Koloff & Gary Hart Chain match
04/15 Asheville, NC beat Ernie Ladd
04/16 Fayetteville, NC beat Tully Blanchard
04/17 Raleigh, NC lost to The Assassin
04/21 Greensboro, NC lost to The Assassin
04/22 Savannah lost to The Assassin
04/22 Charlotte, NC beat The Assassin
04/27 Richmond, VA lost to The Assassin
04/29 Toronto, ON beat Great Kabuki
04/30 Greenville, SC w/. Angelo Mosca Jr., lost to Ivan Koloff & Don Kernodle
05/01 Columbia, SC w/. Angelo Mosca Jr., lost to Ivan Koloff & Don Kernodle
05/06 Asheville, NC w/. Angelo Mosca Jr., lost to Ivan Koloff & Don Kernodle
05/10 Sumter, SC w/. Angelo Mosca Jr., lost to Ivan Koloff & Don Kernodle
05/13 Toronto, ON w/. Angelo Mosca Jr., beat Ivan Koloff & Great Kabuki
05/19 Greensboro, NC beat The Assassin
05/20 Charlotte, NC lost to The Assassin
05/24 Sumter, SC drew The Outlaw
05/24 Norfolk, VA lost to The Assassin
05/25 Richmond, VA lost to The Assassin
05/26 Greenville, SC lost to The Assassin
05/27 Toronto, ON beat Ivan Koloff Chain match
05/30 Tampa, FL beat Mike Rotundo
*Won the NWA Southern title
06/09 Jacksonville, FL beat Mike Rotundo
06/10 Toronto, ON beat The Assassin by DQ
06/12 Tampa, FL w/. Ron Bass & Black Bart, beat Mike Rotundo, Mike Graham, & Joe Lightfoot
06/17 Orlando, FL w/. Billy Graham, lost to Billy Jack Haynes & Mike Rotundo
06/20 Miami, FL beat Joe Lightfoot
06/23 Sarasota, FL drew Mike Rotundo
06/24 Toronto, ON w/. Jimmy Valiant & Buzz Sawyer, beat Kamala, Assassin & Paul Jones
06/26 Tampa, FL w/. Dick Slater, beat Mike Rotundo & Joe Lightfoot
06/28 Ocala, FL drew Mike Rotundo
06/30 Miami, FL w/. Ron Bass & Black Bart, lost to Wahoo McDaniel, Junk Yard Dog, & Jimmy Valiant

07/01 Orlando, FL beat Mike Rotundo
07/03 Tampa, FL w/. Kevin Sullivan, beat Barry Windham & Joe Lightfoot
07/07 Lakeland, FL drew Mike Rotundo
07/08 Orlando, FL w/. Kevin Sullivan, lost to Blackjack Mulligan & Joe Lightfoot
07/09 West Palm Beach, FL w/. Kevin Sullivan, beat Blackjack Mulligan & Joe Lightfoot
07/11 Fort Lauderdale, FL w/. Ron Bass, beat Barry Windham & Joe Lightfoot
07/15 Orlando, FL w/. Kevin Sullivan, beat Blackjack Mulligan & Joe Lightfoot
07/16 West Palm Beach, FL lost to Mike Graham by DQ
07/18 Miami, FL w/. Black Bart, lost to Blackjack Mulligan & Joe Lightfoot
07/21 Fort Lauderdale, FL lost to Blackjack Mulligan Lumberjack match
07/22 Orlando, FL w/. Ron Bass, drew Blackjack Mulligan & One Man Gang
Leaves the Florida territory still recognized as Southern Champion in July.
10/07 Toronto, ON w/. Sgt. Slaughter, beat Nicolai Volkoff & Iron Sheik
10/09 Ottawa, ON lost to Paul Orndorff by DQ
10/21 Toronto, ON beat The Iron Sheik
10/31 Kitchener, ON w/. Andre the Giant, beat Iron Sheik & Kamala
11/03 Calgary, AB lost to Iron Sheik by DQ
11/04 Edmonton, AB w/. Sika & Afa, lost to Iron Sheik, Adrian Adonis & Dick Murdoch
11/05 Vancouver, BC lost to Iron Sheik by count out
11/07 Winnipeg, MB vs. Iron Sheik
11/20 New York, NY beat Mr. Fuji
11/21 Buffalo, NY beat Bobby Bass
11/22 Landover, MD lost in a 20-man Battle royal
11/23 Hartford, CT lost to Greg Valentine
11/24 Providence, RI beat Mr. Fuji by DQ
12/06 Vancouver, BC beat Iron Sheik
12/09 Toronto, ON beat Iron Sheik Texas Death match

1985
08/03 Honolulu, HI w/. Andre the Giant & Steve Collins, beat King Kong Bundy, Kevin Sullivan & Mark Lewin
12/26 Pickering, ON beat Karl Krupp Cage Match

1986
02/26 Hamilton, ON Promoted wrestling card under banner of "Mosca Mania"
03/14 Toronto, ON w/. Angelo Mosca Jr., beat Karl Krupp & Sweet Daddy Siki
05/19 Montreal, QC beat Man Mountain Moore
12/26 Thornhill, ON Won a Battle royal

1987
02/15 Hamilton, ON beat Pez Whatley
06/14 Toronto, ON drew Sweet Daddy Siki

—Compiled by Vance Nevada for *SLAM! Wrestling*

Index

A

Abdullah the Butcher 215
Afflis, William 178
Agro, Johnny 120
Allard, Don 49
Anderson, Gene 203, 211
Anka, Paul 118
Armstrong, George 161, 177
Atkins, Doug 64
Atkins, Margene 139
Atlas, Charles 45
Avruskin, Milt 216
Auger, Eddy 113
Azzopardi, Mario 218

B

Back, Len 74
Backlund, Bob 207
Baker, Art 130
Baker, Mike 77
Ballard, Harold 220, 223
Barrow, John 12, 80, 89, 105–6, 120, 133,
    143, 150
Baun, Bobby 135
Beckett, Mel 100
Berra, Yogi 135
Bethea, Willie 130, 138, 140, 143, 154
Bevan, Eddie 80
Bower, Johnny 135
Braley, David 220, 222–3
Brennan, Terry 55, 57, 60
Brenner, Al 154, 169
Bright, Johnny 185
Brito, Gino 182
Brody, Bruiser 195

Brody, King Kong 195
Brower, Bulldog 182, 187
Brown, Jim 61, 135
Brown, Paul 98
Brown, Tom 130, 133, 138
Bruggers, Bobby 200
Buchanan, Dave 156
Buchanan, Ed 121
Bundy, King Kong 195
Butts, Wally 16, 63

C

Campbell, Hugh 147
Campbell, Milt 97
Carme, Mike 5, 25
Cartwright, Hoss 83
Cassata, Rick 159
Cavanaugh, Martin 45
Ceppetelli, Gene 87, 97, 130, 133, 143–6, 175
Cherney, Aaron 230
Cherney, Helen 228–9
Cherney, Mark 229–30
Cherney, Nathan 229–30
Cherney, Ryan 230
Clair, Frank 94, 116–7, 121
Coffey, Tommy Joe 143
Cohen, Dr. 52
Cohon, Mark 224
Coleman, Wayne 184–5
Cosentino, Frank 125, 128
Counts, Johnny 138
Crockett, David 199
Crockett, Jimmy 199
Crump, Donald 223–4
Cudmore, Beverly 53

Cureton, Hardiman 111
Custis, Bernie 156
Czaja, Emile 195

D
Daigneault, Doug 118
Danychuk, Bill 87, 143, 199
Davis, Ernie 61
Dekkar, Paul 120
DeMarco, Mario 100
Dempsey, Jack 45
DeNobile, Geno 80
Devaney, Bob 63
DiMaggio, Dom 33
Dinapoli, Fiona 35
Doerr, Bobby 33
Dorow, Al 153
Duncum, Bobby 112, 177
Dunnell, Milt 134
Dylan, Bob 110

E
Ealey, Chuck 125, 154, 156–8, 169
Etcheverry, Sam 124

F
Faloney, Bernie 80, 89, 92, 94, 99–100, 106,
     117, 120, 123–5, 128, 140, 229–31
Faloney, Jan 89
Ferguson, John 219
Flair, Ric 199–200, 215, 217
Fleming, Dave 143–4, 154–6, 164, 169–70
Fleming, Sue 144
Fleming, Willie 84, 130–3, 135, 138, 177
Floyd, Otis 130
Ford, Alan 148
Ford, Whitey 135
Foxcroft, Ron 222, 225–6
Funston, Farrell 108

G
Gabler, Wally 154, 156–7
Gabriel, Tony 154–5, 169
Gagne, Vern 186, 205
Gaines, Gene 137
Gaudaur, Jake 75, 122, 131, 224
Geremia, Frank 55
Gilchrist, Cookie 90, 144
Giralumo, Tom 44
Goldston, Ralph 99, 101, 120
Golla, Jimmy 79
Goodrich, Darlene 61
Grant, Bud 139–41
Grant, George 228
Grant, Tommy 137, 143, 159

Green, Pumpsie 23
Gretzky, Wayne 146
Guglielmi, Ralph 51

H
Halter, Sydney 127, 139, 223
Hanley, Bob 75
Harding, Ken 47
Harris, Wayne 152
Hart, Owen 183
Hart, Stu 183, 185, 187
Hawkins, Ronnie 110
Heenan, Bobby "The Brain" 195
Heffer, Bull 208–9
Henley, Garney 97, 126, 143, 154, 162
Hercules, Mighty 176
Hodgson, Bill 117
Hogan, Hulk 204, 210
Hohman, Jon 143
Holleback, Mike 119
Hornung, Paul 59, 61, 151
Horton, Tim 135, 161, 177
Howe, Gordie 135
Huffman, Dick 220

I
Inskeep, Gary 154–5, 161, 177
Ivy, Pop 80

J
Jackson, Russ 12, 117–8, 137, 139, 222
Jacobs, "Indian" Jack 75, 91
James, Gerry 108
Jenkins, Fergie 135
Johnson, Dan 216
Johnson, Rafer 98
Jones, Cal 100
Jones, Paul 213
Jurvavinski, Charlie 219
Just, Jim 55

K
Kapp, Joe 129, 132
Kelley, Harold 44, 160
Kelly, Ellison 87, 143, 159
Kelly Twins 216
Kiniski, Gene 185
Kirk, King Kong 195
Knight, Bobby 225
Kolov, Nikita 216
Kosmos, Mark 154
Kramer, Bob 220
Krouse, Bob 129, 154
Kruschev, Krusher 216
Kuntz, Bobby 125, 130, 138, 144

Kwong, Normie 185

L
Lacey, Barb 227
Ladd, Ernie 112, 177
Lampman, Harry 100
Lancaster, Ron 118, 147, 159, 169
Lanza, Black Jack 177
Leahy, Frank 57, 59–60
Ledyard, Hal 94
Lee, Harold 110
Lewin, Mark 212
Lewis, Leo 99, 126
Locklin, Billy Ray 87, 148
Love Brothers 184
Lyons, Billy 184

M
Macdonald, David 228
Mann, Dave 94, 140
Marconi, Joe 176
Marshall, Bob 64–5, 67–8
Marshall, Norm 75, 108
Martinello, Marty 76, 175
Mathias, Bob 98
Matson, Ollie 94
McCrae, Earl 166
McDaniel, Ed "Wahoo" 112, 166, 178, 202–3
McDougall, Gerry 90, 108, 144
McGregor, Father 62
McMahon, Vince Jr 186, 194, 205–6, 208,
    213, 217, 228
McMahon, Vince Sr 185, 205–206
McNeeley, Tom 49
McQuay, Leon 153
McRae, Earl 131, 166, 196
Michener, Governor-General Roland 162
Miksza, Chet 80
Minihane, Bob 127
Mitchell, Doug 5, 221, 224
Mitchell, Scott 5, 222
Montana, Joe 146
Moore, Dickie 135
Mosca, Agnes 168
Mosca, Angelo Jr 5, 21, 53, 109, 165, 167, 211,
    216, 230
Mosca, Becky 21, 39
Mosca, Darlene 62, 64, 66–9, 77, 109, 112,
    151, 178, 198, 231, 236
Mosca, Gino 5, 221, 230
Mosca, Gwen 196–9, 215, 219, 226–8, 231
Mosca, Helen 5, 10–12, 27–8, 109, 168,
    228–31, 233–4, 237–8
Mosca, Jolene 64, 66–7, 77, 109, 151, 211,
    230–1

Mosca, Mike 40, 229
Mosca, Nathan 221
Mosca, June 40
Moss, Perry 121
Mulligan, Black Jack 112, 177, 200
Munsey, Bill 138

N
Nagurski, Bev 105
Nagurski, Bronko Jr 12, 53–6, 87, 104–105,
    185, 237
Nagurski, Bronko Sr 53, 178, 185

O
Oliver, Greg 182

P
Padillo, Porky 65
Paikin, Marnie 225
Palermo, Mike 5
Paletta, Angelo 160
Paquette, Don 110, 124
Parilli, Babe 118
Parker, Jackie 126
Patterson, Floyd 49
Patterson, Hal 123–4, 131, 137, 154
Patterson, Pat 190, 206
Peters, Kris 231
Piper, Roddy 218
Pitts, Alan 108
Pitts, Ernie 99
Plimpton, George 219
Ploen, Ken 99–100, 107–8
Poirier, Joe 118
Polak, Jo-Anne 222
Powers, John 184
Presley, Elvis 110
Proudfoot, Tony 121

Q
Quinn, Bernie 5
Quinn, Big John 184
Quinn, Eddie 111–113, 115, 177, 182, 213
Quinn, Pat 161, 177

R
Rauhaus, Norm 99
Reddell, Bill 146
Reed, George 147, 159
Restic, Joe 51, 128, 151–2
Reynolds, Jim 87
Rhodes, Dusty 215, 217
Richard, Henri 135
Richard, Maurice 135

Road Warriors 216
Roberg. Carol 5, 40, 10, 33, 36, 167
Robertson, Dewey 184
Robinson, Jackie 23
Rockne, Knute 57
Rossettani, Vic 216
Rote, Tobin 118–19
Roussimoff, Andre "the Giant" 201, 204
Ruddick, Steve 222

S
Sanderson, Sandy 96
Sauve, Dave 177
Savoldi, Angelo 113–5, 181
Savoldi, "Little Jumping Joe" 113
Saxon, Gene 55
Sazio, Ralph 68, 75, 87, 91, 98, 104–5, 116,
        128–31, 136, 137, 139–40, 146–7, 149,
        151–3, 157, 178, 221
Schaaf, Jim 56
Scott, George 199–200
Scott, Vince 79, 89, 100, 108
Selinger, Jerry 147–8
Shack, Eddie 219
Shaw, Rick 154
Sheik, Iron 194
Shepard, Charlie 108, 126
Shepherd, Tom 169
Shire, Roy 189
Shull, Don 120
Silly, Jack 153
Simpson, Bobby 118–19
Simpson, Jimmy 96
Sinclair, Gordon 219
Slaughter, Sergeant 216–17
Skrein, Joe 131–2
Smith, Larry 224
Smith, Steven T. 238
Smythe, Bill 117
Stallone, Sylvester 204
Starkweather, Charles 65
Steiner, Bob 87, 157
Sternberg, Gerry 154
Stevens, Ray 190
Stewart, Ronnie 117–8
Storey, Red 135
Stover, Smokey 146
Strube, Martin 64–5, 67
Studd, John 204
Sutherin, Don 127
Sullivan, Kevin 212
Suminski, Dave 80, 107
Sunter, Ian 158, 169
Swift, Bob 138

T
Taylor, Bobby 155–6
Theismann, Joe 154, 156
Thelen, Dave 118
Trimble, Jim 68, 74–5, 78, 80, 89–91, 93–4,
        96, 98–9, 104–5, 109, 111, 116, 123, 125,
        128, 137, 153, 156
Trudeau, Pierre Elliott 86, 238
Tucker, Julius 63, 66–68, 75, 237
Tucker, Whit 139
Turner, Charlie 143
Twitty, Conway 110

V
Vachon, Maurice 165
Valentine, Johnny 199–200
Valiant, Jimmy 215
Van Pelt, Jim 99–100, 107
Vaughan, Kaye 117–9
Ventura, Jessie "The Body" 213, 217
Verachioni, Frank 51
Viola, Fern 76
Viti, Dave 87

W
Wade, Sonny 152
Walker, Gordie 133–4, 159–60
Walker, Hal 134
Walker, Terry 160
Walton, Chuck 87
Washington, Vic 139
Watkins, Ted 146, 148
Watson, "Whipper" Billy 184
Wheeldon, Ralphie 25
Wilkinson, Tom 220
Williams, Gina 231
Williams, Jerry 153–8
Williams, Ted 33, 135, 238
Wituska, Bob 56
Wolfe, Louise 5
Wood, Agnes 21
Wood, Wallace 30
Woods, Tiger 109
Woods, Tim 200
Wotton, Gwen 151

Y
Young, Bob 5, 226

Z
Zeno, Joe 48
Zili, Jack 58
Zuger, Joe 84, 123, 125–6, 128, 130, 140, 143,
        148, 156
Zullo, Tony 41, 48, 90

Postscript

I am fond of this story written long ago.

Every day is a gift as long as I open my eyes.

Old age is like a bank account — You withdraw in later life what you have deposited along the way.

So my advice is to deposit all the happiness you can in your bank account of memories.

Thank you for your part in filling my account with happy memories, which I continue to fill.

My simple guidelines to happiness:

1) *Free your heart from hate*
2) *Free your mind from wrong*
3) *Live simple*
4) *Give more*
5) *Expect less*

— Angelo Mosca